THE
RIGHT TO KNOW

The Rise of the World Press

By the same Author

General

War by Revolution
Democracy's Battle
The Triple Challenge
Ernest Bevin: Portrait of an Englishman
Press Parliament and People
Dangerous Estate: The Anatomy of Newspapers
The American Invasion
A Pattern of Rulers

Fiction

No Man Is An Island
A Provincial Affair
The Richardson Story

THE
RIGHT TO KNOW

The Rise of the World Press

Francis Williams

Longmans

LONGMANS, GREEN AND CO LTD
London and Harlow
Associated companies, branches and representatives
throughout the world

© Lord Francis Williams 1969

First published 1969

SBN: 582 10862 4

Printed in Great Britain by Hazell Watson & Viney Ltd.,
Aylesbury, Bucks

To Jess With All My Love

Author's Note

This book owes much to newspapermen who are my friends all over the world. I cannot expect them to agree with all of it and in a book with so wide a span in both time and territory no doubt they will find some errors of fact, although I have tried to avoid them. But I hope they will accept it as a tribute to our common trade and its importance in the world. Because it is meant for general reading I have kept free of footnotes. Sources are acknowledged in the text itself. My debt to many of the volumes in the bibliography printed at the end is great. Also to many private sources both written and verbal. But the opinions are, of course, my own.

Finally I must thank my secretary, Mrs Irene Jackson. This book has been an unconscionable time growing and she and I have grappled with it for a long, long time. I cannot thank her too much.

CONTENTS

CHAPTER ONE

Barometers of Their Time

Newspapers are unique barometers of their age. They indicate more plainly than anything else the climate of the societies to which they belong.

This is not simply for the obvious reason that they are a source of news about their time but because the conditions in which they operate, the responsibilities they are expected, or allowed, to fulfil, the pressures they have to meet, their circulation and economic base, the status of those who write for them and their relationship to their readers, all provide a direct insight into the nature of their communities.

Because its business is news, the newspaper operates in what is at once the most universal and the most sensitive area of public interest. It reflects in what it prints not only the common curiosities of mankind but also the extent to which authority at every level is prepared to disclose its purpose or can be cajoled or bullied into revealing its intent. 'A community,' Rebecca West has remarked, 'needs news for the same reason that a man needs eyes. It has to see where it is going.' Yet it is rare for this function to be exercised without challenge. The secrecies of governments, the self-preserving mechanisms of bureaucracies, the pressures of great interests, the compulsions of political ideologies, stand in its way. So, to an increasing extent, do the terms of reference accepted by many newspapers for themselves. The pressures of economic circumstances are often as dangerous, if less openly acknowledged, deterrents to freedom as are the compulsions of political philosophies.

I

The Right to Know

The press has traditionally three linked responsibilities: to collect and publish the news, to interpret and comment on it, to act as a guard dog of the public interest in areas of public concern where executive power may be arbitrarily used. Its business, in the words of Delane of *The Times* a hundred and fifteen years ago, is 'to obtain the earliest and most correct intelligence of the events of the time and instantly, by disclosing them, to make them the common property of mankind'; to 'print the news and raise hell' as Wilbur Storey of the *Chicago Times* said a few years later.

These linked responsibilities are recognised even in communist countries, except as regards the higher level of authority. Indeed, the extent to which the third is considered a necessary part of press responsibility in Soviet Russia is indicated by the fact that *Izvestia* commonly receives some 300,000 readers' letters a year which are examined and analysed by a complaints department of the newspaper.

Of course, the press has other functions than these in all countries. It provides entertainment. It transmits gossip. It criticises the arts. It recommends racehorses and football teams, tells women what to cook and what to wear (even *Pravda* now has its fashion page). But it is on its responsibility as an agency of public information, inquiry, and protection that the traditional case for the freedom of the press rests. With this, as the *Economist* has said, goes the requirement to provide serious and continuous intellectual argument over all the issues of the day even when to do so may attract acute controversy or dislike. New forms of communication have not diminished this. On the contrary they may well have increased it.

In a short time space satellites are likely to be in orbit capable of simultaneously transmitting a volume of news some four hundred times as great as that of the most modern trans-Atlantic cable and more than 160 times greater than existing communications satellites can transmit. Three or four such satellites strategically sited could blanket the world with an unending service of quick and voluminous news. Moreover, not only is it becoming possible for anything happening anywhere to be relayed immediately in vision via space satellites to domestic television stations and thence to television sets in millions of homes, but in the foreseeable future, possibly indeed within so short a period as ten years, it will be technically feasible to cut out the intermediary of the local television transmitter and service home television sets direct from space satellites. The television set in the sitting-room could then become a window on the world in a sense far surpassing anything that has been known so far.

This is no doubt an exciting prospect—if national interests ever let it happen. But it is also an intimidating one. Instant news, raw and in bulk, is an indigestible commodity. It needs processing. The editorial processes of newspapers provide weight and perspective to public happenings; they enable them to be presented in terms that fall within the experience and judgment of readers differing widely from newspaper to newspaper and from country to country. If space communication should ever bypass this editorial process the world will be in danger of becoming punch-drunk with too much instant news, surfeited with an excess of flickering images that will make men not more but less well informed than they are now.

So far from diminishing the newspaper's responsibilities modern systems of communication may well increase them. For the purposes of civilisation it is necessary that words should move constantly across frontiers. But it is no less necessary that they should do so in forms comprehensible and assimilable. In this respect those who write for newspapers are likely to remain among the most serviceable ambassadors of ordinary men and women.

However, they are increasingly ambassadors under pressure, plenipotentiaries of regimes in a state of flux. Not since steam printing, the rotary press, mechanical setting and the electric telegraph made a popular press a practical possibility in the mid-nineteenth century has there opened before newspapers the possibility of such far reaching technological advances as now. But this opportunity for technical innovation of a kind that could alter the whole shape and scope of the press comes at a time when in most economically developed countries newspapers face problems more varied and potentially perhaps more formidable than ever before. Moreover because newspapers mirror so accurately the societies of which they are a part, they are today to be found functioning at almost every level of historical development in one part of the world or another. Free and unfree newspapers operate almost alongside each other; the journalistic process that finds contemporary expression in great conurbations of news and entertainment in Britain, the United States, Japan and other highly industrialised societies finds expression also in a form no less contemporary in the regimented informational news publications of Soviet Russian and other European communist countries, in the violent wall newspapers of communist China, and in the fugitive short-lived news and opinion sheets of many parts of Africa and the Middle East.

This immense diversity of newspaper development and status would matter less if there were a greater common body of agreement as to what the responsibilities of the press in society really are: a standard against which each could measure itself and be measured. Such a body of principle once existed. In so far as it still does it is constantly eroded by the fact that even where ideological differences do not arise the course followed by the press in advanced countries often seems to those seeking to establish newspaper freedom in countries less advanced not only inapplicable to their own conditions but actually hostile to the values they believe important.

Where concepts of democracy differ it is no doubt natural that ideas as to the function and status of the press should differ also. It is not sensible to presume that newspapers can stand so far outside the values governing their societies that their functions and status can, or should, be the same whether they operate in highly sophisticated industrialised communities or in under-developed and still mainly agrarian ones; in nations settled in their modes of life or at a stage of difficult transition; in political democracies or authoritarian societies. Nevertheless certain basic assumptions about the purpose and responsibilities of newspapers, although not always honoured in practice, were until recently accepted as part of the common formula of civilisation, as was the thesis that a free and uncensored press was an element of a good society, not, it should be said, because of any special privilege attaching to owners and editors of newspapers but because this freedom was a part of the public interest.

This is no longer always the case. Let me quote as an example, no more, a letter I received from a distinguished Rhodesian journalist in the early days of the Rhodesian crisis. 'It might be

thought,' he wrote, 'that people of any Western country would
resent any tampering with the freedom of the press. But this is
certainly not so in Rhodesia. The average European in Rhodesia
today is angry when he sees blank spaces in his daily paper—but
his anger is directed against the editor, not the censor. He watches
the shackling of the press with quiet satisfaction, if nothing more.'
That this should be so was, argued my correspondent, 'the
predictable consequence of the failure of the press in other parts
of the world to inspire people with an urge to defend its freedom.
Rhodesia,' he went on, 'is not the first country to have its press
freedom curtailed or imperilled ... yet nowhere, as far as I can
see, have the people of these countries resisted the first inroads
made against their essential freedoms.'

This Rhodesian journalist was writing in the middle of the
traumatic experience of a press censorship that he had expected
to set alarm bells ringing throughout the country, but which had
instead been greeted with public enthusiasm. But he did not
greatly exaggerate. Even in Britain which has the longest tradition
of press freedom in the world the extent of the antagonism that
had developed towards newspapers was shown in 1963 in the
popular reaction to the sending of two British reporters to prison
for refusing to disclose their sources of information to the Vassall
Tribunal, in the widespread conviction, in the words of *The Times*,
that 'whatever may have been the role of newspapers in the past
they have long since forfeited any right to confidence or respect'.

Nor, it would appear, was this feeling merely transitory; a
reflection of a particular mood at a particular time. Some three
years later, in May 1966, the House of Lords debated on the Press
and the Law following a joint report by the British Committee of
Justice, an international association of lawyers and the British
Committee of the International Press Institute which recommended reforms in the laws affecting libel and official secrets. Of
this debate the Parliamentary Correspondent of *The Times* wrote:
'The Press Gallery of the House of Lords is never a comfortable
place; the cushions are too hard, the desks too narrow. Today it
became almost uninhabitable but for quite a different reason.
From the benches below came a wave of criticism, a barrage of
contempt, a fusillade of unconcealed dislike. Their lordships were
debating the press.' Few who heard or read the debate would

challenge this description. As one who took part in it and sought to resist the majority view I certainly would not. Nor is it easy to deny the *Sunday Telegraph*'s subsequent observation that most of the debate was 'marked by a tone of animosity to the newspapers distressing in its intensity and short sightedness'. This animosity was by no means simply the reflection of the prejudices of a largely hereditary House. The most pungent critics of the press were life peers, among them two of notably progressive outlook: Baroness Gaitskell and Lord Goodman, Chairman of the Arts Council. Nor can it be doubted that they reflected the attitude of a large body of British opinion.

Regard for the press stands somewhat higher in the United States. There it is still probably true, as Henry Brandon, Chief Washington Correspondent of the *Sunday Times*, reported at the time of the Vassall Tribunal, that although public opinion is often critical of the performance of newspapers it is still anxious to see their freedoms upheld while much British public opinion no longer cares if these freedoms are curtailed and in some cases would positively like this to happen. But even in the United States there has been remarkable apathy about the growing inclination of governments to 'manage the news' and on occasion the press itself has shown a readiness to roll on its back before authority that would have shocked American editors of half a century ago. Yet without free, independent and efficient newspapers the public right to know what its rulers are up to, which is at the heart of the democratic system, will always be thwarted.

In most of what are commonly called free enterprise societies — societies politically democratic or moving towards political democracy but in which the predominant economic mode is that of private enterprise — there would seem to be four main stages of press development.

The cycle runs like this.

First there is a period of censorship and licensing. This is characteristic of early political development in all national societies whether in the eighteenth century or now. However, as society grows more fluid and new political and commercial groupings emerge such controls become more difficult to maintain. The public appetite for news increases. The demand for free expression of opinion grows. Licensing controls are resisted or circumvented.

Censorship is defied. Newspapers are started, suppressed, re-started.

In this guerrilla war between the press and authority, men of political passion and journalistic integrity often find themselves in alliance with touters of cheap gossip, place hunters, bribe takers and blackmailers. It is rare for the regiments of freedom fighters to be wholly composed of the noble. One cannot choose one's heroes. Yet although harried by law and hounded by authority the guerrillas make ground. They have public opinion behind them: they can live on the country. As their ranks extend the second stage of newspaper development begins.

At this stage governments find themselves compelled to accept an independent press as an unavoidable evil to resist which would provoke public opinion too much for comfort. But although authority withdraws from what were formerly its main positions, a series of rearguard actions are commonly fought. Licensing and censorship are abandoned but the laws of libel, sedition and contempt are mobilised in their place. To contain the newspaper forces and restrict their field of advance newspaper taxes are introduced. Any stratagem that will put newspapers beyond the reach of the mass of the people and restrict their distribution to the few is adopted. As the late A. P. Wadsworth, editor of the *Manchester Guardian*, pointed out in an admirable paper to the Manchester Statistical Society in 1955, 'Newspaper Circulations 1800–1954', much of the history of the British press in the first half of the nineteenth century derived from the conviction that 'the lower orders were not to be trusted' and that newspapers should be kept from them.

These rearguard actions commonly continue in one form or another for a considerable time. Sometimes they become part of a much wider attempt to slow down the advance of popular democracy in which the press itself becomes an ally of authority. Having achieved acceptance newspapers are often found ready to compromise their freedom for respectability and economic security. They become the propagandists of governments or political parties, or great social or economic interests in return for commercial advantage and political and social recognition. They dine at the tables of the great, but well below the salt, and bargain at side doors for honorariums fitted to their station. Robert Walpole spent £50,000 on secret hand-outs to the press in the last ten years of his administration. Regular stipends to compliant newspapers of £500 or £600 a year were regarded as a matter of course by most English administrations of that time.

However, with the growth of political literacy and commercial enterprise, this stage, too, passes. Newspapers begin to find themselves less dependent on bribes, more able to sustain themselves by sales and advertising. A time comes when, as Lord Liverpool told his Cabinet in 1815, the only newspapers that can be bought are no longer worth buying. The third stage of newspaper development has begun.

This commonly expresses itself in the emergence of a number of strong journalistic personalities: we have arrived at the age of the predominant individual. At first these predominant individuals are usually editors, or if publishers, publishers who think of themselves primarily as editors and joyfully undertake the daily chores of editorship. It is the editorial impact of newspapers that counts most at this time, the influence of the press as a public service that is considered most highly. However, as the scale of newspaper enterprise expands, talents other than editorial ones come to be required. Publishers and capitalisers take over: impresarios of journalism who dictate policy but do not themselves engage in the daily rigours of editorship. Newspapers become means to fortune and power. Both attract, but at this stage the pull of power tends to be greater than that of money.

Finally—or at least finally so far as we have yet gone—the age of the press as business arrives. The businessmen who come to the front at this stage are not to be confused with the press barons of the preceding one. To the press barons a newspaper was a weapon even more than an investment. It was the power to influence opinion that held them. The financial rewards of success in owning newspapers were important. But they came second to the sense of power. In the fourth stage they move up to first place. This is the stage to which we now seem to be moving.

It marks, or could mark, a much sharper break with the past than any preceding one: a change not only in emphasis but in purpose.

The role of the predominant individual in journalism began with Barnes of the London *Times* in the early days of the nineteenth century. It may well have ended with the death of Beaverbrook in 1964. Both were British newspapermen and, although the United States, as we shall see, has produced more than its share of great editors and maverick proprietors, it is not inappropriate that they should be. For reasons both historical and geographical the British press often tends to illuminate changes in the situation of newspapers more sharply than elsewhere. Circulations are bigger, concentrations of newspaper power greater. The newspaper industry is the only British industry to outrank the American in the size of its units and the number of its millionaires.

Yet although the two differ in many ways, the British and American press, and especially a number of their more prominent individuals, have jointly stamped a conception of journalism on the world that is still widely accepted. The question that now has to be put is whether it is still valid and still possible.

CHAPTER TWO

Barnes and Bennett And the Start of Independence

The tradition of the politically and economically independent newspaper owing allegiance to none but its readers has drawn on many sources, but two men, an Englishman and an American, have the strongest claim to being its founding fathers: Thomas Barnes of the London *Times*, James Gordon Bennett of the *New York Herald*. One took over a newspaper already commercially established, the other started his own. One was a hired man given his head by a far-seeing publisher, the other a publisher-editor who had to fight his own financial battles as well as his editorial ones. They were very different kinds of men in very different societies and their conception of journalism differed greatly. So did their practice. But they established a claim for the newspaper as an independent power—a fourth estate—which whether challenged or endorsed, seen as a call to public service or distorted to serve private ambition has coloured all subsequent thinking about the press.

Barnes was an exponent of the journalism of opinion. He directed his newspaper to men of influence, although as it happened the conditions of the age made it also the most widely circulated newspaper in the country—a national popular newspaper with a circulation superiority over its rivals far greater than that of the most successful mass circulation newspaper today.

Barnes and Bennett and the Start of Independence

Bennett was a man of the people. His aim was mass circulation. He sought the interest of the man in the street and the woman in the kitchen, and was not over-much concerned as to how he got it. His purpose was to excite, to stimulate and to entertain. He would also have liked to influence, but in this he was less successful.

In describing Barnes and Bennett as the founding fathers of independent journalism and as such still worthy of examination one must, of course, be careful not to claim too much. They did not operate in an historical vacuum. Although they gave the daily press new direction and authority they were innovators, not creators; beneficiaries of a long struggle for the right to print.

When Barnes entered *The Times* office as a young man newly down from Cambridge to serve it successively as dramatic critic, parliamentary reporter and leader writer before becoming its Editor in 1817 at the age of thirty-two, the position of the press was already well established in British society. More than a century before, Daniel Defoe had given political pamphleteering a new dimension by his political reporting and Steele and Addison had shown in the *Tatler* and the *Spectator* that periodical journalism could influence the manners of an age. Half a century before Barnes arrived at *The Times*, Junius and Wilkes had made the freedom of political comment a great issue. William Cobbett had already given the mob a voice in the *Political Register* and Perry of the *Morning Chronicle* and Stuart of the *Morning Post* had shown that it was possible for serious political journals to be commercial successes. But although Barnes stood, as all men do, on the shoulders of his predecessors he was the first to ally a newspaper to the feeling of the country irrespective of such party alliance as Perry and Stuart had depended on and to demonstrate that journalistic independence had an absolute value of its own.

He was fortunate in his period, or perhaps uniquely representative of it, as the great journalist must always be. A moderate reformer by temperament, he came to the editorial chair of *The Times* at a time when Cobbett and his *Political Register* had helped to make parliamentary reform a burning popular issue and when Cobbett's unique capacity for bringing politics alive to ordinary people had created a public avid for news and comment. The days of licensing and censorship were over, the teeth of the worst of the libel laws, so often used in the past to intimidate those papers bold enough to criticise governments, had been drawn, the freedom to report Parliament accepted. The newspaper stamp tax was, it is true, still in force. But this did not weigh so heavily on a newspaper directed, as Barnes intended *The Times* should be, to the middle classes, as it did on Cobbett's *Political Register* with its appeal to the masses. Nor did the notorious Six Acts passed in 1819, two years after he became editor of *The Times*, hamper his progress. Conceived in the haunted atmosphere of anti-Jacobinism that followed the French Revolution and provoked by the fear of popular insurrection, these Acts marked, as Professor Aspinall has said, 'the high water mark of legislation restricting the press'. But their weight fell less upon the daily newspapers than on radical pamphleteers. It was writers and publishers like Henry Hetherington with his *Poor Man's Guardian*, 'established contrary to Law to try the power of Might against Right', and Richard Carlisle, the British publisher of Thomas Paine's *Rights of Man*, who suffered— in Carlisle's case with a total of nine years' imprisonment—rather than those who owned and published daily newspapers and who were by now themselves men of property, as anti-Jacobin as the government.

Cobbett appealed to the new industrial workers and landless labourers. Barnes, less radical and more practical, set himself to capture the mercantile middle classes. As yet these classes lacked parliamentary power. But their time could not be long delayed. To Barnes who came of this class himself, they represented what was most stable and valuable in the community. To speak for their interests was to him to speak for the best interests of the whole nation.

It was also, it turned out, a highly profitable thing to do.

Barnes was a great editor. But unlike Perry and Stuart before him—and unlike James Gordon Bennett—he did not own the newspaper he edited. He was a professional journalist, an employee, the first of the great editors to be so, and as dependent as any modern editor in like position upon the goodwill of his publisher. He carved out his own policies but he was able to do so and to establish both for himself and his successors on *The Times* unquestioned editorial independence only because those policies proved not only politically influential but commercially viable.

When it had been founded thirty-two years before by John

Barnes and Bennett and the Start of Independence

Walter I, a failed Lloyds underwriter who had acquired from a London printer the patent for an improved system of typography and thought a morning journal would provide him with a shop window for it, *The Times* had eked out existence, according to the common practice of the times, by 'suppression fees', 'contradiction fees', government subsidies and payments for puffs under editors no more scrupulous in such matters than was the founder himself. But although John Walter I was a good deal of a rogue he was also an extremely shrewd man of business with the wit to recognise quicker than most the traumatic effect of the French Revolution on public opinion and the appetite it had created—as all crises do—for hard news. When he handed the paper over to his second son, John Walter II in 1803, *The Times* was already a successful journal with an excellent news service from the Continent and a more attractive typographical lay-out than most. Under John Walter II it improved in every respect, winning considerable reputation for itself twelve years before Barnes became editor by getting news of the Battle of Trafalgar to London well ahead not only of all its newspaper rivals but the government couriers.

Not yet a great paper, it was already a considerable one; its position firmly based on good management and sound commercial principles; rejecting, under the son, the government subsidies the father had so eagerly canvassed, although it remained a supporter of the Addington Ministry. But John Walter II was neither a journalist nor a politician. He was a businessman and a printer and having found in Barnes an editor he could trust he gave him his confidence and from the start a considerable degree of editorial discretion. This with success developed into an acceptance of the editor's primacy on all issues of public policy, establishing a publisher-editor relationship that was to become a settled *Times* tradition. This independence, both of the editor in relation to the management and of the paper in relation to political parties, developed out of, and was conditional on, commercial profitability. If Barnes's policy had brought financial loss he could scarcely have kept his job, still less his editorial independence. The impact *The Times* was able to make on its age was the reward of commercial success.

Barnes was helped by journalistic good fortune. Three years after he became editor, poor mad George III died, to be succeeded by the Prince Regent who at once made himself the centre of immense public controversy by repudiating his wife, Queen Caroline, and seeking by Act of Parliament to dissolve their marriage and deprive her of her royal position. It was an issue that split the country. On the surface *The Times*'s interests were the King's. Its readers lay mainly among politicians and members of the court circle. Its most solid subscribers were on the King's side. Cobbett had rushed to defend the Queen. But Cobbett was a radical and a troublemaker, contemptuous of the aristocracy and the financial interests. He had nothing to lose. *The Times* had.

Barnes lacked Cobbett's intuitive understanding of mass opinion. But he felt as a good many of the middle classes felt and when it became plain to him that a great body of ordinary middle opinion shared his sympathy for the Queen he made *The Times* her chief champion. In so doing he placed it in jeopardy with its court connections but tapped a whole new reading public. Within a few weeks its circulation had doubled from 7,000 to 14,000 a day. Moreover by putting *The Times* on what proved to be the winning side in this matter over the Queen, Barnes did much more than simply increase its circulation. He made it a rallying point for anti-Ministerial feeling throughout the country and took the first step towards fulfilling his ambition to turn it into the chief spokesman of the middle classes. Even before the Queen Caroline case he had gone a good way to put it at the head of the movement for political reform. It was the first newspaper to publish a full account of the massacre of Peterloo when cavalry with drawn sabres charged a peaceful demonstration of 80,000 people in St Peter's Field in Manchester. Its reporter, Mr Tyas, was where all good reporters should be, at the very centre of affairs, standing on the platform beside 'Orator' Hunt when the cavalry charged. He was arrested along with Hunt but managed to talk himself out of the hands of the military in good time to send off his report.

Barnes was a journalist of opinion. He taught, urged and thundered their duty to the new middle classes until, as the *History of The Times* justly records, 'they recognised themselves as the largest and most coherent body in the State'. But although he made *The Times* into a national institution he did so by never forgetting that it was a newspaper. He was a skilled organiser of news and one of the most able supervisors of every section of his paper journalism has ever known. Although he made *The Times* famous for its views, its strength and circulation derived in the first place from the comprehensiveness of its news service and the quality and uniqueness of its sources of information. He did not so much seek to form public opinion—although he did much to do so —as to discover and express it.

He believed that a newspaper should draw its authority not from the opinions and ambitions of any one man or group of men, but from its representative character. For this reason he freed *The Times* of all party alliances, expressing in resolute practice throughout his editorial life the principles later enunciated in a famous *Times* leader by his successor, Delane: 'We cannot admit that a newspaper's purpose is to share the labours of statesmanship or that it is bound by the same duties, the same liabilities, as that of Ministers of the Crown. The purpose and duties of the two powers are constantly separate, generally independent, sometimes diametrically opposite. The dignity and freedom of the press are trammelled from the moment it accepts an ancillary position. To perform its duties with entire independence and consequently with the utmost public advantage the press can enter into no close or binding alliance with the statesmen of the day, nor can it surrender its permanent interests to the convenience of the ephemeral power of any government.'

The rewards in influence, circulation and advertising revenue were so great as soon to still any doubts felt by John Walter II, who like his father, although less subserviently so, had originally conceived of the paper as supporting the government. When Barnes became editor *The Times* was still publishing only four small pages a day as it had when founded thirty-two years previously as the *Daily Universal Register* by John Walter I. When Barnes died in 1841 it was regularly publishing an issue of eight large pages, swollen three or four times a week by advertising supplements of the same size and had a circulation twice as great as that of any other three newspapers combined. On the foundations he built it achieved under his successor, Delane, a circulation nearly three times as great as all the rest of the British press put together. For close on forty years the history of the press in Britain is for all practical purposes the history of this one newspaper.

The achievement belonged to Barnes and then to Delane. But

it could not have been won in such measure without the strongest commercial support. Barnes made *The Times* the most powerful political force in the country. John Walter II made it the most businesslike and mechanically advanced newspaper in the world. It was the first to introduce steam printing, without which, indeed, it would have been impossible to meet the circulation demands Barnes' editorial genius created, and the first to use a rotary press—invented for it in its own works by Ambrose Applegarth. John Walter II put it in the lead in all publishing techniques and ahead of all others in the exploitation of advertising possibilities. As always in the newspaper industry the combination of great editor and superb businessman proved irresistible. Yet there is no evidence that the two men were ever personally close or that either John Walter II or John Walter III who succeeeded him in 1847 were much attached to Barnes' memory or appreciated what he had done for them and for journalism.

Barnes lived wholly for *The Times*. He was never a dining Editor like his successor, Delane, who although he declared himself 'to have the bad taste not to greatly admire the society of Dukes and Duchesses', put up with their company a good deal and rarely missed a fashionable occasion. Barnes had no liking for such things. He lived a quiet domestic life with an affectionate mistress and occasionally entertained a few friends of whom Leigh Hunt was the closest. But most of his life was spent in Printing House Square. He did not seek out the rich or powerful. He was confident that those whose information or judgment he valued would seek him out in his own office. He supervised every department of his paper, wrote or shaped every leading article in it, sought no satisfaction other than it gave, wanted no personal fame. He edited *The Times* for just on a quarter of a century, but the only time his name appeared in it was on the occasion of his death. A two line obituary notice announced the event in the Births, Marriages and Deaths column. It did not mention that he had any connection with the paper.

A very different man in a very different society began the tradition of independent journalism on the other side of the Atlantic.

James Gordon Bennett emigrated from Scotland to Canada as a youth. He had a succession of odd jobs in Halifax, Nova Scotia and in Boston where he went at the age of twenty-four but none of them did much more than keep him just above the starvation line although they taught him to feel for the underdog and hate those whom he called the money men. Finally after several badly paid jobs on the fringe of publishing he landed a job as a newspaper reporter in Charleston. From there he progressed to a New York Sunday scandal sheet, the *Courier*. Here he made a sufficient reputation for himself with a series of articles on business sharp practice to be offered a post on James Watson Well's *Enquirer* when that paper found itself with a vacancy by reason of the killing of its Associate Editor in a duel. When the *Enquirer* and *Courier* were merged a little later Bennett went off to Washington as the new paper's Washington Correspondent—one of the first in American journalism.

He was a vivid writer with a penetrating eye for the follies of polititicians and a talent for the small revealing detail in descriptive reporting and he did well. But he had a conscience. When the *Courier* and *Enquirer* which had supported Jackson and the Democrats switched to the Whigs, persuaded to do so according to Bennett by a bribe from the Bank of the United States, he found this more than he could stomach. He resigned and went to Philadelphia to run a pro-Jackson party newspaper there. However, the constraints of party journalism proved uncongenial and he soon threw up the Philadelphia job and returned to New York. There with five hundred dollars as capital he rented a basement in Wall Street. With a broken-down press, some decrepit type and a plank laid across two empty flour barrels for an editorial desk he set himself up as a newspaper publisher.

On a May morning in 1835 the *New York Herald*, price one penny, was born. Its principles Bennett set out in a prospectus on the second page: 'Our only guide shall be good sound practical commonsense, applicable to the business and bosoms of men engaged in everyday life. We shall support no party, be the organ of no faction or *coterie* and care nothing for any election or any candidate from President down to constable. We shall endeavour to record facts on every public and proper subject, stripped of verbiage and colouring with comments suitable, just, independent, fearless and good-tempered . . .'

Bennett's *Herald* was not the first popular daily in America any more than Barnes' *Times* was the first for an educated public in England. It had already been preceded by the publication of a compositor from Springfield, Massachusetts, named Ben Day, who two years before had started a four page penny daily with a page size only eight inches by ten which he called the *Sun*. Day made a startling success out of reporting in a quick staccato way all the fires, burglaries, suicides and court cases in New York with humorous, dramatic and pathetic anecdotes to add depth to the product which was then sold by newsboys on trains, steam boats and in the street. But although Day exploited the popular market ahead of him, Bennett's was the first paper in American history to run up the flag of absolute political independence and nail it firmly to the masthead. Bennett kept it there as stubbornly as Barnes kept the flag of independence flying at *The Times*.

Like Barnes, Bennett had a specific public in mind, although a very different one. Barnes had recognised the growing importance in British society of the middle classes to which he himself belonged and in return for a newspaper that spoke for their interest and gave them the political and commercial news they needed they gave him influence on the grand scale. Bennett saw the growing significance in American society of the teeming, poverty stricken, immigrant masses of the cities, the have-nots of whom his own youthful struggles had made him feel himself a part. He gave them a newspaper they could afford to buy, written in a language they could understand, about the things that interested them. They could not give him political influence in return, for, unlike the middle classes in Britain for whom Barnes catered, their time was not yet, but they gave him immense journalistic success and a circulation greater than that of any previous American newspaper, although the *Sun* came near to it, and far, far greater than any English one. Within fifteen months of its first issue from the basement in Wall Street, the *New York Herald* was selling between thirty and forty thousand copies a day.

No less than Barnes, Bennett was, of course, the inheritor of a long struggle for the right to publish. The journalism into which his *Herald* erupted was still partisan and vituperative. It had its roots in colonialism and the reaction from colonialism.

The first American newspaper had been published in Boston in 1690 by a radical bookseller named Benjamin Harris. It was suppressed by the Governor of Massachusetts after one issue.

Barnes and Bennett and the Start of Independence

There was no successor until the opening of the new century. This time what was produced was safe, cautious and official, fit provender for governors and governed. It was the brain child of a Scottish bookseller named Campbell who had a contract as Postmaster of Boston under the new postal law passed to improve colonial communications. His *Boston News Letter* modelled on the *London Gazette* and published 'Under Authority' appeared in April 1704. He distributed it to subscribers weekly through the postal service and paid no mailing fee on the grounds that it was a public service. When in due course the Boston postmastership went to another, Campbell took his newspaper with him. The new Postmaster started his own, the *Boston Gazette*, and had it printed by James Franklin, older brother of Benjamin. When yet another change of Postmasters lost Franklin the printing contract he started a paper of his own, the *New England Courant*, thus becoming the first independent editor-publisher in the colony.

The pattern set in Boston was copied elsewhere. Well placed to hear what was going on and to supplement it from overseas newspapers and other unsealed correspondence, postmasters became the parents of American journalism. When they lost their postmasterships their printers took over their papers or started new ones. By 1740 Newport, New York, Philadelphia, Annapolis, Williamsburg and Charleston had all followed Boston. The newspapers produced by the postmasters stuck for the most part, as one would expect, to what colonial officialdom approved. The printers' papers—notably those published by the two Franklin brothers—took a more independent line, providing a forum for the younger dissident elements in the colony who wrote for them under innumerable pseudonyms—Timothy Turnstone, Tom Penshallow, Ichabod Henroost, Silence Dogood (Benjamin Franklin's first pen name) and the like. If one paper was closed down, its contributors took themselves and their pseudonyms to another.

From the seaports and provincial capitals the press spread inland with the tide of colonial settlement. Every itinerant printer carried a newspaper in his knapsack. Such newspapers were not long in reflecting the mounting popular temper that was to erupt in the War of Independence. To voice such discontents had political dangers for a printer. But it had its commercial advantages

The Right to Know

too. It allied him with the most active and prosperous classes in the community, increasingly hampered in their enterprises by the stiff restrictionism of colonial bureaucracy and the obscurantism of imperial power. To these classes the newspaper was important as a source of news and also a medium for commercial advertisement. Their interests and those of the printer coincided. Moreover if the worst came to the worst and authority struck at him the printer could always hope for an independent minded jury like that which tried John Peter Zenger, publisher of the *New York Weekly Journal*.

Zenger was charged with criminal libel on the order of an unpopular Governor, William Crosby, whose administrative incapacity and personal extravagancies the *Weekly Journal* had exposed. The paper, however, was backed by substantial merchants and landowners, well able to afford the services of a lawyer to defend their printer when he was arrested. They chose a noted liberal lawyer, Andrew Hamilton, of Philadelphia, then in his eighties. Contemptuously brushing aside the letter of the law by which Zenger, as the admitted publisher of lampoons against officials, was undeniably guilty, Hamilton appealed to the jurors not to be browbeaten by legal authority, which appeared before them in the person of a youthful crony Crosby had appointed Chief Justice over the protests of the New York Bar. Their duty, he cried, was to serve the cause of Liberty. 'I make no doubt,' he told them, 'that your upright conduct this day will not only entitle you to the love and esteem of your fellow-citizens but every man who prefers freedom to a life of slavery will bless and honour you as men who have baffled the attempt of tyranny and by an impartial and uncorrupt verdict have laid a noble foundation for securing to ourselves, our posterity and our neighbours, that to which nature and the laws of our country have given us a right—the liberty both of exposing and opposing arbitrary power (in these parts of the world at least) by speaking and writing—truth.' The jury were proud to accept his invitation. They found Zenger not guilty. By their verdict they not only demonstrated the limitations of unpopular colonial power which much as it might seek to subvert the jury system dared not abolish it, but also encouraged newspapers everywhere to be bolder and juries to support them when they were.

It was not an atmosphere to encourage moderate opinion or

Barnes and Bennett and the Start of Independence

objective reporting. Newspapers were instruments of war, as yet undeclared but soon to become open. Their belligerence was sharpened by the Stamp Act. Imposed from London this put a tax of a halfpenny per 'half sheet' on all publications and not only provided one more flagrant example of taxation without representation, but brought into alliance with the anti-colonial commercial interests even the most cautious of newspaper publishers and printers. Such men previously hesitated to put official printing contracts at risk by too open a support for anti-British sentiments. With their livelihoods threatened, they became bolder.

Some newspapers were forced to close but others, giving as many public farewells as prima-donnas, published a succession of last numbers edged with black and denounced their official murderers in each. Others openly defied the new law and continued to come out on unstamped paper. All helped to create so great a furore about press freedom as to make it for the first time a positive political issue stirring strong public emotions. In such an atmosphere newspapers inevitably became more violent in language and more propagandist in intent as their printers and publishers moved closer to the centre of insurrection. It was in a back room of the *Boston Gazette*, dubbed 'Monday's Dung Barge' by a royalist editor, that the Boston Tea Party is reported to have been planned.

There was even less place for objectivity and moderation when the war of words became a war of arms. Where the British ruled, patriot papers were closed down and their editors arrested or forced to fly; where the patriots were in control the offices of Tory newspapers were mobbed and their editors burnt in effigy.

There were thirty-seven newspapers in the American colonies when the War of Independence started. Seventeen were forced out of existence almost at once. But thirty-three new ones took their place and although only fifteen of these survived, the total at the end of the war was not appreciably different from that at the beginning. The press had taken root. Its importance was recognised in the constitutions of nine states which by guaranteeing its freedom prepared the way for the first amendment to the Constitution of the United States itself whereby Congress was restrained from in any way 'abridging the freedom of speech or of the press'.

Newspapers had played a formidable and vehement part in bringing the Revolution to success. They had mobilised and unified public opinion. Now they were turned into battlefields of warring ideas on the future of the country, becoming in the process less and less adjuncts of the postmaster's office or the jobbing printer's shop and more and more platforms for men who thought of themselves as journalists and shapers of opinion; usually passionately so. In the clash of ideas and interests that inevitably accompanied the birth of the republic the press had a powerful and pervasive role. So did it in the growth of a society on the move, for, as Professor Weisberger has written in his excellent historical study *The American Newspaperman*, it was 'part of this growth, responding to it and nurturing it. The newspaper, being a form of social communication, went wherever society was going, to the very limits of settlement. . . .' Above all, the era of the Revolution made the newspaper a forum of political controversy. The newspaperman was no longer primarily a printer but an editor, the publicity arm of a political faction in the process of crystallising into party. The best known journals from 1789 to 1816 were partisan organs— more partisan at this time than party. As Weisberger says, for a time they 'gave the United States the nearest thing it ever had to a journalism of political debate. And if the debate was often muddied by insult it was nonetheless conducted often enough with literary grace and intellectual boldness.'

That it should be so conducted was natural. Men such as Thomas Jefferson and Alexander Hamilton, James Madison and John Adams were engaged in it, glad to use the newspapers in their struggle for the minds and souls of their fellow-countrymen: Hamilton and Adams through the *Gazette of the United States* which Hamilton established to be the organ of the Federalists, Jefferson and Madison through the *National Gazette* which they founded to further the Republican cause.

The issues that were debated were great ones on which men felt passionately, for they concerned the basic principles of the Revolution and were to set the mould of American politics for the future.

It has been justly said that the constitution framed at Philadelphia in May 1787 was the greatest ever struck from the hand of man. But it concealed rather than illuminated the real nature of the internal struggle. For the most part the leaders of the Revolution were not revolutionaries and certainly not egalitarians. Yet it generated a revolutionary dynamism of its own in spite of them.

Barnes and Bennett and the Start of Independence

Depending on the people and owing victory to them it gave birth to aspirations directly opposed to the aristocratic conservatism of Washington, Hamilton and the Federalists. Their chief desire was to establish a system of society and government that should be as nearly as possible an independent American replica of that of England. To Jefferson and those who thought as he did this was to betray the Revolution and dishonour the Declaration of Independence of which he had been principal draughtsman.

Washington's first Cabinet was thus a congeries of disparate philosophies held together only by the need to avoid a disintegration into factionalism that might place the whole of the new political order at risk. Under a different constitution the clash of principle among ministers might have been carried to the legislative assembly. From the debates of legislators empowered by their votes to select the head of government and determine the broad pattern of government policy a workable pattern of party might have evolved. But by constitutional design the President was independent of the legislature and his Ministers were no more than his personal advisers, neither members of nor with a voice in the legislative assembly as was the case, for example, in the British parliamentary system. Because the President's authority derived directly from the States, and through them from the people, the functional logic of the new Constitution itself required that policy arguments should be carried to the electorate—to the people themselves.

In these circumstances it was natural that both sides in the great debate should turn to the press which, during the war and the years that led up to it, had been firmly established as a forum for public opinion. It was natural also that called upon to take so leading a part in so great a debate the press should become more, not less, partisan, for what was involved were the deepest emotions and moderation seemed like treachery.

Naturally the debate had its compromises—all political debates do. It was affected, as it could not help but be, by the federal system and by the existence of opposing interests within and between the States that transcended political ideologies. Moreover, both Federalists and Republicans had their right and left wings so that Hamilton and Henry Adams intrigued against each other no less virulently than both did against Jefferson and Madison. It was

Adams, not Jefferson, who destroyed the Hamiltonian dreams of empire when he had the good sense to avoid war with France after becoming President despite Hamilton's opposition in 1789. And when Jefferson defeated Adams three years later the great Republican's inaugural speech as President won more approval from Hamilton than it did from his own left wing.

Nevertheless, despite the leavening effect of office on extreme opinions the debate between the two sides was intense and fundamental. Although often, as Professor Weisberger has said, conducted with great nobility, vitriol was sometimes more in evidence than nobility at the lower levels of press debate. Even the President did not escape its sting. 'If ever a nation was debauched by a man, the American nation has been debauched by Washington,' wrote Benjamin Franklin Bache, grandson of Benjamin Franklin, in the *Aurora*. 'If ever a nation has suffered from the improper influence of a man the American nation has suffered from the influence of Washington. If ever a nation was deceived by a man the American nation was deceived by Washington.'

Nor were the other early Presidents more fortunate. Adams was subjected to a tirade of newspaper abuse greater even than Washington had had to bear and reacted to it less philosophically. With the public hysteria arising from the expectation of war with France to help he introduced in the Alien and Sedition Acts penalties of up to two years' imprisonment for 'false, scandalous and malicious writing' against the President, Government or either House of Congress, tending to bring them into 'contempt or disrepute' or excite against them 'the hatred of the good people of the United States'. As for Jefferson, despite advocacy of press freedom on many occasions and his often quoted declamation that 'were it left to me to decide whether we should have a Government without newspapers or newspapers without Government, I should not hesitate a moment to prefer the latter' (although he did add the proviso, often forgotten: 'provided every man should receive those papers and be capable of reading them'), he was forced to initiate two prosecutions for seditious libel against editors during his Presidency. At its close he could only take comfort from the thought that the 'great experiment' of press freedom had shown that an administration 'conducting itself with integrity and commonsense could not be destroyed even by the falsehoods of a licentious press'.

Barnes and Bennett and the Start of Independence

As the country expanded so did the press. Wherever new communities established themselves newspapers were born. By 1830 the 35 newspapers that existed in 1781 when the British surrendered at Yorktown had grown to at least 700, 65 of which were dailies. Moreover most of these new publications were much more specifically newspapers than their forerunners. New or growing communities needed news. The commercial interests to which the newspapers turned for advertising revenue, and often for their initial finance, needed it for business reasons. Ordinary readers, proud of the new townships they were building and avid for gossip of their neighbours, needed it too. These new newspapers were the official boosters and public relations officers of their communities, publicising without cessation the opportunities they offered compared with less forward towns. And they were also the propagandists of particular groups determined to see to it that civic authority should rest with those that backed them.

As partisanship solidified into party, it was natural that these local journals should become party sheets, elements in the organisation and mobilisation of voters and the management of political affairs. The decentralisation of the American political system, the constant run of State, county and local elections, the dependence upon popular votes to fill administrative offices from the highest to the lowest, all helped to shape the newspapers' role.

Similarly in Washington, the political capital, and New York, the commercial capital, party newspapers became accepted institutions. These newspapers were not more nor less partisan than those in the earlier days of the Republic. But they had a different character. Although often subsidised, the journals through which Jefferson, Hamilton and their followers conducted their controversies were edited by men of principle who could not be bought and sold. Their language might often be violent, but they were concerned with the most fundamental issues of political philosophy. Written for the propagation of ideas among the few they were almost irrelevant in terms of mass communication for which the only real instrument available at that time was the post office. It was by the distribution of private correspondence through the mails, not by the influence of a party press, that Jefferson won victory for the Republicans in the 'political revolution' of 1804.

By 1825, however, this victory had had its effects on the organisation of both politics and propaganda. With the arrival at the White House of General Andrew Jackson, the first President not to have graduated from Harvard, Princeton or William and Mary, popular party politics had arrived. So also had a party press.

Aiming at a far larger and less literate audience than had the protagonists of the original great debate, this party press was more concerned to produce slogans and catchwords for the multitude than philosophic essays for the few. Its purpose was practical not theoretical, the winning of votes rather than of minds, and it did much to win votes for Jackson.

Jackson did not hide his gratitude. Nor was he niggling in rewards. They provoked from John Quincey Adams, his defeated predecessor in the White House, the bitter but not unjust observation that 'the appointments, almost without exception are conferred upon the vilest purveyors of slander during the last electioneering campaign and an excessive disproportion of places is given to editors of the foulest press ... every editor of a scurrilous and slanderous newspaper is provided for.' Jackson's reliance on the press did not end with victory. No sooner was he installed in the White House than he summoned his chief newspaper aides, Francis P. Blair and Amos Kendall of the *Kentucky Argus of the Western World* and Isaac Hill of the *New Hampshire Patriot* to serve along with Blair's partner, John C. Rives, in his Kitchen Cabinet. A $50,000 a year contract for Congressional and Departmental printing was arranged to provide Blair with the money to launch a new journal, the *Washington Globe*, as the Administration's mouthpiece.

It was into this world of extreme party journalism that Bennett broke with his *New York Herald*. It may be that the independent tone of the *Herald* was due as much to Bennett's liking for being his own man as to high-minded idealism. But despite, or perhaps because of, his brash egotism, he proved as durable a defender of the principle of press freedom as did the more sober Barnes.

He could not have succeeded in being so unless he had possessed a similar flair for news, although of a different order. The news values that guided him were no more like those that moved Barnes than the teeming multitudes of city have-nots who were his readers were like the solid commercial middle classes making their slow way up the hierarchical ladder of British society for whom

Barnes wrote. But both men were alike in their newspaper professionalism and it was this professionalism, aided by the new
printing methods that were opening the way to mass circulation,
that brought them their success. Both helped to shape their
societies. But they did so by working with the grain, never against
it. They gave their publics what they wanted. Their genius
lay in their ability to perceive these wants before the public
itself did.

Bennett was not, as already said, the first to perceive the immense
potentialities for a cheap popular daily paper offered by the
teeming immigrant population of New York. But although he
copied Day and his *Sun* he went further than he did and he was
more independent and more professional. Early on he published
in the *Herald* an outline of his habits of work, for he always
believed in taking his readers into his confidence, especially if he
could do so to the detriment of his rivals.

'We do not as the Wall Street lazy editors do,' he told them,
'come down to our office about ten or twelve o'clock, pull out a
Spanish cigar, take a pair of scissors, puff and cut, cut and puff for
a couple of hours and then adjourn to Delmonico's to eat, drink,
gourmandise and blow up our contemporaries. We rise in the morning at five o'clock, write our leading editorials, squibs, sketches, etc.
before breakfast. From nine till one we read all our papers and
original contributions, the latter being more numerous than those
of any other office in New York. From these we pick out facts,
thoughts, hints and incidents sufficient to make up a column of
orginal spicy articles. We also give audience to visitors, gentlemen
on business and some of the loveliest ladies in New York who call
to subscribe—Heaven bless them! At one we sally out among the
gentlemen and loafers of Wall Street—find out the state of the
money market, return, finish the next day's paper—close every
piece of business requiring thought, sentiment, feeling or philosophy, before four o'clock. We dine moderately and temperately,
read our proofs, take in cash on advertisements, which are increasing like smoke, and close the day by going to bed at ten o'clock,
seldom later. That's the way to conduct a paper with spirit and
success.'

His territory was the city of New York: over-crowded, pulsating
with life and incident, with crime, corruption, poverty and success,

constantly expanding as the immigrants from the old world filed in off every boat, avid for freedom in the land of opportunity. He gave them the news of New York in all its rawness and variety. 'If any man were to ask me what I would suppose to be a perfect style of language,' Daniel Defoe had written in London more than a century before, 'I would answer that in which a man speaking to five hundred people all of common and various capacities should be understood by them all.' Except that he thought not of five hundred but five thousand and very soon fifty thousand, Bennett wrote for his readers in language of which Defoe would have approved: blunt, unvarnished, racy, contemptuous of generalities and always conscious of the value of detail.

Courtrooms, hospitals, fires, accidents, the city jails and precinct houses, political rallies, the gossip of the theatres, religious revival meetings, Wall Street and the business centres, gave him his material. As his paper prospered he took on a staff of reporters to cover the city, each with a regular news beat. But although local news was his stand-by, his conception of news was much wider than even New York with all its tumultuous variety could give. He was ahead of all others in organising fast packets to intercept off Sandy Hook ships bringing dispatches from Europe and in 1838, three years after launching the *Herald*, set sail for Europe himself, there to organise a six-man team to cover European news for him, the first time an American newspaper had opened a foreign bureau. He was the first man, also, to organise a Washington News Bureau and arrange for his staff regularly to cover sessions of Congress and the first to appoint staff men right across the country, supplementing their work by that of special reporters sent wherever big news broke, from the Californian gold fields to Mexico, from the Canadian north to South America.

When the electric telegraph arrived to speed communications he became its biggest client in America. Helped by a managing editor, Frederick Hudson, who joined him in his teens and was as hungry for news as he was himself—it was said of Hudson that 'The whole world was to him a Reporter's district and all human mutations plain matters of news'—he scoured New York, the United States, Europe and the world for anything that would interest his readers. Bennett sensed the possibility of civil war long before any of his contemporaries and set to work to organise

28

news from the South well in advance of hostilities. Wherever anything happened a *Herald* man was on the spot.

But he also put into his paper the political essays, the commercial advice, the literary and dramatic criticism on which more specialised publications had previously depended. The *Herald* was a great compendium. It could well have adopted, and with better right, the publicity slogan used more than a century later by the London *News of the World*: 'All human life is here.'

News and features were flanked by opinion no less spicy, crisp and to the point. Bennett was in thrall to no man or party. He said what he felt about anything and everything and said it in no less blunt a way than he had taught his reporters to report. He had a talent for invective and picked his victims as he pleased, irrespective of party. Denounced and derided by churches, political institutions and newspaper rivals, he thrived under every attack. His conception of the power of a newspaper was boundless. 'What,' he asked, 'is to prevent a daily newspaper from being made the greatest organ of social life? Books have had their day—the theatres have had their day—the temple of religion has had its day. A newspaper can be made to take the lead of all these in the great movements of human thought and of human civilisation.' He liked to flatter himself that 'a newspaper can send more souls to Heaven and save more from Hell than all the churches or chapels in New York—besides making money at the same time.'

His ambition, he said, was 'to make the newspaper press the great organ and pivot of government, society, commerce, finance, religion and all human civilisation'. It was an excessive ambition but not a mean one. Instead he finished up rich, self-willed, megalomaniacal, spoiled as many who came after him in the same trade were to be, by the money he had once despised and the personal notoriety he had always coveted.

To Barnes, Bennett must have seemed, if he ever thought of him, a brash and vulgar upstart. To Bennett, Barnes, if he ever thought of him, must have looked a grey, anonymous figure, not his sort of fellow at all. But between the two of them they set newspapers on a new course. They gave them independence.

CHAPTER THREE

Swelling Tide of Freedom

The journalism of Barnes and Bennett had large consequences on the press of their own countries and the world. But it took time.

Before *The Times* could become a pattern for serious independent journalism across the world the political conditions indispensable to journalistic independence had to exist.

Before popular journalism on the *New York Herald* model could succeed, the social and economic conditions favourable to the rise of a mass circulation press were necessary.

In neither instance was this at first the case. Nowhere outside the United States, for example, could be found the combination of political freedom and mass population that made New York journalism possible. Not until thirty years later did the first popular daily on the Continent arrive, *Le Figaro* of Paris, and even in Britain it was not until the last of the stamp taxes had been removed in 1855 that the American popular newspaper revolution began to have an impact. Even then its influence was at first small. Traces of it were to be found in what *The Times* was pleased to think of as the 'yellow journalism' of the *Daily Telegraph*, but it did not really amount to much: somewhat larger headlines than had been usual, a more dashing and colloquial style, a greater readiness to go beyond plain facts, that was about it. The fact was that although the *Telegraph* called itself a paper for 'the millions', Britain was much too class ridden for such a thing to be possible. Only the Sunday newspapers, and especially those like *Lloyds Weekly News*, the *News of the World* and *Reynolds's News* which dated from the cut in the stamp tax to a penny in 1836, had a chance of reaching a mass market. These were the true descendants of the early news-sheets with their executions and horrid murders and of the radical pamphleteers with their unlicensed attacks on authority. They spoke in much the same mixture of sensationalism and radicalism as did Bennett and his competitors on the other side of the Atlantic. The fortunate conjunction of the Jack the Ripper murders and its installation of the first American Hoe rotary printing press in Britain made *Lloyds Weekly News* the first newspaper in the world to reach a million circulation.

If popular newspapers had to wait on events, so did independent serious journalism. The international impact of *The Times* was at first no larger than that of the *New York Herald*. It was admired in liberal circles on the Continent, but could not be emulated because the political and economic conditions necessary were lacking.

There were, of course, many newspapers on the Continent appealing to an educated public. In this respect Britain had started late. Two centuries before Barnes became editor of *The Times* the *Frankfurter Journal*, the first genuine newspaper in the world, offered the commercial and educated classes of Germany a regular weekly service of serious news. The *Frankfurter Postzeitung* appeared the following year and the *Magdeburgische Zeitung*, which survived until 1955, ten years later. The first daily newspaper in the world, the *Leipziger Zeitung*, was also German. It made its appearance in 1660.

Nor, although the German press led, were others far behind. France had the weekly *Gazette de France* in 1631 — although it did not get its first daily, the *Journal de Paris*, until nearly a century and a half later. The first newspaper in Spain, the *Gazeta* of Barcelona, was published in 1641. In Sweden, the *Ordinarie Post-Tidende* of Stockholm appeared in 1643, and in Holland, the *Courant* of Haarlem, in 1656. The *Weiner Zeitung* of Vienna, the oldest surviving newspaper in the world, its long record of continuous publication interrupted only by the Nazi occupation of Austria, appeared more than eighty years before John Walter I founded *The Times*. The *Der Hamburgische Correspondent* of Hamburg, the first paper in the world to have a resident foreign correspondent (a French refugee journalist in London), started publication seventy years before *The Times* began. So also did the Italian *Diario di Roma*.

By the time *The Times* appeared even Russia had had newspapers for more than three quarters of a century, led by the *Vedomost*, which Peter the Great ordered to be published to report Russia's war on Sweden. (China had been several centuries ahead of everyone with *Yi Chau* a regular news-sheet first published in the eighth century A.D.) Denmark had known newspapers since 1666 starting with the *Den Danske Mercurius* of Copenhagen and followed, three decades before *The Times* appeared, by the *Berlingske Tidende*, still in active publication and still in the possession of the family that founded it. Thirty-seven years before Barnes became editor of *The Times* the *Zürcher Zeitung* of Zurich had already, although at first only as a weekly, started on a career that was to make it one of the great informational newspapers of the world—helped thereto, ironically enough, by a censorship that prohibited publication of local Swiss news and compelled it to specialise from the start in the reporting and interpretation of foreign news: a function it carried out brilliantly under an editor recommended to its owner, Johann Henrich Füsili, the son of the great historian, by Johann Strauss. 'It will not,' it announced modestly in its first number, 'be possible for us, any more than for other writers of newspapers, to announce world events before their occurrence or even before foreign newspapers have reported them. But we have made arrangements with the best French, English, Italian, Dutch and German newspapers and with reliable private correspondents in order always to receive and publish news as early as any other of our neighbours do.'

In making *The Times* a vehicle for the serious world-wide information required by a commercial people Barnes did no more than was being done by many newspapers on the Continent and had already been done in Britain itself by Perry's *Chronicle* and Stuart's *Morning Post*. What was new was his complete political independence. His equivalents on the Continent were for the most part either unable, like the *Zürcher Zeitung*, to exercise direct political influence on affairs in their own countries because of domestic censorship or had, like the *Berlingske Tidende*, to submit to a good deal of government interference, including interference

with editorial appointments, in return for official news and advertisements and for the right to use the mails.

Over most of the Continent newspapers were compelled either
to keep away from domestic politics or faithfully to reflect what
their governments wanted them to say. Independence as Barnes
understood it did not begin to take root to any significant degree
until some twenty years after his death.

Even in Britain itself *The Times* remained at first an isolated
phenomenon. Under Barnes and Delane it imposed an image of
journalism so firmly on the educated classes that even today many
think of what was, in truth, the product of a unique marriage of
men and circumstance in the first half of the nineteenth century
as the journalistic norm and everything that differs from it as a
fall from grace. But even in its own country *The Times* was more
admired than copied. It was a great oak in whose shadow nothing
else prospered. For nearly four decades it monopolised so large a
share of the market for daily newspapers—accounting by 1850 for
some eighty per cent of the daily newspaper circulation in the
country—that not enough standing room was left for anyone else.
It was a model of what could be, not an exemplar for others.

Try as they would, the *Morning Post*, the *Morning Chronicle*,
the *Morning Herald*, the *Morning Advertiser* and, later, the *Daily
News* could not challenge it either in influence or circulation. Only
two of them, the *Morning Advertiser* (trade paper of the licensed
victuallers) and the *Daily News*, sold as many as 5,000 copies a
day, the rest not much more than half that, at a time when *The
Times*'s circulation was over 60,000. None could rival its command
of information of the most confidential character. 'The degree
of information possessed by *The Times* with regard to the most
secret affairs of State,' wrote Lord John Russell to Queen Victoria
in 1854, 'is mortifying, humiliating and incomprehensible.'

Not only was Barnes the initiator of truly independent political
daily newspaper journalism but during the first half of the nineteenth century he and Delane alone sustained this tradition. It was
a specifically middle class one. Although Barnes held that 'a
newspaper is not an organ through which the Government could
influence the people but an organ through which the people could
influence the Government', his idea of the people did not go much
beyond that of the commercial and property owning classes. He

would have considered the mid-twentieth century slogan 'Top people read *The Times*' vulgar. But he would not have disagreed with it as a statement of fact.

The exercise by one newspaper of so unique an influence would have been impossible in a more democratic, less oligarchic society. It was because the government of Britain was still in the hands of a small, ingrown and largely self perpetuating group, all of whom could be reached by one newspaper and for the most part read no other, that *The Times* was what it was. This, too, was the reason for the paper's command of the most confidential information. In the coalition of interests that governed the country there were always those anxious to pass information to *The Times* in the hope of forwarding their own interests or blocking those of others. Where government by log-rolling prevails, secrets are seldom kept. When politics coalesced into parties and mutual self-preservation replaced the pleasure of dishing a colleague, the ability of *The Times* to disclose cabinet secrets sharply declined.

The near monopoly of *The Times* was, in any event, running contrary to the grain of an expanding society by this time. It had helped to give the middle and commercial classes a voice but as they consolidated their position they outgrew its tutelage and were ready to join with the old oligarchy in toppling it from its eminence.

To do so required the end of the newspaper tax, for so long as this existed *The Times* by reason of its dominating position in circulation and advertising had a built-in advantage over all rivals. What was a liability to most was to *The Times*, with its country-wide subscription sales, a positive asset, for stamped newspapers were carried free through the post. Provincial morning newspapers, compelled by the tax to sell at about the same price although they neither used nor needed to use the mails to the same degree, could not match its twelve or sixteen pages daily, plus regular advertising supplements. The most their economic position enabled them to offer was six or eight pages. As for the rest of the London press, lacking a comparable revenue from subscription sales and advertising revenue, they could neither match *The Times* in size and news coverage for a quality market nor, so long as their price was artificially inflated by the tax, hope to find alternative markets for cheaper papers as had been done so successfully on the other side of the Atlantic. 'So long as the penny lasts,' declared Richard Cobden explosively in 1850, 'there can be no daily press for the middle or working classes. Who below the rank of a merchant or wholesale dealer can afford to take a daily paper at fivepence?'

He believed the governing classes would continue to resist the removal of this tax, not, as he explained, 'on account of the loss of revenue—that is no obstacle with a surplus of two or three millions —but because they know the stamp makes the daily press the instrument and servant of the oligarchy.' In this, however, he proved wrong. In the end the oligarchy's fear of what the *Edinburgh Review* called the 'extraordinary and dangerous eminence' of *The Times* and Queen Victoria described as 'the reckless exercise' of its 'anomalous power' came to outweigh even their fear of popular opinion. Not only was the tax repealed, it was repealed in such a way as to strike directly at *The Times*. Under the new legislation, newspapers that went through the mails were required to pay a postal frank on which there was a surcharge for all newspapers above four ounces in weight. And *The Times* was the only paper to exceed this weight.

It was thus compelled either to reduce its size or increase its price. It chose to do the latter, deliberately opting out of the circulation race in order to maintain its character. It was not virtue alone that made it so choose. Although there was pride of quality in the decision there was also a good deal of arrogance. *The Times* had 'very little opinion of the sagacity of uneducated people,' Mowbray Morris its manager told the Select Committee on the Stamp Tax, and when he was asked by Cobden whether he really considered it in the public interest that the ownership of newspapers 'should be limited to a few hands and be in the hands of parties who are great capitalists', he replied sharply that he did. By the mid-nineteenth century those in charge of *The Times* had become incapable of recognising the emergence of new powers in political and social life, as Barnes had done in his day. They were altogether uninterested in the new newspaper public knocking on the door. Secure in their conviction that *The Times* was a unique public institution, they stood contemptuously aside from the forces that were to shape the journalism of the future.

With the end of the newspaper tax an iceberg melted. Almost overnight new daily papers sprang into existence all over the country. On a strict commercial consideration it might have seemed that the end of the tax would do no more than allow a reduction in the price of newspapers by a penny or so to 4*d*. or 3*d*. Instead new papers began to appear in increasing numbers at 2*d*. and before long at 1*d*. A psychological as well as a commercial barrier to cheap newspapers had gone. So long as the tax was there and the position of *The Times* seemed unchallengeable, it had seemed impossible to think of daily newspapers other than on its terms. Now it became possible.

Before 1853 there had not been a single English morning or evening newspaper outside London, only one in Scotland. With the end of the newspaper stamp tax in that year, Manchester, Liverpool, Bradford, Birmingham, Leeds, Newcastle, Nottingham, Edinburgh, Aberdeen, Sheffield, Darlington, Plymouth and Belfast all became possessed of vigorous organs of local opinion, many of which were to make great names for themselves in the history of British journalism. The effect on London journalism was hardly less remarkable. Twenty-four hours before the formal ending of the stamp tax the *Daily Telegraph* was launched at 2*d*., later to be reduced to 1*d*. Within six years it had more than double *The Times*'s circulation. The *Daily News*, which had started disastrously in 1846 with Charles Dickens as its Editor, although he lasted only three weeks, and which by 1853 had lost its original capital of £50,000 four times over, now began to flourish. A new radical daily, the *Morning Star*, followed it. Soon afterwards came a galaxy of evening papers lighting the London sky with a radiance never seen before or since: the *Pall Mall Gazette*, the *Westminster Gazette*, the *St James's Gazette* and the *Globe*, all erudite and cultured, all brilliantly written.

None of the new morning papers whether provincial or metropolitan sought to do what *The Times* did. They did not and could not challenge it in news coverage or bulk. Nor did their readers, earnest but busy men, wish them to do so. What nearly all of them took over from *The Times*, however, was its creed of journalistic independence. They were not so politically uncommitted as Barnes and Delane had been. They lived in a different age. Parties had moved to the centre of the political stage. There was a sharper division of principle that found its parliamentary expression in the great conflicts of Gladstone and Disraeli. The new editors, therefore, were party men. But although their papers commonly supported one party or the other, they were men of principle, as ready to denounce as to praise the parties they allied themselves to when political conscience required it. C. P. Scott of the *Manchester Guardian*, the greatest and longest lived of them all, was a Liberal to the core of his being. But he vehemently opposed his party on two major issues, woman's suffrage and the foreign policies that led up to the First World War, and on many minor ones.

Nor did those who, unlike Scott, were not in the fortunate position of being the publishers as well as the editors of their papers consider themselves the servants either of political organisations or their employers. They were their own men. When Sir Alfred Mond, later Lord Melchett, Chairman and Chief Proprietor of the *Westminster Gazette*, was so presumptuous as to send two signed letters to that paper on successive days, its Editor, J. A. Spender, rounded on him sharply. Such a habit, he said, would do him no good and the paper much harm, for the British public very properly had 'a rooted objection to any newspaper influence which it conceives as personal'. If owners insisted on interfering with policy, editors resigned. It was the least their conception of journalistic independence would allow them to do.

Unfortunately this independence too often rested, particularly among the brilliant group of London evening newspapers of which the *Westminster Gazette*, the *Pall Mall Gazette* and the *St James's Gazette*, were such shining stars, on nothing more substantial than a rich man's readiness to spend his money on a newspaper instead of a yacht or a mistress. The editors of these newspapers had learned political independence from *The Times*. But apart from Scott of the *Manchester Guardian* who never forgot it, few of them recognised as Barnes never failed to do that political independence has roots in shallow soil without economic independence.

Nor did most of them have any better nose than the controllers of *The Times* for the new public coming along. They were happy to go on catering for a public very much like that of *The Times* itself, although by now larger in number and more widely based. They left the newspaper revolution started by Barnes unfinished, for they were unable, or unwilling, to 'teach, urge and thunder' its duty to the new public waiting in the wings in the way that he had for the new public of his day. To do so became the perogative of other men with different ideas about journalism, the makers of the 'new journalism'.

In his *Study of History*, Professor Toynbee claims that this new journalism when it arrived polluted the 'pure river of enlightenment' the extension of popular education had caused to flow. Whether it did or not the old and the new 'quality' newspapers and their editors did little to affect the matter either way. The stream forked but they were content to keep in traditional waters.

There was no such dividing of the waters in the United States. There they spread out in all directions from the beginning unconfined by either stamp tax or social hierarchy.

The immigrant masses of America were hungry for news, excitement and reassurance. Bennett and his contemporaries gave them all three. They collected news for them from the teeming sidewalks of their own city of New York, then from all across the States and soon from all across the world. Above all Bennett brought them the excitement of recognising themselves part of a vast community whose achievements and tragedies, successes, failures, romances and peccadillos were also theirs. He clapped them on the back and fought giants for them. 'As to intimidating me or changing my course,' he roared in the boldest type he could find, 'the thing cannot be done . . . I may be attacked, I may be assailed, I may be killed, I may be murdered, but I will never succumb. I never will abandon the cause of truth, morals and virtues.'

When he fell in love he told them about it in his biggest headlines: 'To The Readers Of The Herald: Declaration Of Love: Caught At Last: Going To Be Married: New Movement In Civilisation.' The lady, he assured them, had a fortune: 'I sought and found a fortune—a large fortune. She has no Stonington shares or Manhattan stock but in purity and uprightness she is worth half a million of pure gold. Can any swindling bank show as much? In good sense and elegance another half million: in soul, mind and beauty millions on millions equal to the whole specie of all the rotten banks in the world.' It was personal journalism, yellow journalism, of a kind to make the gentlemen of England wrinkle their noses. Noses wrinkled also in New York, Washington and New England. But every attack on Bennett confirmed his position with his readers and brought him new ones. He gloried in his independence and they gloried in it for him—and for themselves as well.

But although Bennett showed American newspapers and American readers the way to independence, the newspaper revolution in the United States was too big to be charted by him alone as it had been by Barnes in Britain. There was no possibility of one newspaper dominating the American, or even the New York, scene as *The Times* dominated the British.

The structure of a country's press always reflects its community. The British daily press of Barnes's day accurately reflected a hierarchical society formalised and enclosed. The doors of this society were slowly opening, but carefully and cautiously, inch by formal inch. The new arrivals were like guests at a subscription dance in a great house: their tickets were scrutinised in the hall before they were allowed to move upstairs to join those already there as of right who had dined beforehand. In America, however, the doors were wide open, a restless moving mass spilled over the whole house. Within this mass there were static islands of birth and privilege, all the more conscious of their position for being delineated by lines invisibly drawn and not publicly acknowledged. But even the inhabitants of such islands could not altogether escape the nudge in the ribs, the tread on the toes that signalled the arrival of the new men moving in. The party was not, perhaps, quite as free-for-all as it seemed and was to become less so as money drew new frontiers. But is was sufficiently so to make most people feel statisfied that it was.

The American press mirrored this society as closely as the press of Barnes's day mirrored British society. It was diverse and numerous. Long before the British press it reflected both a 'quality' and a 'popular' readership.

Bennett was one of the entertainers not, much as he would have liked to be, one of the persuaders. For all their liking for the news he brought them, Bennett's readers seldom took their opinions from the *Herald*. Perhaps he was too much one of themselves. Perhaps he was too vehemently against too many things to be accepted as a positive guide to any. Perhaps he offered his readers too much and in too great variety so that they fell into the way of thinking of the *Herald* as a dime store of journalism with something for everyone but nothing solid and permanent for anyone. Perhaps the public he attracted was itself too fragmented in political and economic interest to follow any single guiding line, even if he had had one to offer. Whatever the reason he was among the first to demonstrate the curious journalistic paradox that circulation and persuasion may run in inverse ratio to each other, that the more you sell, the less you may influence.

There was only one newspaper in New York contemporaneous with his own that had any significant influence on the city and the nation. This was the *Tribune*, founded by Horace Greely four years after Bennett started the *Herald*. Greely was no more endowed with the world's goods than Bennett but what he possessed in abundance was an inexhaustible stock of idealism and moral earnestness. He was born and brought up in poverty on a Vermont farm, became an apprentice printer at an early age and when he was twenty arrived in New York with ten dollars in his pocket and a Bible— the main source of his early education—in a bandanna over his shoulder. He found work on the first penny paper in New York, the *Morning Post*, which closed down three weeks later, and then attracted the attention of a New York State political boss by some vigorous pieces in a struggling Whig weekly, the *New Yorker*. He was given the job of editing campaign papers. By frugal living he saved $1,000 by the time he was thirty and with this and a similar amount that he managed to borrow started the *Tribune* in April 1841 as a 'New Morning Journal of Politics, Literature and General Intelligence' dedicated to lighting the path of progress and promoting 'the Moral, Political and Social Well-Being of the People'.

Like Bennett, who had six years' start on him, Greely put his greatest faith in a mass public. But he thought more highly of its intelligence and its faith in moral principles than Bennett did and opened his paper to wide ranging discussions of religion, politics, philosophy and literature, turning it into a forum for serious intellectual discussion on a level rarely seen in a popular paper, before or since. A great man for panaceas, practical and impractical, he crusaded for a medley of causes from co-operative ownership of land to teetotalism and vegetarianism, from anti-slavery to spiritualism, from the promotion of trade unions and high tariffs to the abolition of capital punishment and found each political party in turn wanting in seriousness about one or the other of them. The *Tribune* never rivalled the *Herald* in circulation or news coverage and the news it gave was often coloured by its editor's highly idiosyncratic opinions. But by 1854 it had thirty-eight regular out-of-town and overseas correspondents and a staff of fourteen reporters in New York plus ten associate editors at work on a great variety of features, articles and reviews.

Greely had one of the most essential gifts of a great editor. He respected sincerity and intellectual power in others, even when he disagreed with them, and, eccentric and catholic in his own interests, encouraged a similar catholicity in those who wrote for him. He attracted to the *Tribune*, in consequence, the most brilliant and independent minded staff in the American journalism of his day.

What above all gave the *Tribune* its influence was the sincerity of its editor and the encyclopaedic range and humanity of his interests. He was often wrong headed but his heart was always in the right place. Moreover, although his platform was New York, he comprehended America as a whole. 'Go West, young man,' he declared in a famous message to the young, but he did not simply tell others to do so, he went there himself, travelling across the States to California, talking and listening and reporting, his moon face with its fringe of whiskers and general air of rustic benevolence aglow with interest, his eyes, owl-like behind his spectacles, bright with an inexhaustible curiosity. Bennett was a man of the city, Greely essentially, despite his urban base, a man of the country-side. He reflected in his own personality the conflicts inherent in the transition from a rural to an industrial society and the clash of urban and rural moralities. He was the old American trying to come to terms with the new. Because of this, because he reflected so many of the doubts and aspirations of ordinary Americans, their confidence in the future and nostalgia for the past that was dying before there had been time fully to savour it, their anxiety for moral certitudes and their awareness of impending change, their longing for simple solutions and their confrontation by ever new complexities, his influence spread far beyond New York into the rural communities of New England and the Middle West, where the weekly edition of the *Tribune* had a circulation of nearly 200,000. 'It was,' said Clarence Darrow speaking of his childhood in just such a rural community, 'the political and social Bible of our home.'

The *Tribune* differed from the *Herald* in moral earnestness and respect for its readers. It differed even more from the general clutter of papers. With the exception of the *Evening Post*, now the sole survivor of that rich crop which had some of the *Tribune*'s own seriousness and literary flavour, these fought for the attention of the new mass audience with every twist of sensationalism they could find. But although the *Tribune* was a paper of ideas it was hardly more like the solid journal of information and opinion that Barnes had fashioned out of the London *Times* than were its more sensational competitors. For such a journal New Yorkers had to wait until 1851 — and the *New York Times*.

The *New York Times* did not seek to compete with either the *Herald* or the *Tribune*. Nor was its co-founder and first editor, Henry Jarvis Raymond, cut to the pattern of either Bennett or Greely although he had had his first training in journalism on Greely's *Tribune*. Bennett and Greely were personal and paternal editors. The *Herald* was Bennett, the *Tribune* Greely, even when success put them in a position to engage able associates.

Raymond made of the *Times* a newspaper with its own personality. No doubt this was somewhat like his own, for he was a calm, quiet man with a disciplined and orderly mind, a graduate of the University of Vermont who had consciously set out to turn himself into a fully professional newspaper man. But from the beginning the *Times* stood on its own feet, a newspaper in its own right, not the reflection of the character of one man. That was the way Raymond wanted it and the way the public he had in mind wanted it also. It was a public not unlike the one Barnes had secured for the London *Times*: the public of the solid, successful commercial classes who needed a newspaper to bring them the facts they required for the conduct of their private and public business and to interpret those facts without heat. 'We do not mean to write as if we are in a passion unless that shall really be the case; and we shall make it a point to get into a passion as rarely as possible.' So wrote Raymond in his opening declaration of editorial intent. He kept to that principle and made it into a tradition.

Until the *New York Times* the commercial classes of New York had depended on two newspapers specifically mercantile in their appeal, the *Journal of Commerce* and the *Courier and Enquirer*, on which latter paper Raymond served part of his journalistic apprenticeship. These brought them news of activities in world markets and of public events likely to affect those markets. They reported on changes in tariffs and commercial legislation, on the movements of ships, money rates and the rise and fall of commodity and bond prices. They were moral in tone as befitted newspapers serving serious men but their field of interest was essentially practical and limited. They were ungainly in size and high in price.

What Raymond envisaged—and what he achieved—was a cheaper, handier, more readable general newspaper that would give this public the commercial news it needed but against a larger background: a newspaper for public men of all sorts, commercial, professional, political. Appropriately whereas Bennett had started the *Herald* with $500 and Greely the *Tribune* with $2,000 the *New York Times* required an initial capital of $50,000. For help in raising this Raymond turned to a banker friend, George Jones, who had been in the business office of the *Tribune* with him and had subsequently moved to a bank in Albany. Aided by another business friend, Edgar Wesley, they floated the *New York Times* as a public corporation with a nominal capital of $100,000, of which half was paid up, the first American newspaper to break into big business.

Like Bennett and Greely, Raymond was a young man when he achieved his ambition of starting a newspaper of his own. He was thirty. But he was a middle-aged young man and he founded a middle-aged newspaper, careful and considered in tone, sedate in style: a good grey newspaper as was subsequently to be said of it almost *ad nauseam*, but of formidable staying power.

By the middle of the nineteenth century New York thus already enjoyed an infinitely greater variety of daily newspapers than London. Instead of one great Everest of a newspaper there was a whole mountain range. Nor was American journalism concentrated in one city as British journalism was until 1855. There were more newspapers in New York than any other city but when Britain outside London was still a wasteland so far as the press was concerned the United States was alive with newspapers of all sorts and sizes. These newspapers expressed both in their numbers and their diversity the spirit of a society bursting at the seams with energy, optimism and conflict. That the political capital, Washington, should rival New York as a press centre was natural enough.

But outside New York and Washington the *Philadelphia Public Ledger*, the *Baltimore Sun*, the *Boston Herald* and the *Boston Times*, the *Louisville Journal*, the *Detroit Free Press*, the *Chicago Tribune* and the *Chicago Times* were all flourishing, several of them with circulations of 40,000 or more when England still had no daily press outside London. And these were only the giants. Up and down the country there were close on 400 daily newspapers as well as a multitude of weeklies. Most of these dailies had circulations of only a few thousands, but all were active energisers of their communities. Not every editor took his profession as grandly as Samuel Bowles of the *Springfield Republican* who proclaimed the newspaper's 'brilliant mission' as that of 'the high priest of history, the vitaliser of society, the world's great informer, the earth's high censor, the medium of public opinion and the circulating life blood of the whole human mind'. But even those who did not put their place in the world as high as he did were in no doubt that they and their newspapers were essential elements in a great society, ladles to stir the melting pot of a new democracy. Nor did their readers doubt it either.

Outside America it was the British model that most influenced newspaper development in the second half of the nineteenth century except for some of the newer countries like Australia and Canada where conditions approximated to those in the United States even if only on a minor scale.

As the settled commercial communities of Europe became subject to political and social forces similar to those that had made *The Times* possible in Britain it was natural that their newspapers should take a similar course, all the more so in that a long tradition of serious newspapers of information for the professional and commercial classes already existed. Political independence for newspapers had had to wait on the movement of events but when it came it had strong professional foundations to build on. In Germany the *Frankfurter Zeitung* first published in 1856, in Paris *Le Temps* which appeared in 1861 and in Milan the *Corriere della Sera* which began in 1870 all offered concrete evidence of the advance towards political independence. So on a smaller but no less significant scale did the *Aftonbladet* and the *Dagens Nyheter* of Stockholm, the *Aftenposten* of Oslo, the *Algemeen Handelsblad* of Amsterdam and the *Nieuwe Rotterdamse Courant* of Rotterdam.

Nor was it only in Europe that serious independent journalism of information and opinion now began to express itself. In the unlikely climate of South America, in Buenos Aires, *La Prensa* was launched in 1869 with a resounding declaration from its founder Dr Jose Clemente Paz, whose direct descendants still own and edit the paper, that it would acknowledge no obligation, political or commercial, other than 'Independence, respect for the private citizen, reasoned attack on the public man and not on the individual personality'. It was with the words *'Verdad, Honor, Libertad, Progreso, Civilizacion'* at its masthead that what was to become the premier Spanish language newspaper in the world and one of the finest in any country began, its record of independence interrupted only when it was taken over for four years by the Peron Government in 1951. In India the *Hindu* of Madras was founded in 1878 by a group of young Indian intellectuals to cater to the political awakening of the Indian middle classes and provide a vehicle for the thoughtful expression of nationalist sentiments. A year later Japan made its contribution to the serious press of the world with *Asahi* (today an immensely popular daily with a circulation of over 6,500,000 but still essentially serious in its approach and serving what it likes to describe as a 'mass elite'). Founded in Osaka in 1879 as an independent non-party newspaper by merchant families specialising in imports from the West, *Asahi* won middle class support but official disapproval by campaigning for an elected Parliament.

In Australia and Canada, struggling to free themselves from the grip of colonialism, the journalistic response was understandably closer to the American.

The editor of the first Australian newspaper, the *Sydney Gazette* founded in 1803, conducted himself, it was said, as though 'his situation had been that of a mastiff to His Excellency'. When the interests of the developing commercial classes collided with those of colonial authority and the city masses began to demand voice in their own affairs the mastiffs, however, became less tame and authority itself less assured in its use of the whip. Censorship was ended in 1824. Opposition newspapers started up. There were attempts to check them by licensing and a stamp tax. Neither succeeded and, although the stamp tax was to remain in Britain for another quarter of a century, it ended in Australia in 1830. By mid-century at least eleven Australian dailies were being published. For the most part they confined themselves to local news with tit-bits of foreign intelligence when the clippers arrived. With a judicious combination of politics and crime they constituted, according to one contemporary judge, 'the only literature published in the Australian Colonies'. Within a few years another writer was to declare that in a country 'where Society is imported and wealth not yet fully organised' the newspapers represented the 'best if not the greatest institutions in the country'.

Such claims need water added to them before swallowing, as Mr Henry Mayer of the University of Sydney has pointed out in his admirable study, *The Press in Australia*. But there was some truth in them all the same. The early Australian newspapers were as rough and raw as the society of which they were a part and in a society without much literature or culture of its own they provided most of the available reading matter. Two of them, the *Sidney Morning Herald* which became a daily in 1840 and *The Age* which was launched in Melbourne fourteen years later, not only took their journalistic responsibilities very seriously but carved out for themselves positions of considerable political influence.

Inevitably geography and the spread of population along the rim of the continent made the Australian press regional: the *Herald* and *Empire* in Sydney, the *Age* and the *Argus* in Melbourne, the *Register* and *Southern Australian* in Adelaide, the *Courier* in Brisbane, each was compelled by a restricted circulation area with a small population to offer something for everyone. They were unable, even if they had wished, to find economic viability by appealing to a small but influential group in national society as *The Times* did in Britain.

The press grew with the country, expanding as it expanded. It boomed with the gold boom. Between 1848 and 1852 the circulation of the *Argus* increased nearly tenfold from a few hundreds to over 5,000 and its advertising revenue rose from a mere £13 a week to £800. As city populations expanded such papers as the *Sydney Daily Telegraph* and the *Sydney Evening News* and weeklies like *Truth* emerged to meet the popular demand for what the *Telegraph* described as 'something that takes little trouble to master'; entrenched Sabbatarianism prevented the growth of Sunday newspapers and it was such newspapers as these that took on the job performed by the Sunday press in Britain of providing sex, sensationalism and excitement for the masses. The Australian press was less literate than the British, less flamboyant, forceful and influential than the American. But it had a great deal of rude energy. In all of which it reflected its society.

In Canada press developments naturally followed closely on those in the United States—although in a reducing mirror. With a sparse and widely scattered population strung out over a vast distance from east to west in a narrow strip alongside the American border, newspapers could not be other than regional—and often regional on a particularly local and domesticated scale. But, as in Australia, a few newspapers of greater substance did arise in the larger cities of Ottawa, Montreal (with a powerful French speaking press), Toronto, Winnepeg and Vancouver. Paramount among them was the *Winnipeg Free Press* which had the incalculable advantage of taking to its bosom at the turn of the century, to reign over its destinies for forty years, the greatest editor Canada had produced, John W. Dafoe, an editor made in the mould of a Barnes or a C. P. Scott. But if the *Winnipeg Free Press* led the way, the *Ottawa Journal* came only a little behind. It spoke for conservatism in the east with a voice scarcely less independent than that of the *Free Press* for liberalism in the mid-west.

In South Africa the press took a different, a more imperialist course. As in America, Canada and Australia, it came up in the first instance the hard way, fighting colonial authority in the Cape. James Fairbairn, the editor of the first general newspaper in the territory, the *South African Commercial Advertiser*, was twice suspended by the Governor and was forced to go to London to fight for more press freedom—enlisting both Barnes and the London Missionary Society in his support. He got what he was after in a new Press Law in 1828 and made his *Advertiser* the chief campaigner for more representation in government. He paved the way for several small sheets in English and Dutch although the first Afrikaans paper did not begin until 1875.

By 1857, as Rosalynd Ainslie shows in her excellent and painstaking study of press developments throughout the African continent, *The Press in Africa*, the need for a more sophisticated newspaper voice had become clear to the rapidly developing commercial and agricultural interests of the Cape. They took the

British press, just freed from the stamp tax, as their model. The *Cape Argus* founded in that year was not only designed to be as like a serious English newspaper as possible, but imported editorial staff from London to see that it was. It began as a weekly, became a tri-weekly, and then in 1880 a daily, to meet the competition of the *Cape Times* started four years earlier.

Both *The Argus* and the *Times* were highly professional newspapers backed by substantial capital. Both spoke for the commercial and financial interests of the territory and when gold was discovered in the Rand in 1886 the *Argus* went there too. It bought a small news sheet, the *Johannesburg Star*, pumped capital into it and made it the voice of mining interests anxious to take mining policy out of the hands of President Kruger and his Afrikaans Republic. Its readers were the English-speaking 'Uitlanders', the 'aliens' who had flooded in with the gold rush and it fought hard for them—it was soon to be deeply implicated in the Jameson Raid.

Behind the *Argus* and *Star* and their controlling company, the Argus Printing and Publishing Company, were the towering figures of Cecil Rhodes, Barney Barnato, Solly Joel, all the great names in gold mining together with the commercial and shipping interests of the Union Steamship Line and Imperial Cold Storage and the financial and insurance interest of the Syfret group. When Rhodes and his British South Africa Company went north looking for gold and land the *Argus* group went with them to launch in 1892 the *Rhodesia Herald* and two years later the *Bulawayo Chronicle*. In South Africa the empire of the press went hand in hand with that of commerce.

These newspapers did not, as *The Times* of Barnes had done and as most of his disciples across the world were doing, establish themselves as independent forces, sympathetic to, but not controlled by the expanding commercial interests in their society. Nor did they arise to meet the needs of immigrant masses as the independent American press had done. They were the direct instruments of financial and commercial power springing fully armed into the arena: the ancillaries of commerce, not its mentors.

Originally the *Argus*, it is true, had had a different complexion. It had been started as an independent, although strongly pro-British, journal by two English born residents of the Cape, Bryan

Swelling Tide of Freedom

Henry Darrell, a member of the recently formed Legislative Assembly, and a former London journalist, Richard William Murray. It was printed by another member of the Assembly, a dwarf named Saul Solomon, who owned the principal printing works in the Cape. When he acquired control a few years later he made the *Argus* briefly into a markedly pro-African and anti-British publication. Such policies soon landed him in business difficulties. At this point Cecil Rhodes moved in. He provided the *Argus* editor, Francis Joseph Dormer, with the capital to buy out Solomon, the 'negrophilist', and set the paper on a new course.

Neither the *Argus* nor the *Star* were indigenous products in the sense that most newspapers elsewhere were. The Africans were still, for the most part, illiterate. They had no press of their own and none even to speak for them once Solomon was gone. Even the Boers had no Afrikaans press of any sort until 1875 when a small paper, *Die Patriot*, was started by Di Genootskap van Reyte and they did not get a substantial one until 1915 when *Die Burger* was founded. In so far as they were readers at all they tended to be magazine rather than newspaper readers. Yet although to a degree not paralleled in the press of either Canada or Australia, the main South African daily newspapers were the instruments of great commercial interests drawing much of their financial power from London, they could not help, by the very nature of their trade, from becoming in the end much more than this.

Newspapers are made as much by their readers as by those who own or edit them. They must live up to their readers' expectations if they wish to prosper. As the British Royal Commission on the Press (1947–49) observed, each has a personality and tradition of its own 'compounded not merely of its physical appearance and its political policy but also of its tone and style, its unspoken assumptions and its subtle relationship with its readers'. This personality is self-induced and self-perpetuating. It can only, as Northcliffe was to find with the London *Times*, be turned into the vehicle of another personality within limits set by its own. Each day's edition is a palimpsest on which can be read the history of all those that have preceded it.

Although the South African press was the product of a deliberate process directed to a particular financial and commercial purpose nevertheless the very necessities of journalistic existence forced it to acquire a life independent of its promoters. In so far as it sought to defend and advance its shareholders' interests—and, of course, it did—its ability to do so was affected by the extent to which these interests were accepted as part of the general interest—or at least that of the English-speaking European population. Nor can any newspaper in a free society remain unaffected by the international press climate. The second half of the nineteenth century had accepted press freedom as one of its principles. No more than the press of any other country could that of South Africa avoid some of the attendant obligations.

CHAPTER FOUR

Hearst, Northcliffe and the Popular Press

By the last decades of the nineteenth century there had thus been established in most literate parts of the world a tradition of journalism that, although it varied a good deal from place to place, had a common pride in independence and a common confidence in its importance as a vehicle of the public interest. Outside the United States, Canada and Australia few daily newspapers spoke directly to or for the masses. Elsewhere they catered primarily for the official, professional and commercial elements in society, although in Britain, because of the popularity of reading rooms and mechanics' institutes, they were read more widely by the working classes than their circulation figures suggested and popular Sunday newspapers had begun to sell in immense numbers. Outside North America and Australia the daily press, although somewhat brighter in make-up than formerly, was still mainly one of opinion, concerned much more with the quality of its readership than its size, much less in interesting and entertaining a large public than in providing information and argument for a few. In some instances this 'quality press' paid its way out of sales and advertising revenue. In others it was subsidised by rich men. Very rarely was it run primarily for motives of profit, although it was steadily becoming more commercial in size and organisation.

Newspapers expanded most rapidly in the United States because American society itself grew more rapidly than any other. Changes in the character of the press were most obvious in

Britain because the transition between old social structures and new was sharpest there.

The British press had led the world in political awareness and influence in the nineteenth century. Now, as a general habit, it became much less political than the Continental press. New interests of an a-political sort opened out before ordinary people in Britain and it was these the newspapers reflected.

In the United States the press had been close to the mass of the population from the beginning. There was no sharp break between the old journalism and the new. Newspapers became larger. There were more of them. Their owners became richer, less involved in the shirt sleeve, day-to-day running of their newspapers. But basically the American press remained what Bennett and his contemporaries had made it. There was no major change of direction.

Even the Civil War brought few radical alterations in the character of the American press, although it increased circulations as wars do. One change it did bring was to give new status to the reporter as the man on the spot, the eyes and ears of the public. He became a legendary figure, more significant in popular journalistic mythology even than the editor: a folk hero unabashed by authority, undeterred by threats, committed only to the public right to know. This conception of the reporter, the man who goes out and gets the news, as the key figure rather than, as was often the case in Britain, the man who sits at home and comments on it, had an invigorating effect on American journalism. To millions of ordinary Americans it confirmed the position of the press as an independent arm of democracy, an essential investigatory element in the American way of life.

Under the stimulus of the Civil War newspapers multiplied and went on doing so. In 1880 the number of English language dailies in the United States was around 850. By 1900 it was close on 1,970. The number of weekly newspapers trebled. At the same time the afternoon paper read after work and with a strong appeal to the whole family began to take over from the morning paper—except in a few great centres like New York and Washington. By 1890 two-thirds of all daily papers in America were afternoon publications concentrating particularly on local affairs and drawing heavily for their revenue on local advertising.

Hearst, Northcliffe and the Popular Press

James Gordon Bennett had died in 1872, Horace Greely in the same year a few weeks after running unsuccessfully against Grant for President on a Liberal Republican ticket. Henry Raymond of the *New York Times* had died in 1869.

But although the founders were dead their newspapers lived on. The *Herald* climbed to new heights, or depths, of sensationalism and extravagance under James Gordon Bennett Junior. The *Tribune* moved to a more respectable and safe Republicanism under Whitelaw Reid who had first made his name as a war correspondent in the Civil War and was backed financially in his purchase of the *Tribune* by Jay Gould, famous as a Stock Exchange gambler and railroad tycoon. Under Raymond's partner, George Jones, the *New York Times* added to its reputation as a paper of record a crusading bite when it exposed and smashed 'Boss' Tweed, the corrupt head of Tammany Hall, who before the law caught up with him, offered Jones five million dollars to call off the hunt—probably the biggest bribe ever offered to and refused by a newspaperman.

But the *Herald*, the *Tribune* and the *Times* were only three of the many newspapers New Yorkers had to choose from. The *Sun* under Charles A. Dana, one of whose city editors, James Bogart, coined the famous maxim, 'If a dog bites a man it's not news; if a man bites a dog it is', was challenging the *Herald* in 'human interest' reporting and finally beat it in circulation; the *Evening Post* owned by a famous *Herald* reporter of the Civil War, Henry Villard, who had made a fortune in the post-war railroad boom, wielded such extraordinary influence under its scholarly editor, Parke Godwin, that every editor, politician, college president and church minister felt compelled to read and quote its editorials. There were plenty of others for every kind of taste, all competing for circulation.

In the closing decades of the nineteenth century this journalistic maelstrom was stirred to a new fury by the arrival on the New York scene of Joseph Pulitzer, a Hungarian-Jewish immigrant who had made a great success out of merging two St Louis newspapers into the *St Louis Post Dispatch*, and turning the new paper into a notable crusading journal. In 1883 he bought the almost dying *New York World* from Jay Gould who had picked it up accidentally as part of a package railroad deal. Within three years he had raised its circulation from 15,000 to over 250,000. He did so by a remarkable mixture of sensationalism and idealism, a synthesis of everything likely to attract readers, or that had attracted them in the past: scandal, sex and violence at one end of the scale, serious campaigning, intellectual discussion and liberal politics at the other. This hold-all formula, which was similar to Bennett's in its aim of making the best of all worlds, was brilliantly presented with great wit in headlining and prodigious energy in the pursuit and display of news. It was given dizzy momentum by a never-ending series of stunts and crusades which included titanic battles against the Standard Oil Trust and other monopolies and the raising of 100,000 dollars in nickels and dimes to build a pedestal for the Statue of Liberty which had been sent as a gift to the United States by the people of France and left lying in a packing case because Congress had forgotten to appropriate any funds for its erection. Nor was it only liberty that was the *World*'s concern. To the poor of New York it gave free coal and Christmas dinners.

Not only did the New York press offer a frenetic exhibition of journalistic energy but all across the States newspapers expanded at a rate that made the progress of the press in other parts of the world seem curiously muted.

In the Middle West the newspaper tone was set by the incredible Wilbur F. Storey of the *Chicago Times* with his jocular headlines like 'A Drop Too Much' and 'Jerked to Jesus', on reports of hangings and his ceaseless stream of vituperation and slander. Even when newspapers began to take on a more civic role under the leadership of men like Medill of the *Chicago Tribune*, who became mayor of the city as well as its most successful newspaper publisher, they did not abandon sensationalism. They believed in reporting rather than editorialising. Their weapons were investigation and exposure and with these weapons men such as Stone and Lawson of the *Chicago Daily News* and Rockill Nelson of the *Kansas City Star*, who almost single-handed brought some sense of civic morality to a wide-open city famous for corruption and mobster rule, did much to help civilise the Middle West.

Newspapers were proving themselves essential ingredients of a developing society in every part of the country. In the South two newspapers, the *Atlanta Constitution* under Henry W. Grady, a rich, well connected young man from Georgia who had studied law before turning journalist, and the *Louisville Courier-Journal* under Henry Waterson, son of a wealthy congressman from Tennessee who had cut his infant teeth on politics and was, despite his service in the Confederate Army, a great admirer of Lincoln, preached the need to replace the shattered feudalism of the old South by the beginnings of a more liberal and commercially progressive spirit and did something at any rate to heal the desolation that followed Appomattox.

In the far West journalism, like the climate and the people, came hot and crude. In Denver, Colorado, Frederick Gilmer Bonfils and Harry Heye Tammen, the one the son of a Probate Judge who graduated to journalism by way of land speculation and professional gambling, the other an ex- bar-tender and confidence man, turned the *Denver Post*—'The Paper With a Heart and A Soul'—which had been dying on its feet when they bought it, into a roaring success by scandal, sensation, exposure, libel and stunt journalism on a scale never before seen even in the brashest days of New York and Chicago journalism.

From further West still, from San Francisco, came journalism's gaudiest contribution to the American scene—William Randolph Hearst. Hearst had the *San Francisco Examiner* as a gift from his father who made a vast fortune out of the Constock Silver strike and then acquired even vaster ones from the Anaconda, Ontario and Homestake mines and had taken over the *Examiner* in part payment of a bad debt. It proved useful in pushing his claim for a seat in the U.S. Senate but he found it of little other interest to a man who liked real money. Not so his twenty-four year old son, who had got himself a job as a reporter on Pulitzer's *World* after being expelled from Harvard for presenting all the members of the Faculty with inscribed chamber pots and thought of little else but newspapers.

William Randolph Hearst was to become the most notorious example in American history of newspaper ownership at its most megalomaniacal but in his first days in San Francisco he showed a good deal of aptitude for being on the side of the people and much courage and talent in cleaning up cesspools of corrupt administration along the way. He was a master of 'Gee Whiz' journalism: journalism based on the thesis that a newspaper should aim to make its readers exclaim Gee Whiz when they saw its front page, Holy Moses when they turned to the second and Great God Almighty when they came to the third. He was in no doubt that the man who mattered most on a newspaper was the editor, not, as some of the businessmen who had moved into newspapers were inclined to think, the manager. He demonstrated his belief, as W. A. Swanberg notes in his biography *Citizen Hearst*, by rapidly changing the notification 'W. R. Hearst, Proprietor' printed under the title when the paper was handed over to him by his father to 'W. R. Hearst, Proprietor and Editor' and then two days later to 'W. R. Hearst, Editor and Proprietor'. Nor was he only editor in name. He took off his coat and worked on the news desk and in the composing room personally directing the setting of the sensational headlines that erupted from his brain like fire-crackers. The *Examiner* was his paper down to its last lurid line and he worked from 7 o'clock in the morning until 2 o'clock the next day to make sure that it would explode like a bomb when it hit the streets.

San Francisco journalism had always been tough and rough like the city it served. One of the brothers de Young who founded its best and most respected newspaper, the *Chronicle*, had been shot dead a few years before Hearst arrived by a member of the so-called Workingmen's Party who did not like his editorials and he himself had earlier shot and wounded the same party's candidate for Mayor. Editors had to be quick on the draw, reporters had to learn to get news the hard way. However, things were settling down by the time Hearst turned up. H. de Young who took over when his brother Charles was killed had a great admiration for Rockill Nelson's *Kansas City Star* and he turned the *Chronicle* into a civic force on the same model and an excellent paper for straight and honest news.

Hearst had other ambitions. He cared little for news of the ordinary kind, news the others had. Although he recognised such news was a necessary ingredient of a newspaper and increased the *Examiner*'s local coverage and bought the *New York Herald*'s syndicated service to demonstrate that it was in the big city league, what really excited him was the news he could make or make into something different.

An *Examiner* reporter was assigned to get himself committed to an insane asylum and write a searing account of his experiences, a 'sob sister' was told to dress up in old clothes and collapse in the street to see what the hospital services did for her. Another girl reporter was told to make friends with the most notorious madam in town and describe life in San Francisco's plushest brothel, although she was not actually required to take up the profession herself. Another reporter was ordered to jump off a ferryboat to see if the crew knew what to do about a man overboard, another to catch a grizzly bear and bring it back alive in order to prove that they still existed in California. Yet another, noted for his drinking habits, was ordered to take a cure and describe what it was like to be 'dehydrated'. In a more romantic vein a young couple were persuaded to go up in a balloon with the *Examiner*'s name plastered all over it, there to be married by a publicity-eager clergyman swaying above the city as cameras clicked.

Personally Hearst was a shy man, incapable of easy contact with people. He derived his main social pleasure from crude practical jokes. Black print and large headlines enabled him to put himself over in a way he could never do in person. In the process he exposed many abuses in the muck-raking tradition of the time and campaigned valiantly against the Southern Pacific Railroad which had acquired a tight grip on Californian politics. But what he chiefly contributed to American journalism was the conception of the newspaper as a non-stop vaudeville show, the biggest razzle-dazzle act on earth. He was a rich man's son who threw wild papers instead of wild parties. He loved banging about and gathered around him a barnstorming crew of talented newspapermen who painted the town red with printer's ink, confident that neither threat nor bribery need deflect them because Hearst was behind them and behind Hearst were his father's millions. The *Examiner* was sent spinning like a garishly painted musical top that would have collapsed immediately if it had ever stopped. But it never did stop. Hearst whipped it on with maniacal energy, self-hypnotised by the need to startle, amaze and stupefy.

Nevertheless there was a certain attractive innocence about those early San Franciscan days, a wild purposeless pleasure in the sheer excitement of making a noise that had its own mad poetry. It was like the beginning of a drunken party before alcoholism sets in. The innocence did not last. The raw spirit took over, deceiving Hearst into the belief that what he held in his hands was power, power to make the millions dance to his tune and through them to dominate governments and command policies. So long as his father lived there was some rein on his ambitions. Hearst senior had the purse strings. Although the *Examiner* soared in circulation it got little solid advertising and Hearst senior by no means approved either of Willie's extravagance or his cavalier attacks on the rich and established. So little did he approve, in fact, that when he died he left all his millions to his wife with not a penny to his son. He hoped by so doing to curb his son's extravagance and force him to run the *Examiner*, if run it he must, on a commercial basis.

But Mrs Hearst was a doting mother. She sold the Hearst interests in the Anaconda Mine to Rothschilds of London for $7,500,000 and handed the money to her son.

Hearst, the alcoholic of power, now had a licence to spend as he liked and do what he wanted. He had enjoyed himself in San Francisco but for the sort of spree he could now contemplate only New York would do. He dispatched his business manager, C. M. Palmer, to the big city in a hurry to find out what was buyable. The *Times*, the *Advertiser*, and the *Recorder*, reported Palmer, could all be got at a price but for a real bargain the best bet was the *Morning Journal*, once owned by Joseph Pulitzer's brother when it was known as the 'Chambermaid's delight', but since fallen into respectability and decrepitude under the control of John R. McClean, publisher of the *Cincinnati Enquirer* who had paid $1,000,000 for it and succeeded in reducing its circulation to 77,000. McClean offered Hearst a half interest for $360,000. Hearst, through Palmer, countered with a bid of $180,000 for an outright sale and McClean, who would probably have been glad to get clear for much less, accepted. Hearst who never doubted his own ability to transform any newspaper property he acquired had a New York stand. The stars of his San Franciscan gee whiz troupe were summoned east, the price of the paper cut to one cent and with all journalistic guns firing Hearst set out to show New York and his old hero Pulitzer what was what. Within twelve months he had put the *Journal* above the *Times*, the *Sun*, the *Tribune* and the *Herald* in circulation, although it still ran behind Pulitzer's *World*.

Hearst, Northcliffe and the Popular Press

'What is frequently forgotten in journalism is that if news is wanted it has to be sent for ... the public is even more fond of entertainment than it is of information,' he proclaimed in an article of self praise on the first anniversary of his proprietorship of the *Journal*. It was not only news he sent for, it was talent also. Paying salaries far above all rivals he raided every newspaper, but particularly the *World*, for staff. When the editor of the *Sunday World* hesitated he bought up the entire staff of the paper to keep him company. Although the *Journal* gathered readers it lost money. Advertisers did not like it. However, this did not bother Hearst. So long as he had a private fortune to draw on he was prepared to pay for his fun and soon he saw a chance of fun on a grander scale than anything the crimes and scandals of New York could offer. He smelled war. The story of Hearst and the Spanish-Cuban war has become a part of newspaper mythology. But it illustrates so graphically the extent and the limitations of newspaper power when exercised by one individual entirely according to his own whim that it is worth recalling in some detail.

In Cuba a handful of patriots were in rebellion against Spain. For Hearst's purposes they were archetypal underdogs; raw material for every tear the *Journal* could cause to flow, every heart it could wring, every pulse it could make beat faster in its circulation battle with the *World*. 'General' Maximo Gomez, the Cuban rebel leader, was proclaimed to be the greatest living soldier, every wounded Cuban a Spanish atrocity.

Despite Hearst's efforts, however, it was not at first much of a war. The rebel forces were no more than a group of ill-organised and ill-armed, although courageous, guerrillas in the interior. Hearst's sympathy for them was genuine; his strength as a propagandist always lay in his ability to be convinced by his own stories. But even he could not turn them into a mass army.

Real news was hard to get. The rebels were in the jungle. The correspondents were at the Hotel Inlaterra in Havana. Passes to the interior were difficult—even for those who wanted them. However, the American public, or that part of it the *Journal* catered for, wanted blood and tyranny and blood and tyranny they got. They were told of Cuban prisoners beaten to death or fed to the sharks, of Spanish soldiers poisoning wells, raping women and roasting Catholic priests alive—atrocity stories, it is interesting to note, which were to recur unchanged, except for the names, in the propaganda stories of the First World War. For Hearst and his readers the Cuban War had nearly everything. It was near enough to America to be exciting, not near enough or big enough to put America in peril. The only thing it lacked, in fact, was authenticity.

'Everything is quiet. There is no trouble here. There will be no war. I wish to return,' cabled the artist Frederick Remington when Hearst sent him to Havana at a salary of $3,000 a month to illustrate stories of battles and atrocities. Hearst was unperturbed. In words that were to become famous as an expression of his journalistic philosophy, he cabled back: 'Please remain. You furnish the pictures and I'll furnish the war.'

For a real war there must, he decided, be American intervention. He began his campaign to bring this to pass with a sensational story of three pretty Cuban girls 'stripped to the skin on an American ship under the protection of the Stars and Stripes'. They had, said the *Journal*, been seized by jeering Spanish policemen who had boarded the American vessel *Olivetti* just as she was leaving Havana for New York. The story was supported by a half page drawing from Remington, who having agreed to stay on in Havana felt, no doubt, that he must earn his $3,000 a month, but proved to be quite untrue when the *Olivetti* docked in New York. The three girls had, they indignantly declared on landing, been subjected to nothing worse than a search in the privacy of their stateroom by women matrons who were looking for incriminating documents. Undeterred, the *Journal* switched to the case of Dr Ricardo Ruiz, a dentist who had returned to Cuba to join the rebel forces after taking American naturalisation and had committed suicide in prison after being arrested for train robbery. American citizens, shrieked the *Journal*, were being wantonly murdered by Spain while the American Government stood by. It demanded an immediate declaration of war.

When American readers proved unwilling to go to war for a dentist Hearst set himself to rally American womanhood in the cause of Señorita Evangelina Cosio y Cisneros, a pretty eighteen year old Cuban girl described by the *Journal* as 'The Cuban Joan of Arc' and 'The Flower of Cuba'. This young lady had been arrested after inviting a Spanish military commander, Colonel

Berriz, to her cottage where he was set on and beaten by a group of Cuban rebels who were lying in wait for him. She was awaiting trial in comparative comfort in the Recopidas Prison in Havana when the *Journal*'s correspondent, George Eugene Bryson, came across her. Under the magic of his pen she became a heroine flung into a prison full of degenerates for defending her chastity against the brutal advances of a Spanish officer. 'We've got Spain now,' roared Hearst in delight when Bryson's story arrived. *Journal* correspondents all across the country were ordered to get signatures of American women to a mammoth petition to the Queen Regent of Spain. Mass meetings were held. Pope Leo XIII was persuaded to give his support. 'This young woman has two clean rooms in the Casa Recopidas and is well clothed and fed,' cabled the American Consul in Havana, an honest official although a strong opponent of the Spanish regime. 'She would have been pardoned long ago if it had not been for the hub-bub created by American newspapers.' There was, he added, 'no doubt that she was implicated in the insurrection in the Isle of Pines. She herself, in a note to me, acknowledged that fact.' 'At least nine tenths of the statements about Miss Cisneros printed in this country seem to have been sheer falsehood,' commented the sober *New York Commercial Advertiser*.

It made no difference. Hearst had discovered the way to promote national hysteria by telling lies with ever increasing emphasis in ever larger print. Nor was it only the ignorant and ill-educated who swallowed what he told them. The credibility of black print backed by absolute assurance swept all before it. The mother of President McKinley, the widows of Grant and Jefferson Davies, the wife of Secretary of State Sherman, a clutch of eminent writers headed by Julia Ward Howe and Frances Hodgson Burnett all signed the petition. In England Lady Rothschild gathered 200,000 signatures to support a campaign which the American Consul in Havana brusquely described as 'tommyrot'.

When the excitement showed signs of diminishing Hearst played his ace. He ordered one of his correspondents in Havana, Karl Decker, to rescue Miss Cisneros from prison and bring her to New York. It was not a mission of great difficulty. She was not under any very strict surveillance and her jailors were readily amenable to bribes. But it had to be done quickly, since the

Spanish authorities were known to be getting ready to release her of their own accord. And it had to be done melodramatically. Decker hired a house facing the prison across a narrow lane and having arranged a time suitable to Miss Cisneros (there was little or no restriction on visits) slid a ladder from the roof of this house to the parapet of the prison. He then crawled along the ladder with a hacksaw and while the prison guards earned their money by going to sleep sawed through the bars of the cell window. When the window was clear Miss Cisneros emerged and joined him. She was then conveyed to a 'secret room' rented by Decker and three days later when the search for her, never very vigorous, had died down was dressed up as a sailor and with a cigar in her mouth to add verisimilitude to the proceedings boarded the steamship *Seneca* for New York. What was, according to the *Journal*'s modest estimate, a feat unequalled since the rescue of Mary, Queen of Scots, had been triumphantly accomplished.

'Evangelina Cisneros Reaches The Land of Liberty' boomed the *Journal* as the *Seneca* steamed into New York harbour to be met by a steam launch packed with *Journal* reporters. Miss Cisneros was installed in a suite in the Waldorf-Astoria and after a quiet night to recover from the horrors of prison life was taken to buy 'a superb trousseau' in Fifth Avenue in readiness for a banquet at Delmonico's. The banquet was preceded by a ceremonial drive in an open carriage with a guard of naval cadets and was followed by an immense open air demonstration in Madison Square where 'The Flower of Cuba' and her rescuer Decker, 'The Modern d'Artagnan', were acclaimed to the music of brass bands and the explosion of fireworks.

It was magnificent. But as it turned out, it was not war. At least, not yet.

Hearst's readers enjoyed Miss Cisnero's adventures. But they were not, it soon appeared, prepared to fight for her. No doubt they felt it unnecessary so long as Hearst had Decker and others like him on his pay roll.

Disillusioned by this public ingratitude Hearst almost lost interest in Cuba. He instructed Decker to turn his attention to planning an expedition to rescue Captain Dreyfus from Devil's Island instead. And then the American battleship *Maine* blew up in Havana harbour. The explosion seems to have been accidental—certainly neither of the subsequent inquiries by America and Spain produced any evidence to the contrary. Nor did the *Journal*'s offer of a $50,000 reward for information. It is just possible that a mine was put under the ship by a group of Spanish extremists. But there was no more evidence to support this than the alternative theory that Cuban rebels had blown up the ship to promote friction between Spain and America or that Hearst himself was behind it—another theory current at the time. The idea that it was deliberately caused by Spanish Government agents was on the face of it the most absurd of all explanations, for there was nothing Spain wanted less than war with America. Not only had a new and more liberal Spanish Government decided to offer Cuba autonomy, but it was leaning over backwards to demonstrate its readiness to recognise American interests there. 'Public opinion should be suspended until further report,' called the *Maine*'s captain, adding that he was receiving every possible assistance and sympathy from the Spanish authorities. 'Clear the front page,' said Hearst. 'This means war.'

There followed a quintessential example of journalism at its most fraudulent and irresponsible. Each morning the *Journal* found some new lie to flaunt on its front page. One seven column drawing showed the *Maine* anchored over a mine with wires leading to a Spanish fort on shore and *Journal* readers were told that the Spanish had deliberately waited until most of the crew were asleep before triggering it off. Jingoism proved an unequalled circulation booster. On many days now the *Journal*'s morning and evening editions sold 1,500,000 between them. To keep in the circulation race Pulitzer's *World* was compelled to rival it in sensational untruths. The reward came when on 19 April 1898, two months after the *Maine* explosion, Congress voted for war.

Probably there would have been war without Hearst. There were others beside him anxious to pick a quarrel with Spain, many good reasons why the United States should wish to see the end of European colonialism on the American continent. But he did not himself doubt whose war it was. 'How Do you Like The *Journal*'s War?' enquired the *Journal* in large type across its front page and offered a $1,000 prize for the best suggestion for getting it off to a good start.

The Right to Know

The bizarre episode of Hearst and the American-Spanish war is worth retelling because it illustrates to an extreme degree the excesses to which the era of the personal proprietor as the predominant figure in journalism lent itself. Hearst was neither the first nor the last of these predominant figures, but he carried the exploitation of newspapers as instruments of personal whim a stage further than anyone had done before or was to do subsequently, despite the achievements of Northcliffe and Beaverbrook in this line. He could not have done so, of course, if he had not reflected the America of his time, which was also that of Phineas T. Barnum. Ready to his hand was a credulous semi-illiterate mass public avid for sensation, willing to believe anything it was told so long as its pride in American power was flattered and its conviction that those in authority were mostly (*a*) crooks and (*b*) trying to do the ordinary man down confirmed. He was uncharacteristic in that he came to journalism as a rich man, not a poor one as Bennett and Pulitzer did. They became rich by recognising and then exploiting developments in popular taste. He spent millions building newspapers in his own image. Newspaper ownership fed their egotism. His newspapers were from the start media for his megalomania and because this megalomania fitted the times, in the end the money he squandered brought another fortune to replace the one he had spent. His excesses went far beyond anything known previously, even in Dana's *Sun*, but the public appetite he aroused was such that even Pulizter had to follow him or be swamped. Later Pulitzer drew back and before he died refashioned his newspapers in a more reputable image nearer to his own conviction of what popular journalism should be. But at the height of the *Journal*'s success he had to follow it or take a beating his vanity could not let him accept.

'Nothing so disgraceful as the behaviour of these two newspapers has been known in the history of American journalism,' Godkin of the *New York Post* wrote of the *Journal* and the *World*. But the *Post* never reached a circulation of more than 35,000. The *Journal* and the *World* each went to beyond 1,000,000. It was an ominous indication of the rewards available to the unscrupulous.

These opportunities were slower to develop in Britain. The English, an essentially insular people, have long tended to credit

Hearst, Northcliffe and the Popular Press

Alfred Harmsworth, later Lord Northcliffe, with the invention of the popular press. The accolade is unwarranted. Although it did not reach its extravagant climax until Hearst bought the *Journal* in 1894 a popular press both good and bad had been flourishing across the United States for well over half a century before Northcliffe's *Daily Mail* was launched on 4 May 1896.

The slower development of popular journalism in Britain exactly reflected the differences between the two societies. Although the *Daily Telegraph*, as already noted, took over circulation leadership from *The Times* after the removal of the stamp tax and to do so borrowed some of the techniques of American journalism, it used them cautiously. It neither sought nor won the kind of mass readership that Bennett, Dana, Pulitzer and Hearst went after. G. P. Sala, its famous descriptive writer, with his verbose and highly coloured style, might have fitted into the American pattern. So, too, might Clement Scott, its dramatic critic, Le Sage, its war correspondent in the Franco-Prussian War and later its editor, or Dr Emile Joseph Dillon, its famous foreign correspondent whose formidable learning, mysterious past and intimate friendship with the great of many countries exactly suited the popular idea of a great foreign correspondent. But the public the *Telegraph* appealed to was a middle class public and despite breaks with tradition that shocked the austere spirits of Printing House Square, the paper was basically middle class in its attitudes and like many other British institutions became more so the older it got. So, too, were the Liberal *Daily News* and *Daily Chronicle* and so, too, in even greater degree were the new provincial dailies led by the *Manchester Guardian*, the *Scotsman*, the *Glasgow Herald*, the *Liverpool Post*, the *Yorkshire Post* and the *Birmingham Post*.

Such newspapers were less comprehensive than *The Times* and in some instances more popularly written. But their purpose was the same, to educate and inform. Like *The Times* — and like the best of the American regional papers — they were animated by a belief in journalism as a high calling. They were written for men already established, or on the way to being established, in their business and professions: top-hatted, frock-coated men with serious minds. Neither women nor the lower classes came within their view.

The Right to Know

Some of the new London evening papers, notably the *Pall Mall Gazette* under W. T. Stead and the *Star* under T. P. O'Connor who had worked in the London office of the *New York Herald*, borrowed more extensively than the morning papers did from American campaigning journalism. But the most famous of all such campaigns in British nineteenth century journalism, Stead's 'Maiden Tribute of Modern Babylon' which exposed the horrors of the traffic in prostitution to which polite society preferred to close its eyes and landed Stead himself in prison for three months for 'procuring' a girl of fifteen, was neither planned as an attempt to raise circulation, nor in fact did so to any significant extent. It was a magnificent piece of journalistic muckraking that in the hands of Dana, Pulitzer or Hearst—especially Hearst—would have brought immense rewards as a circulation booster. It increased that of the *Pall Mall* by only 3,890 copies. But because of it the Criminal Law Amendment Bill was passed.

O'Connor set out more deliberately to attract a popular public. Not, however, by Hearst's or Pulitzer's methods. In many ways his journalism was nearer to that of Godwin's *Evening Post* than theirs. The *Star* was crisp, cheerful, impudent and amusing and it sold for $\frac{1}{2}d$. Bernard Shaw wrote on music for it, A. B. Walkley on plays, a future Lord Chief Justice, W. T. Hewart, wrote its leaders which were kept down to half a column. It had a great variety of short items of news boldly displayed and wonderful racing tips. It was a great breeder of future editors, no less than seven, including H. W. Massingham, later Editor of the *Daily Chronicle* and founder of *The Nation*, Sir Robert Donald who succeeded him on the *Chronicle* and Thomas Marlowe, Editor of the *Daily Mail* for twenty-seven years, were among those who learned their trade at its sub-editors' table. However, although it attracted readers it did not make money and O'Connor's financial backers who consisted of a group of rich Liberals lost confidence in it as a political force and a profit earner and bought him out.

Even when British daily popular journalism arrived in earnest with Harmsworth's $\frac{1}{2}d$ morning *Daily Mail* its form was at first very different from that of American popular journalism. This form was conditioned by the nature of the British market—not a market of teeming immigrants of all races such as New York popular journalism had exploited from Bennett onwards, or of the free-wheeling pioneering communities of the Middle and far West that Storey, Medill, Lawson, Nelson, Bonfils, Tammen and Hearst had catered for in their several ways, but a market of the new black-coated lower middle class born of the Education Act of 1870 and passionate for self-improvement.

The potentialities of this new public had first been exposed in October 1881 by a thirty-year-old Manchester representative of a London fancy-goods firm named George Newnes. He had a liking for snipping interesting paragraphs out of newspapers and magazines and was persuaded by his wife to turn this hobby to practical use by starting a 1d weekly magazine. When he could not find a printer willing to take the risk she opened a vegetarian restaurant and on the profits from nut cutlets the new journalism was launched. *Tit-Bits from all the Most Interesting Books, Periodicals and Newspapers of the World*, soon shortened to *Tit-Bits*, proved an immediate and extraordinary success. It provided exactly what many thousands of the public of the newly educated most wanted—potted, easily assimilated facts about a multitude of different things, pre-digested reading matter for the whole family. Backed by ingenious sales promotion schemes, one of which offered clues to a hidden bag of gold sovereigns in a serial story, the circulation soared to the phenomenal figure of 700,000 in less than three years.

Almost by accident Newnes had uncovered a great new reading public. Newspaper publishers were slow to take advantage of it. Even Newnes himself failed to after *Tit-Bits*. He turned his formula for milking other people's cows to more sophisticated use in the *Review of Reviews*, this time in partnership with W. G. Stead, and had a great middle class success with the *Strand Magazine*—sweet still in the memory of many of the middle-aged and elderly as the birth-place of Sherlock Holmes. But when it came to newspapers he went no further than financing the distinguished but small circulation *Westminster Gazette*. On this for sixteen years he lost with unruffled cheerfulness between £10,000 and £16,000 a year, thinking it, no doubt, a small price to pay for furthering the Liberal interest to which he had adhered since youth, and acquiring a title.

Alfred Harmsworth was a school-boy of sixteen when *Tit-Bits* exploded on the news-stands in its green cover. Socially he was a cut above the lower middle class *Tit-Bits* public. His father was a barrister, although an unsuccessful one given to Micawberish expectations. Fortunately for his family his wife was very far from being a Mrs Micawber. The *Tit-Bits* formula of bitty information in short paragraphs fascinated Alfred's magpie mind. He had an appetite for unrelated facts as insatiable as a competitor in a television quiz show. From being a reader of *Tit-Bits* he became a contributor, selling it short articles at a guinea a column on 'Curious Butterflies', 'Organ Grinders', 'The Making of a Q.C.' and similar matters. Thus launched in journalism he moved on to the editorship of a paper called *Youth* at £2 a week and from there, with a 10s rise, to the editorship of *Bicycling News* published by the Coventry firm of Iliffe.

There could have been no more useful apprenticeship. With the invention of the safety bicycle and the pneumatic tyre, cycling had become for hundreds of thousands of the lower middle class young far more than a form of cheap transport or even an agreeable exercise. It was a magic carpet to wider horizons. Like H. G. Wells's hero, Mr Kipps, they found on wheels the freedom and romance ordinary life denied them. In Robert Blatchford's Clarion cycling clubs the bicycle even became a powerful instrument of socialist propaganda. That, however, was something young Harmsworth did not concern himself with: he was wholly lacking in evangelical political fervour or the crusading passion that brought many early American newspaper publishers into journalism. What he acquired at the cycling club rallies and club suppers he attended on his journalistic business was an unrivalled knowledge of the sort of things that interested the new reading public created by popular education. He came to realise, also, that despite the exclusively male preoccupations of the daily press, this public included women as well as men.

The bicycle had become a potent, if humble, instrument of female emancipation offering the freedom of the road and temporary escape from domestic bondage to those bold enough to ignore the hoots of laughter the appearance of a woman on a bicycle brought to the lips of witty masculine passers-by: sometimes more than laughter, indeed, for some anti-feminists were so outraged by the evidence that women had legs and could propel themselves with them that they threw stones. However, the stoning of a few women cyclists in the interests of masculine chivalry failed to check the lure of mobility. A Women Cyclists' Association was formed. Before long women were participating with men in club rides. Under its youthful, forward-looking editor, *Bicycling News* appointed a woman cycling correspondent.

Although Harmsworth lacked social conscience he had a sharp eye for social change. He was still earning £1 a week from *Tit-Bits* as well as editing *Bicycling News* and was also writing for various other periodicals such as *Young Folks*. But his ambitions were set higher. Unlike the established mandarins of publishing he realised that *Tit-Bits'* success was destined 'to modify in the most profound degree the intellectual, social and political tone of the press as a whole'—as *The Times* put it in its pontifical way in the hindsight of the second volume of its official history. He was determined to be one of the modifiers. In the official biography of him by Reginald Pound and Geoffrey Harmsworth a conversation with a friend in Coventry is recorded. 'One of these days,' he said, 'I'm going up to London to start a penny weekly like Newnes' *Tit-Bits*. Only I shall let the great British public ask the questions.' To another friend he confided, 'This Coventry life is too middling. You are not quite down but you are by no means up. I must be up.'

He got a chance to start on the road up when a young Dublin friend of his mother's family named Dargaville Carr turned up in London with £1,500 to invest in some reasonable undertaking and was persuaded that a partnership with Alfred Harmsworth in a publishing enterprise would provide exactly that. In practice it scarcely managed to do so at first. The new publishing company published several cheap paper-back booklets written by Harmsworth but made little money out of them. However, with the help of another £1,000 from an acquaintance who had married money, and the promise of printing credit from his old employers in Coventry, Harmsworth's long planned raid on the *Tit-Bits* market was started on 2 June 1888 with *Answers To Correspondents* soon to be shortened to *Answers*. *Answers*, its first number proclaimed, would be a universal information provider: 'Anyone who reads our paper for a year,' it asserted, 'will be able to converse on many subjects on which he was entirely ignorant. He will have a good stock of anecdotes and jokes and will indeed be a pleasant companion.'

As in *Tit-Bits* this universal information was conveyed in short brisk paragraphs no more than two or three lines in length. Those who bought the first issue were able to learn 'What The Queen Eats', 'How To Cure Freckles' and 'Why Jews Don't Ride Bicycles', together with a mass of information, useful no doubt to many, on 'Strange Things Found in Tunnels', 'Narrow Escapes from Burial Alive', 'Strange Arrests' and 'Do Women Live Longer Than Men ?'—all provided in reply to fictitious questions written in the office, mostly by Harmsworth himself. *Answers* was factual, philistine and as far as Harmsworth could make it so, exactly suited to the intellectual interests, which were indeed his own, of a lower middle class public avid for information, self-improvement and subjects for family conversation.

Although Newnes paid it the compliment of declaring it to be 'the first real opposition I have had,' *Answers* had none of the immediate success of *Tit-Bits*. It took eight desperately impecunious months to reach a circulation of 30,000. What got it off the ground eventually was not its editorial content, but Harmsworth's genius as a circulation promoter. Like other geniuses he borrowed from others when he could, sometimes copying Newnes quite shamelessly, as when he offered a junior clerkship in the office of *Answers* as the first prize in one competition—although even in this he showed his awareness of social change, for whereas the *Tit-Bits* offer was confined to young men the *Answers* competition was open to young women also. Real success came with an idea he picked up from a tramp on the Embankment (he was always ready to talk to anyone) who said longingly, 'The only prize I want is £1 a week for life.' It was, Harmsworth recognised, the poor man's dream of wealth. He immediately adopted it as the prize in an *Answers* competition for guessing the amount of gold coinage in the banking department of the Bank of England at the close of business on a particular date—information then regularly issued by the Bank. Entries had to be sent on a postcard with the names and addresses of five witnesses—thus making sure that the good news should be widely spread.

It was, shouted *Answers* placarding the good news all over town, 'The Most Gigantic Competition The World Has Ever Seen.'

The public thought so too. The response was immediate and extraordinary. A total of 718,218 postcards was received, each with their ration of five supporting witnesses, and on the date named police reinforcements had to be called in to control the crowds who gathered outside the Bank of England to see the figures posted and special runners were employed by the evening papers to take the news to Fleet Street. The prize was won by a member of the Ordnance Survey staff at Southampton who came within £2 of the correct figure. There could have been no more suitable winner. He was young, respectable, hardworking, and promptly announced that having won he proposed to get married at once. He even saved *Answers* money by dying of tuberculosis eight years later. Harmsworth sent his widow a cheque for £50.

Answers was now firmly on the way to success. Carr, who was no businessman, was bought out and sent back to Dublin as Irish sales representative at a salary of £5 a week and commission. A new company was formed and brother Harold (later the first Lord Rothermere) was instructed by his mother to resign his post as a boy clerk in the Mercantile Marine Office of the Board of Trade and go to the help of her eldest son as financial manager. 'Be wise, Harold, be wise,' urged his civil service superior. 'Never resign except with a pension.' But family feeling was superior to bureaucratic caution and Harold took up his new office. Within five years a string of other weeklies aiming at the same market had been added to *Answers*. There was *Answers* for the family, *Comic Cuts* ('Funny Without Being Vulgar') for the children, *Chips* for the errand boy, *Forget-me-Not* for the factory girl, *Home Chat* for the housewife. Following hard on their heels, came *Union Jack*, *Home Sweet Home*, *Boy's Friend*, *Sunday Companion*, *Half Penny Marvel*—an empire of the semi-literate broadening down from precedent to precedent. Four years after the prize of £1 a week for life *Answers* became a public company with a capital of £275,000. Three years later Harmsworth Brothers Ltd with a capital of £1,000,000 was formed.

Alfred Harmsworth was now ready to demonstrate that the qualities that made cheap periodicals sell would work also for cheap newspapers. By now the existence of a market for such newspapers was a mathematical certainty, only no one but

Harmsworth had bothered to do the adding up. His first opportunity to test his arithmetic came when a Conservative MP who had spent £100,000 in keeping the Conservative *London Evening News* alive as a dullish political journal decided he had had enough and instructed his solicitors to seek other arrangements for its future. Before they could do so he died leaving his executors to dispose of the paper as best they could. This proved difficult until two Fleet Street reporters, Kennedy Jones and Louis Tracey, although as penniless as reporters are apt to be saw a chance to make sure of steady jobs for themselves and talked the executors into giving them a short option with the assurance that their knowledge of Fleet Street would soon enable them to lay their hands on a buyer. Potential buyers proved shy until just as their option was nearly up a friend suggested a call on the Harmsworths who until then they had not thought of as likely to be interested in anything other than more cheap periodicals.

Two strings were attached. One was that Jones and Tracey should be given jobs and a small share interest, the other that the paper should continue to support the Conservative interest. The first presented no great difficulty, although Harold Harmsworth did report sourly to brother Alfred that neither Jones nor Tracey had the journalistic reputation they claimed. The second in Harold's eyes was a more serious bar. This was not because he had any objections in principle to supporting the Conservatives but because he feared, wrongly as it turned out, that such a link might damage their non-political periodicals. However, he advised his brother that the *News* had a useful circulation and if bought cheaply might be made to pay and Alfred decided to plunge. They bought the paper for £25,000 including plant, machinery and fittings and Alfred moved in. 'Good God, man, you're not going to turn into an evening *Answers* are you?' complained Kennedy Jones when he heard what Alfred Harmsworth had in mind. This was exactly what Harmsworth did intend.

New type was bought and the old solid columns broken up into short paragraphs. Everything was bright, snappy and written in short sentences. It was a sub-editor's rather than a reporter's paper: a processing plant for turning the raw material of daily news into pre-digested matter for the compulsorily educated.

Sales were helped by a fortunate run of successful racing tips, and a sensational murder trial came at just the right time. In a matter of months circulation had quadrupled.

Kennedy Jones had been appointed editor and his newsman's expertise was helpful. But it was Alfred Harmsworth who made the paper. His was the drive and imagination, his the formula. Brother Harold looked after the accounts, preventing flair from turning into financial extravagance. But his contribution although substantial was pedestrian. Without Alfred nothing could have been accomplished. He was the Bonaparte of the campaign, Harold no more than Quartermaster General.

Success brought wealth. But more than wealth. Alfred Harmsworth found himself being cultivated by politicians and congratulated by Lord Salisbury, the Conservative leader. For the first time he experienced the pleasure of being an insider, the illusion of political influence.

Temporarily this deflected his real appetite which was always for journalism. He allowed himself to be seduced by the social and political attractions of becoming an MP and accepted nomination as the Unionist Candidate for Portsmouth in the General Election of 1895. Characteristically his first move was to make sure of press support by buying a local Conservative evening paper, the *Evening Mail*—although not until Harold had reported that it could be made into a business success. The purchase is interesting as the first indication of his later settled belief in his right to use his newspapers as instruments of personal ambition. Having got it, he tried to persuade William Le Queux, a popular author of romantic thrillers, to write him a serial story for it to be called *The Siege of Portsmouth*. This was to narrate the trials and heroisms of the people of Portsmouth, identified by actual names so far as possible, in a war with Germany—thus flattering both their patriotism and their vanity and inclining them to vote for a man who thought so well of them. William Le Queux proved unavailable. A young Canadian journalist recently taken on by one of the Harmsworth magazines was then given the job, with a naval historian to look after the technical background and provide local colour. The serial remains an interesting oddity of election literature, but otherwise failed in its purpose, as did also a specially composed patriotic song in praise of dockyard workers sung by a young lady draped in a Union Jack on the stage of the Empire music hall with a hired claque in the audience to shout for an encore. The electorate of Portsmouth turned out to be more politically sophisticated than Harmsworth believed. He was defeated.

The blow to his vanity confirmed him in his temporarily suspended contempt for elected politicians—'Anyway my real place is in the House of Lords,' he remarked when the result was announced—but he had too many other things in mind to let such a minor reverse trouble him for long. Among them was a plan for a chain of provincial papers, a start on which was made the same year with the purchase of the *Glasgow Mail and Record*. But the most important was that for a ½d morning newspaper, the *Daily Mail*. It took practical form early the following year, on 4 May 1896.

Northcliffe was thirty, a few years younger than James Gordon Bennett had been when he started the *New York Herald*, the same age as Horace Greeley when he founded the *New York Tribune* and Henry Raymond when he began publication of the *New York Times*, two years younger than William Randolph Hearst when he bought the *New York Journal* or than Barnes when he became editor of the London *Times*. Journalism was still a young man's trade. In appearance he was fair haired and slight of build, 5 ft 8 in in height and more youthful looking even than his years, with a Napoleonic cast of countenance that he did his best to foster, imperious in manner but with a boyish charm that robbed it of some of its edge. Intellectually he was, as his official biographers confess, even more immature than his looks: his head crammed with 'a bewildering miscellany of factual information', but with little sense of the relation of things: responsive to the living moment but 'almost entirely without the power of sustained thought or abstraction'. Serious discussion drove him to a brooding silence which his satellites liked to think was the gestation of genius, but which was more probably boredom. His sense of humour was juvenile. Like Hearst he enjoyed practical jokes and what he thought of as 'leg pulls'. He was inordinately entertained by two Edison Bell gramophone records, one of sneezing and the other of snoring, that continued to reduce him to helpless laughter long after the joke, such as it was, had gone flat on everyone else.

Hearst, Northcliffe and the Popular Press

In artistic matters, said Sir William Rothenstein who knew him well, he had 'a quite sincere bad taste'. In literature he was fond of Dickens's novels and, which was less likely, of those of Thomas Hardy. But he was incapable of reading systematically. The strongest personal influence in his life was his mother whom no other woman, including his wife, could remotely challenge in his affections and he was inordinately ambitious for all members of the Harmsworth family for whom in his years of greatest influence he acquired honours on an almost Napoleonic scale. He had no legitimate children of his own but several illegitimate ones.

This was the man who was now to become the predominant figure in British popular journalism. Here one comes at once on an important distinction between British and American popular journalism. The makers of American popular journalism—even Hearst in his early days—were all possessed of reforming zeal. They were sensationalists but they were also muck-rakers and crusaders: their eyes on the submerged millions. They might, for the most part, lack a coherent social philosophy but they were against injustice and the exploitation of poor and helpless by the rich and powerful—especially when the rich and powerful happened to be great corporations like Standard Oil or the Southern Pacific Railroad. They were Robin Hoods of the pen.

Harmsworth had no such emotional involvement. His emotional links, such as they were, were with the small shopkeeper and the ambitious clerk, with those who had no complaint against society but simply wished to improve their own position in it, satisfied to feel themselves a cut above the labouring poor and happy to be governed by their betters. Charles Booth's *Life and Labour in London*, Stewart Headlam's *The Bitter Cry of Outcast London*, Henry George's *Progress and Poverty* had all been published in the year he started *Answers*. In that same year the Lords Committee on Sweating heard from no less a person than Colonel Birt, General Manager of the Millwall Dock, of dockers who came to work 'with scarcely a boot on their feet, in a most miserable state . . . without having a bite of food in their stomachs, perhaps since the previous day, they have worked for an hour and earned fivepence their hunger will not allow them to continue . . .' In that year also the Bryant and May match girls' strike aroused the conscience of London with its disclosure of young girls employed

75

for eight or nine shillings a week in conditions that condemned large numbers to early death. None of this was reflected in Harmsworth's journalism. Nor was the social turbulence that produced strikes and lock-outs all over the country in the year the *Daily Mail* was launched.

Harmsworth went lower in the British social scale for his public than any of his predecessors. But he did not get, or try to get, to the foundations. The huge mass public at the bottom of the social and economic pyramid that had provided American popular journalism with much of its public from Bennett onwards had to wait in Britain for nearly another thirty years. The most startling social fact about the Northcliffe revolution, indeed, is that despite, or perhaps because of it, British popular daily journalism avoided right up to the 1930s the kind of mass appeal that gave American popular journalism its strength.

Harmsworth told his staff on the *Daily Mail* to think of its readers as men with £1,000 a year. When the boldest among them protested that this could not very well be so since £1,000 a year was an exceptional income in those days he replied, 'Well they like to imagine themselves like £1,000 a year people and they certainly prefer to read the news of £1,000 a year people.' The reader the *Mail* was after, he amplified, was 'tomorrow's £1,000 a year man, so he hopes and thinks'.

It was as a universal provider to this acquisitive and inquisitive new reader that the *Daily Mail* succeeded. Northcliffe was of like kind to Lever, Lipton and the other new captains of industry who made fortunes out of a mass consumer market. His *Daily Mail* had little either of the sensationalism or the crusading zeal of the American mass circulation press—less indeed than had the *Daily Telegraph* or the *Daily News* in their early days or than W. T. Stead sometimes displayed in the *Pall Mall Gazette*; a good deal less than the popular Sunday newspapers commonly employed. What it offered was news at a bargain price processed for easy assimilation: 'A Penny Paper for One Halfpenny', 'The Busy Man's Daily Journal', as its advertising slogans ran. It was eight pages standard size, with classified advertisements on the front page (although some experiments with news on the front page had been made in preliminary dummy runs) and conservative in make-up. It had more headlines and cross-heads than was then normal but they were small in size. All its news stories were short and it often tended, as Harmsworth's official biographers shrewdly comment, to 'confuse incidents with events'. A group of sub-editors trained in the *Answers* formula made sure that everything printed conformed to his excellent dictum: 'Explain, simplify, clarify.' The long reports of parliamentary proceedings previously regarded as obligatory by all newspapers were drastically pruned; they would merely have bored and estranged potential *Mail* readers. The customary leading article of a column or more was replaced, as in the *Evening News*, by four short opinion comments, statements not arguments. *Mail* readers were held to be more interested in people than principles and both news and comment were written with that in mind. A City column specifically aimed at the small investor picked out the news in company reports and prospectuses and presented it in simple English—a shocking innovation and sadly devaluing to the profession of financial journalism many older hands thought. There were two columns particularly for women: 'Movements in women's world—that is to say, changes in dress, toilet matters, cookery and home matters generally—are as much entitled to receive attention,' announced the paper in revolutionary mood, 'as nine out of ten of the matters which are treated of in the ordinary daily paper.' There were short articles packed with facts suitable for family conversational use, a serial story—a form of reader riveting to which Harmsworth was much addicted all his life—good sports coverage and a racing column by Robin Goodfellow. All the regular features appeared in the same place every day so that they could be found without difficulty by readers going to work on buses and trains. Everything was neat, compact, simple and short, as carefully directed to its market as the numerous other consumer goods that were now flooding the country with their appeal to the desire for self-improvement. Like them it offered excellent value for money.

The first number sold 397,215 copies and within two years the paper had a steady circulation of half a million, which went up to a million during the Boer War, and was making profits unequalled by any paper since *The Times* at the peak of its monopoly position. It was, in fact, probably the only morning paper in the country to be making a profit.

What really signalled the opening of a new phase in British

journalism, however, was not just the fact that the *Daily Mail* sold in large numbers to a new public, but the use to which the circulation was put—indeed the purpose for which it was from the very start conceived. This purpose was not political—that was to come later when Harmsworth's increasing megalomania persuaded him, on the whole wrongly, as was to happen also with subsequent owners of popular newspapers, that control of widely selling newspapers provided both the means to political power and the divine right to exercise it—but commercial. Before the *Daily Mail* all British newspapers, indeed most newspapers in all parts of the world, had been private or family properties valued, to use the words of the first Royal Commission on the Press more than half a century later, 'for the prestige and the political and social influence their possession conferred, rather than as a source of dividends'. Harmsworth turned the press into a business. The *Daily Mail* was the first British daily newspaper to become a public company, the first to invite investors to buy shares in it not because they were interested in political opinions or even in newspapers as such, but simply as a commercial business to earn profits. These profits came in abundance. They could not, however, have been earned simply from the sales of a newspaper selling at a halfpenny, however large its circulation. Indeed the larger the circulation, the larger the loss, for a halfpenny was well below the *Mail*'s production cost. What the Harmsworth brothers knew, for they had learned it from *Answers* and their other periodicals, was that what counted most in a publishing budget was not revenue from sales but revenue from advertising. In the conditions of the new mass market the real importance of a large circulation lay in the direct access to large numbers of potential buyers it could offer to advertisers.

From the days of Perry and his *Morning Chronicle* onwards newspapers had, of course, always looked to advertising to re-inforce revenue from sales. It was advertising that provided the economic foundation that gave *The Times* political independence. The Harmsworths were, however, the first fully to recognise the immense commercial possibilities opened up for newspapers by a mass market and to see that it was by providing advertisement space for those who wished to sell in this market that newspapers could most prosper.

Hearst, Northcliffe and the Popular Press

The position of the masses at the lowest levels of the social scale might move others to radical sympathy. Harmsworth was not interested. Such people had no purchasing power worth bothering about. The new white collar workers had. Not very much individually as yet, but in total enough. They had money in their pockets and they were ready to spend it. They were the new market and whoever could command an entry to that market could command fortune.

It was out of such thinking that the idea of a newspaper deliberately sold below cost to attract a mass public was conceived and the new reading public taught to expect its newspapers at a subsidised price—a lesson it learned only too well for the future health of the newspaper industry. Nor did the Harmsworths simply deal in promises of a worthwhile readership as others did. They produced facts. They published a net sales certificate certified by a chartered accountant and fixed their advertising rates at so much per column inch per 1,000 readers. The *Daily Mail* was the first newspaper to use such a method: it was in some ways Northcliffe's biggest contribution to the future of the popular press.

To say this may seem to write Northcliffe down as no more than a man selling newspapers to a mass market as others sold soap or tea. That would be untrue. Rothermere was the businessman— and when he was left to run newspapers on his own after his brother's death, a pretty mess he made of them. Northcliffe was a major influence in turning the press into a branch of consumer industry and journalism into a trade instead of a calling, but he was much more than this. He was a great journalist. Not great in the sense that Barnes and Delane had been or that C. P. Scott, transforming a small provincial newspaper in Manchester into an organ of world opinion, was, but great in the sense of a man ceaselessly captivated by the surface of news and uniquely sensitive to every ripple on that surface. All successful newspapers must have one quality above all others, they must hold their readers' interest. Whatever other virtues they may or may not have they must possess what the best of show business possesses, the power to attract and excite. Northcliffe brought these qualities to his newspapers in supreme degree.

Although some men make great fortunes out of journalism, few go into journalism simply to make money, any more than they go on the stage for such a reason. Nor do they go into it for power, although some imagine they get it, or even to serve the public, although they may hope to do so. They go into it because its tempo is their tempo and its rhythms their rhythms. This is their life. They are hooked irretrievably, captives of a black magic that commands all their senses. So it was with Northcliffe. He was one of the great impresarios of journalism. Such men may not be admirable but they must have in abundance the power to communicate their own excitement with life to others. Northcliffe was adolescent in most of his interests, naïve in most of his judgments—but then so was his public. A restless, endless curiosity possessed him. He had a marvellous flair for what would interest his readers and a superb nose for the news they would want to talk about. Before he came along almost everything that was the subject of ordinary conversation by ordinary people was left out of the morning paper. He put it in. He finished up as a power-confused megalomaniac but on his own level he was a journalistic genius. If he had not been, not all his brother Harold's hard headed business ways could have made the *Daily Mail* and the newspaper empire that grew from it the success they were. He was fortunate, of course, in that he matched his age. The time, the place and the loved one came together. He put his mark on his society because he reflected in his personality so much that was most characteristic of it.

CHAPTER FIVE

The Financiers Move In

'Like a well stocked store a newspaper should offer in its different departments, known in the profession as columns, everything that its clientele could need,' wrote Hippolyte de Villesmessant, founder and editor of *Le Figaro* of Paris, in his memoirs. In words James Gordon Bennett would have approved, he remarked, 'It is necessary that I please serious people; it is also necessary that I am agreeable to light-hearted people or those who wish to refresh their spirits for a while.' He likened editing a newspaper to giving a dinner party at which both 'harvesters and refined city people' were to be entertained and said, 'Whether one likes it or not it is necessary to give to each of my guests what suits his taste and his stomach and, to return to my comparison of the department store, I expand my columns in order that everyone can find ample supply of what he needs.'

Le Figaro was ahead of most British newspapers in meeting changing public tastes and so also was *Le Petit Journal* whose founder and editor, Marioni, much impressed Alfred Harmsworth when he met him in Paris before starting the *Daily Mail*— especially when Harmsworth found that *Le Petit Journal*'s mixture of lively news, gossip and political attack was selling 650,000 copies a day and making a profit of about £150,000 a year.

Outside Paris the European press remained much closer in character to *The Times* than the *Daily Mail* and a world away from the crusades and sensationalism of the American popular press. However, a lighter touch broke through here and there. In Denmark Christian Ferslaw made a big success of *Aftenposten* by mixing non-political news with how-to-do-it-for-yourself features, and even in Belgium, where newspapers and citizens tended to be equally grave, *Le Peuple* broke ranks and did well with a popular, unpolitical approach to news.

The social forces making for a popular press were much less inhibited outside Europe. In Australia John Norton's *Truth* found a rousing policy of sex, sensationalism and exposure so successful that within a few years its circulation had increased tenfold. 'The demand for sensations,' observed a contemporary writer, 'is on the increase and therefore the supply must be kept up.'

This proved to be the case even in Japan. As that country propelled itself into the modern world the Japanese people displayed a taste for sensational journalism that Hearst himself could scarcely have outdone, although it owed a good deal to him. It began when *Yomiuri* (still the most sensational of Japanese dailies although a good deal less so than it was) heard of what Hearst had done with the *San Francisco Examiner* through the Japanese trading links with the American Pacific coast and decided to try his methods. They were so successful that a 'black third page' devoted to scandal about politicians and businessmen was soon mandatory for every Japanese daily with an ambition for large sales. Government action to check this by prohibiting the publication of matter 'inimical to peace and order or injurious to public morals' was met by the ingenious invention of the 'Jail Editor', a minor member of the office staff whose sole occupation it was to go to prison while the real editor carried on undisturbed with his task of printing the worst about everybody. 'You go back and tell the bastard he can't intimidate me,' Charles E. Chopin, City Editor of the *New York World*, had roared when one of his reporters crawled into the office with a lost tooth and a black eye after being beaten up by a ward politician who objected to his private life being investigated. The Japanese press translated Chopin's instruction into a journalistic philosophy and institutionalised it.

As in the United States muck-raking was not solely inspired by the desire to sell papers. A good deal of it came from a genuine radical protest against bureaucratic abuses, the expression of a popular movement for reform which in the absence of constitutional means to make itself felt turned to the press. In this protest Japanese popular journalism found unexpected allies.

The Financiers Move In

Robbed of their hereditary occupation as unsuited to a modern state, ill fitted by training and temperament to absorption in an industrialised society, and allergic to bureaucracy, dispossessed members of the samurai put aside the sword for the pen and splintered on their military virtues of *esprit de corps* the repeated official attempts to stop the development of a crusading journalism. 'It has never once been found,' wrote John Black, an English journalist living in Japan at the time, 'that when one writer or Editor has been incarcerated there was no man of ability to step immediately into his shoes.'

Over most of Asia, however, illiteracy checked the growth of a popular press. There were important papers of opinion for the educated classes in India but such vernacular newspapers as existed were small, badly printed and for the most part short lived. The same was true of South America, despite the towering stature of *La Prensa* and one or two others.

In South Africa the *Rand Daily Mail*, with Edgar Wallace as its first editor, brought modern popular journalism of the London *Daily Mail* kind to the European mining populations in competition with the more sedate *Argus* and *Star* after the Boer War. Elsewhere on the African continent, there was as yet no place for popular journalism—nor much, indeed, for any journalism directed to native populations.

However, the *Gold Coast Independent* which a Sierra Leonean, James Bright Davies, founded 'to create and foster public opinion in Africa and make it racy of the soil', did manage some sort of breakthrough, by concentrating on general news brought to it from all over West Africa by canoe or by hazardous land journeys through the jungle. And in Lagos a Liberian, John Payne Jackson, the first professional journalist on the West Coast of Africa, who like others of his craft elsewhere combined professional flair with a reputation for hard drinking, established in the 'nineties the *Lagos Weekly Record* as a newspaper of protest against white administration. Jackson had a sharp pen. Sir Frederick Lugard (later Lord Lugard), a favoured and, on his own terms, liberal figure of Victorian colonial mythology, he described as 'a man whose walking stick is a pistol'.

Neither the *Lagos Weekly Record* nor the *Gold Coast Independent* had, or could hope to have, of course, a readership among the illiterate mass of the native population. They were read by an elite only. Nevertheless, through this elite they gave voice to the angers and aspirations of a subject people and by setting their own fierce pride in African culture against the assumptions of Western superiority which came natural to colonial administrators and Christian missionaries alike they had considerable effect in shaping African nationalism. Although directed to a literate minority what there was of the West African press thus served many of the purposes of a popular one.

There were no such indigenous newspapers in East Africa where the *African Standard*, founded in 1902, catered entirely for the white settlers. Or in the Congo where Belgian paternalism had no place for press freedom. In Egypt, however, things were already stirring. *Al Mist*, *Al Waten* and *Al Ahram*, each of which was later to have a significant role in Egypt's struggle against foreign domination, were all founded towards the close of the nineteenth century.

By the end of the nineteenth century, therefore, the popular press was beginning to make itself heard in a good many places, although except in countries where economic advance was rapid and political independence a practical possibility it tended to be unstable and vulnerable. It is to Britain and the United States, however, that one must return to trace the main stages in its development.

Until the *Daily Mail* the British national morning press was firmly set in *The Times* tradition: even the new newspapers that came into existence with the end of the stamp tax felt it prudent to model themselves on that paper. The *Mail* ended all that. By the beginning of the new century when it was the only morning paper in London making a reasonable profit. *The Times*, so long supreme in every field, was in grave financial difficulties. These difficulties had been accelerated by the costs incurred and the damage done to its reputation by its publication of forged letters allegedly written by the Irish leader, Charles Stewart Parnell, implicating him in the Phoenix Park murder of Sir Frederick Cavendish, the Chief Secretary of Ireland, and the Under Secretary, Mr Burke, but actually the production of a down-at-heel Irish journalist named Richard Piggott who committed suicide when about to be arrested in a hotel bedroom in Paris.

The Financiers Move In

Even without the Parnell case, however, *The Times* would have been in difficulties: doomed by its refusal to accommodate to changing tastes. By 1908 it was in imminent danger of having to close down and was only saved from doing so by the intervention of an anonymous Mr X who after some months of mystery and conjecture turned out to be none other than Alfred Harmsworth, raised to the peerage as Lord Northcliffe two years before. There could have been no more significant indication of the changing newspaper scene.

The *New York Times* also fell on difficult times towards the close of the nineteenth century. By 1896 it had dropped to a circulation of a mere 9,000 copies a day. However, it was happier in its rescuer than *The Times* of London, which Northcliffe was suited neither by temperament nor intellectual capacity to understand, although he brushed up its commercial organisation and gave it a strong push into the twentieth century. Adolph Ochs who bought the *New York Times* for $75,000 was untouched either by Northcliffe's mania for personal power or his commitment to popularisation. He was content that the newspaper he published should be 'clean, dignified and trustworthy'. With the slogan 'All the news that's fit to print' at its masthead, he not only restored it to a position in public esteem equal and in the end exceeding that it had first won under its founder, Henry Raymond, but tripled its circulation in a year and established it permanently as one of the great newspapers of the world, safe from future misadventures.

He was helped by a public reaction against journalistic excesses of a kind as yet unknown in Britain. By the close of the century Hearst and Pulitzer between them had brought the era of sensational personal journalism in the United States to so gaudy a climax that a large body of the middling public no longer wanted any part of it. In Britain a sharp distinction between quality and mass journalism was already beginning to develop. In the United States, however, as Bernard A. Weisberger observes in *The American Newspaperman*, 'the laurels went to the man who did not confine himself to one appeal, in American society the inexorable market test was passed best by the journal that resisted categorisation'. Every paper was for everyone and in following Hearst during the Spanish-American war and after, the *World* inevitably estranged some of its more serious readers. Its loss was the *New York Times*'s gain.

When he had first bought the *World* Pulitzer had set out his philosophy of the press in these words: 'An institution that should always fight for progress and reform, never tolerate injustice or corruption, always fight demagogues of all parties, never belong to any party, always oppose privileged classes and public plunderers, never lack sympathy with the poor, always remain devoted to the public welfare, never be satisfied with merely printing news, always be drastically independent, never be afraid to attack wrong, whether by predatory plutocracy or predatory poverty.' It was a noble philosophy and although under the stress of competition Pulitzer fell a good way below it, in his old age he hankered after it and, half blind, nervously ill, constantly on the move, editing his newspaper by telephone and telegraph from wherever he happened to be, he refashioned the *World* into one of the best American newspapers there has ever been. By then, however, the *New York Times* under Ochs had established itself as beyond compare the serious-minded paper for serious-minded people: the great American equivalent of the specifically quality newspapers of Europe.

The highly personal journalism initiated by James Gordon Bennett and Horace Greeley and copied by Pulitzer, Hearst and others in the great expansionist age of the American press had outlived its time. It had been a very paternal journalism. Although they by no means despised the money their success brought them its editors and publishers were men with a mission, often indeed several. Their readers looked to them not only as purveyors of news and opinion but as counsellors and guides, constant campaigners in their cause. As American society became more stable and more institutionalised this paternal element declined. In a society on the move newspapers had been independent outriders shooting from the hip. Such newspapers still lingered here and there, but for the most part the American press became part of American business, its owners men of commerce far removed from their shirt sleeved predecessors, their editors managerial executives. Only the star reporters remained to carry on the old personal tradition and sustain in their by-lines the waning image of the newspaper as the investigatory instrument of a watchful democracy.

The Financiers Move In

By the opening of the twentieth century most of the editor-publishers who had given the nineteenth century press of America its special character had gone. Hearst, it is true, remained, but even he had moved on from the direct, night by night control of a newspaper as his personal instrument, to the creation of a vast trans-continental newspaper and magazine chain. His newspapers continued to speak with the Hearst voice and reflected the Hearst megalomania. But the voice was no longer concentrated in one frenetic daily bellow and as it grew less radical and more reactionary it made consistently less impact, retaining the sensationalism of the early years without the capricious social crusading that had sometimes compensated for it.

American journalism did not, of course, lose all its individualists. The maverick tradition stayed bright in the hands of men like Colonel Robert R. McCormick, grandson of Joseph Medill, who turned the *Chicago Tribune* into an even more vituperative, xenophobic journal than his grandfather had done, and those of his cousin Captain Joseph Medill Patterson who launched the tabloid *New York Daily News* and made it the most ruthlessly successful purveyor of sex and sensationalism ever seen in America or anywhere else: a paper, as was well said, appealing 'to the more elementary emotions of a truck-driver and to the truck-driver in everyone'. There were some others. But these men, like Hearst in his later years, were anachronisms, biological sports unrepresentative of the main evolutionary stream of American journalism.

More typical of the twentieth century trend was Frank Munsey who made a fortune out of popular magazines and another out of a grocery store chain before he turned to newspapers. He held that 'The same law of economics applies to the newspaper business that operates in all important business today. Small units in any line are no longer competitive.' Munsey never achieved his ultimate ambition which was to own a chain of 500 newspapers—or came remotely near it. But he bought and merged many famous ones, including the *Sun* and the *Herald* which he put under one masthead, the *Globe* which he merged with the *Evening Sun*, and the *Mail* which he merged with the *Telegraph*. He tried to buy the *Tribune* and when its owner, Ogden Mills Reid, refused, sold him the *Herald* instead—a marriage that neither Bennett nor Greeley would have been likely to contemplate with pleasure but which made the *Herald-Tribune* one of America's great newspapers for several decades. Munsey fell far short of what he set out to do. But he did enough in the way of killing off and merging newspapers to deserve the memorial tribute William Allen White of the *Emporia Gazette* paid him: 'Frank A. Munsey contributed to the journalism of his day the talent of a meat packer, the morals of a money changer and the manners of an undertaker. He and his kind have about succeeded in transforming a once noble profession into an eight per cent security. May he rest in trust.'

Nevertheless although Munsey had little feeling for the character and traditions of the newspapers he merged he was more in tune with the spirit of the times than his critics. The open frontier for the press had ended. In most of the great cities of the U.S.A., Chicago, Boston, Philadelphia, Baltimore, Milwaukee, San Francisco, Detroit, Los Angeles, consolidation of newspaper ownership was becoming the accepted theme. Formerly, individual and often highly eccentric and egocentric newspapers founded and run by publishers who were newsmen by training and aptitude had made up the dominant newspaper pattern. Outside all but the greatest centres of population this now became the newspaper chain.

Hearst moved in this direction early and at his peak owned forty-two daily newspapers across the States. But in this as in so many other things he over-reached himself: he had begun as a young man in love with his own prejudices, he ended as an old man doting on them and it was a gimcrack empire he left behind.

It was far otherwise with his chief rival as a chain maker, Howard W. Scripps. Much more than Hearst, Scripps was the true father of the newspaper chain, devising principles of group ownership that even the great multiple proprietors of our own day, like Thomson and Newhouse, cannot ignore—although he went about the business with a great deal more journalistic passion than they commonly bring to it, and less preoccupation with profit.

He was a man very different from Hearst, hewn out of much the same timber as Bennett, Greeley and other early American newspaper publishers. A poor man who had climbed to the top, he was to the end moved by the radical emotions that, to a degree never duplicated in British daily journalism, inspired so much early newspaper activity in America. He was the thirteenth child of a poor farming family and began journalism as a boy of eighteen on a small neighbourhood paper in Detroit run by his elder brother. Four years later he started his first paper, the *Penny Press*, in Cleveland on borrowed money. It did well. Within five years he acquired a second, this time in Cincinnati. In Cleveland he had been fortunate enough to get hold of an excellent newspaper manager, a Scotsman named Milton McRae. He persuaded McRae to come to Cincinnati as his partner with a contract that gave him one-third of the profits for tending things in the office while Scripps looked around and did what pleased him. What pleased him most was to buy other newspapers, usually small and mostly losing money, and put them on their feet. Within a few years the Scripps-McRae League had added to its Cleveland and Cincinnati properties newspapers in Akron, Des Moines, Toledo, Kansas City, Houston and San Diego. In the end it had twenty-three newspapers as well as its own news agency which was later to develop into the United Press, and its own feature syndicate, the Newspaper Enterprise Association.

Scripps's method when he bought newspapers was to choose energetic young men as editors, offer them a ten per cent stock holding in the paper they were invited to edit, with a loan at six per cent to buy it with if they needed the money, and give them a blanket instruction to build a profitable newspaper by honestly serving their communities. He believed in local autonomy but local autonomy according to his ideas and held indoctrination sessions for his editors at his home, Mirimar Ranch, sixteen miles outside San Diego. Here he sought to instil into them efficient management techniques and a sound journalistic philosophy. His basic attitude in life, publicised on any and every occasion much to the irritation of his fellow publishers who considered him disloyal to their rich man's club, was 'to make it harder for the rich to grow rich and easier for the poor to keep from growing poorer'. He was, he said, prepared to do everything for the poor except live like them. His journalistic philosophy was most cogently expressed during a session with the newly appointed editor of his Houston paper and was subsequently printed as *Letter to a Young Editor*.

The Right to Know

It reads oddly in a world that has come to believe that the viability of newspapers depends on their attractiveness to advertisers, but it made a success of his newspapers and it made him rich and it may not be without some relevance even today.

'I would advise you,' he wrote, 'to begin your course as editor of this paper with one object and only one object in view, and that is to serve that class of people and only that class of people from whom you cannot even hope to derive any other income than the one cent a day they pay for your newspaper. Be honest and fearless with them, always without regard to the goodwill or ill will of the so-called business community. . . . Be diplomatic, but don't be too diplomatic. Most men fear to speak the truth, the bold, bold truth to any man or community because they fear that the man or the community is not prepared to endure such frankness. I think this is a mistake. It is rare indeed when the circumstances are such that a conscientious man can lose anything by fearless, frank speech and writing.'

Howard Scripps was a newspaper genius who bought newspapers for the fun of it. He neither wanted them as vehicles for his personal prejudices, as Hearst did, nor as means of making a great deal of money as most modern multiple owners do—although he managed to make quite a lot. He wished them to be of service to their local communities and he saw to it that they were run by men in touch with ordinary people who would have the courage to speak for their interests, even if they fell foul of the rich and powerful in doing so. Editorially he was able to show that membership of a group could mean commercial strength and freedom from local intimidation. But he was also a shrewd businessman and he ably exploited the advantages offered by chain ownership in bargaining with suppliers of newsprint, with large advertisers and with those who had syndicated editorial material to sell.

Others who lacked his free-wheeling attitude to financial and commercial interests and were much more concerned than he ever was with maximising profits soon learned from him just how considerable those advantages could be. At the turn of the century there were twenty-seven newspapers in chain ownership in America. Most of the newspapers were small and individual chains rarely exceeded two or three newspapers. Ten years later a dozen newspaper chains controlled some sixty newspapers. By the end of another twenty years the number of newspaper chains had grown to fifty-nine and they controlled between them 325 daily newspapers accounting for about a third of the total newspaper circulation of the country. Most of these chains copied Scripps's methods— although not his philosophy. They operated for the most part in small and middle sized towns and usually enjoyed a certain amount of local autonomy. But they were first and foremost business operations seeking to maximise profits and they increasingly drew on advertising rather than sales as their main source of profit, often looking for eighty per cent or more of their total revenue from this one source.

In its beginnings the regional press of America had been notably idiosyncratic and iconoclastic. It had often gone to extremes, some admirable, some gross. But it had reflected the communities it served, even in its eccentricities. Now a pall of anonymity settled over most of the regional landscape. A few great newspapers withstood the prevailing winds, the *St Louis Post-Dispatch*, the *Philadelphia Public Ledger*, the *Boston Transcript*, the *Kansas City Star*, the *Milwaukee Journal* and the *Louisville Courier Journal* among them. A few small town owner-editors continued to go their individualist way. But for the most part it began to be the case that you could travel across America and apart from local news written to offend no one—or at any rate no one of importance—read the same agency news and the same syndicated features wherever you went in the same way as you bought the same branded goods in a chain store.

The American newspaper public continued to get a good deal of information from its newspapers. It also often got a greater variety of opinions on national issues in one newspaper than the people of most other countries, since the regionalism of the press and the wish to give a more cosmopolitan gloss and variety to local products encouraged syndication of Washington columnists. But in local matters grey conformity became the wear as business managers assumed the role of publisher and editors looked over their shoulders at absentee directors who cared nothing for local issues but much for local advertising, or governed their editorials by the need not to annoy local bankers and businessmen whose support was needed. Not only locally but over the whole span of the press the era of the predominant individual, whether editor or publisher, that had stamped itself so firmly on American newspapers in the nineteenth century was passing, had indeed for the most part already passed. It was later to return with some force in magazine publishing, notably in the case of Henry Luce and *Time Magazine*. But in most of the daily press the corporation mind and the salaried executive were moving in. Hearst was the end of a line.

In Britain, on the other hand, Northcliffe was the beginning of one. So far from reaching its end, the era of the predominant individual had still to make its full mark on British journalism.

This difference in pattern, or perhaps more correctly in rhythm of change, was partly because the British press had still a good deal to do that the American press had already done. It had to become a people's press.

In so far as the history of the British press in the first part of the twentieth century reflects the discovery and satisfaction of a mass audience it represents a repetition of American experience several decades late. But there were important differences. American conditions favoured regionalism and the development of newspaper chains in which each link was multi-social. British conditions encouraged the development of national uni-social newspapers appealing to similar groups all across the country. Because of its size the United States was made up of a multiplicity of markets each of which had, as it were, to be cut vertically to satisfy all tastes. In Britain there was one huge national cake which could be cut horizontally layer by layer. This British cake was shaped like a pyramid. The small triangular piece at the top represented the quality press, the broadening layers below the various gradations of popular journalism down to the base. At the base was the vast mass public of the working classes but as yet no one bothered about that. Nor were they to do so until the *Daily Mirror* of the thirties and forties.

British conditions led not only to a sharper distinction between quality and popular newspapers than in America but also to a much more intense battle for circulation. Instead of being spread over many regional markets the greatest newspaper effort was concentrated on the one national market. The fight was bitter, the slaughter heavy. The *Daily News*, the *Daily Chronicle*, the *Morning Leader*, all of which were in good health when the *Mail* was launched, bore the first brunt of the attack. They suffered so badly that the *Daily News* and the *Morning Leader* were almost immediately forced to merge. In 1906 a new Liberal answer to the *Mail* arrived—the *Tribune* which was to provide the background for Sir Philip Gibbs's novel of Fleet Street, *The Street of Adventure*. It lasted only two years. Nor did the much older *Morning Standard* do much better. It was compelled to turn for financial security to Sir Arthur Pearson who owned a string of cheap popular magazines very similar to those of Northcliffe and Newnes. He poured new money and talent into it. But the blood transfusion did not work. Within six years he was forced to sell after making substantial losses and although the *Morning Standard* lingered on for a time, it never again became a viable proposition. Nor did Pearson have much better luck with the *Daily Express* which he started in 1900. With news on the front page and a clever American Editor, R. D. Blumenfeld, it began with a splash as the brightest of the *Mail*'s rivals. But it failed to establish itself and after a zig-zag run of seventeen years was headed for bankruptcy when Blumenfeld persuaded Lord Beaverbrook to buy it in the middle of the 1914–1918 war.

Even Northcliffe could not repeat his *Daily Mail* success when he backed his belief in the importance of women as newspaper readers by starting a daily paper, the *Daily Mirror*, specifically for them. With advance publicity on a scale never previously attempted, the *Mirror* began well with an initial circulation of 265,000. Within three months this had fallen to 25,000. Dispatching one of his young lieutenants, Hamilton Fyfe, to sack all the women staff and turn it into a picture paper (as which it soon became a success) Northcliffe growled that it had taught him two things: 'Women can't write and don't want to read.' Nor, it seemed, did the solid respectable working classes. The *Daily Citizen*, which was launched with the financial backing of the trade union movement to give a voice to the aspirations of the moderate Labour movement, lasted a bare three years. Even at that it was much more successful than W. T. Stead's venture into morning journalism, the *Daily Paper*. This survived only about the same number of weeks.

Looking on that stricken field it could not but seem at first that the rise of the *Daily Mail* had been a false dawn so far as a popular press in Britain was concerned. The myth of an immense flowering of the popular press once the *Mail* had shown the way—applauded or deplored according to taste—is nothing but a myth. For twenty years or more the *Mail* was nearly as unique as *The Times* had been in its day. In fact, although Northcliffe had discovered and exploited with great success a new public among the lower middle classes, the total British market for popular journalism still remained small. The press could not run ahead of social conditions. Edwardian England, which glows so nostalgically in the memories of its ageing middle-class survivors, was still too much the prisoner of a social system that not only treated the mass of the population as congenitally inferior to the few but saw to it that both culturally and economically they were kept so, for it to provide the turbulent flux in which a popular press could take root as in America. The masses read newspapers on Sunday. Not until the golden Edwardian afternoons among the tea cups and cucumber sandwiches were over, did the potential demand for popular daily papers begin to reveal itself.

It is significant that when it did the first challenge to the *Daily Mail* came from a man bred on the other side of the Atlantic, the Canadian Max Aitken, later Lord Beaverbrook. The war shattered the old social pattern. But it did not, as many had feared, and a few had hoped, bring a new society in its place. Except in one economically backward country, Russia, and there more by the accident of war than genuine mass revolution, the Red Peril proved a non-starter. What war left behind it in Britain was not socialism, but opportunism. In such a society Beaverbrook, the outsider, 'the little Canadian adventurer' who went wherever money would take him, was a natural impressario of news. Simply by following his own bent he responded to both the iconoclasm and the credulity of the post-war world. He was against the old aristocratic order and took an impish delight in discovering how much of it was corruptible by publicity. This contempt of his was genuine, the contempt of a man who had made his own way in the world and wanted elbow room. He liked to think of himself as a radical and his radicalism was genuine. too. But it was neither economic nor political but social. He was a plastic surgeon, his concern was with the surface of things, not their foundations. He was not against inequality, but he thought it should be an inequality of money and talent, not birth. Nor did he hanker after a more just society, only a more open one, more suited to men of his own gifts. It is wrong to think of him as without principle, for he was guided all his life by fidelity to the romanitic and unrealistic principle of Empire Free Trade that had caught his loyalty in youth. However, although guided by principle personalities would keep breaking in and he never failed to follow where malice and curiosity beckoned.

Northcliffe's *Daily Mail* had been the ambitious young clerk of the beginning of the nineteenth century writ large. Beaverbrook's *Daily Express* was the post-war flapper generation writ even larger. It had a popular appeal that cut across social frontiers to an extent no other British newspaper had previously done or has ever done since. In its handling of news the *Express* tended to be both more polished and more superficial than most American journals, but in the universality of its aim it followed the American mode. It was a cocktail mixed by men who knew that the suburbs had developed a taste for the West End.

In one sense Beaverbrook's success in journalism was accidental. Northcliffe had seen himself as a man of Fleet Street from the beginning, for him that was always where the pot of gold lay. But Beaverbrook went into journalism because he thought the fortune he already had could buy him political power there. Northcliffe began as a journalist and finished as a propagandist seduced by his own headlines, Beaverbrook travelled the road the opposite way. He began as a propagandist and finished as a journalist, although his taste for propaganda unfortunately never quite left him. He did not find political power, although he often deceived himself that he had. But in the rootless society of the twenties, his newspapers gave him what was almost as good and usually more amusing, social pull and a fruitful field of patronage.

He had already made use of the *Daily Express* on several occasions before he bought it. The first occasion had been in 1911 when he loaned the paper £25,000 in return for, or at any rate coincidental with, a promise by its editor, R. D. Blumenfeld, to support Bonar Law, that grey man for whom Aitken (as he then was) had so curiously strong a public admiration and personal affection. He continued a tenuous and somewhat secretive connection with Blumenfeld thereafter and was for this reason the natural person for Blumenfeld to turn to when it looked as though the *Express* had finally come to the end of its run in late 1916 or early 1917 — Beaverbrook who delighted in small mysteries always refused to put a firm date on his purchase of the paper and produced contradictory ones at various times. He bought it for £17,500 and an undertaking to pay its debts which were considerably more and included £40,000 owing for newsprint. His purpose at the time was entirely political. He saw it as a prop to those ambitions and intrigues in which he so delighted. He had had a large hand in replacing Asquith as Prime Minister by Lloyd George with Bonar Law's backing and if his reward had been what he expected he would have been well content to use the *Express* for such political purposes as he required without involving himself in its general direction. But Lloyd George was not a man to allow gratitude to stand in his way and when he found how unpopular young Max Aitken was with the stiff necked Tories whose support he needed he forgot his promise of a seat in the Cabinet and offered him the sugar plum of a peerage instead. It has subsequently been argued, and Aitken himself believed, or pretended to believe, that in accepting this he destroyed his chances of a major political career: an innocent colonial trapped by a wily Welshman. This is almost certainly nonsense. The only political offices put permanently outside Beaverbrook's grasp by going to the Lords were the Premiership and the Treasury and his chances of either were so minimal as to be for all practical purposes non-existent. It is impossible to conceive of any circumstance then or later in which he would have been acceptable to the Conservative Party as its leader. Even the peerage was touch and go. The King, whose instincts were profoundly affronted, objected strongly and was only persuaded to approve it when Bonar Law managed to persuade him that much difficulty and scandal would follow if it was withdrawn after being promised. In these circumstances Lord Beaverbrook, reluctant peer, was born.

He was a reluctant press baron also. He had never intended to devote most or even a large part of his time to Fleet Street. It was only at the end of the war when he started the *Sunday Express*, to share the printing overheads of the daily, and found himself faced with such losses that it began to look as though the fortune he had brought with him from Canada would soon all run away down the gutters of Fleet Street that he became in his own words 'a full blooded journalist'.

What began as a rescue operation ended as a life time passion.

The Financiers Move In

The top floor of the Express building in Shoe Lane was converted into an apartment furnished like a film set with a wide window looking across the roofs of Fleet Street and Ludgate Hill to the dome of St Paul's and the temples of Mammon in the City beyond. Here, small, gnomish, voice rasping and cooing by turn, inexhaustible in energy, maddening in egotism and malicious in mischief, but with a charm to lure birds from the trees and win loyalty from the initially antagonistic (a loyalty, it is right to say, often, although by no means invariably, abundantly returned) he set about bullying, cajoling, bribing and driving his staff until the two *Expresses* took form as an expression of his own impish and tireless curiosity, and provided much of the new post-war public with a champagne cocktail of news, gossip and extravagant opinion that exactly suited their palates—even although they did not take the opinions very seriously.

Although the sales of the *Daily Express* rose it was still running well behind the *Daily Mail* whose circulation went to 1¾ millions at the beginning of 1922. However, in August of that year Northcliffe died, broken in health and mind, convinced that he was surrounded by enemies, a revolver under his pillow, a telephone, the wires of which had been cut, at his side down which he shouted impossible orders; murmuring at the last, 'Tell mother she is the only one.' With Northcliffe gone, genius left the *Daily Mail*. The way ahead opened for the *Express*.

Moreover, within a few months of Northcliffe's death Beaverbrook found fresh cause to divert his energies to journalism from politics when what had looked like being one of his most successful political intrigues boomeranged. He had intrigued to make Lloyd George Prime Minister in 1916. In 1922 he intrigued to turn him out and put Bonar Law in his place. The manoeuvre succeeded although success owed as much to a very different sort of man, Stanley Baldwin, as it did to Beaverbrook. But six months later, Bonar Law, a sick man who had been persuaded only by his loyalty to the Conservative Party to allow himself to be put forward as Lloyd George's successor, died and the Beaverbrook palace of poker cards collapsed. So long as Bonar Law was at Downing Street, Beaverbrook, his old friend, could hope to exercise great influence. Now to his amazed horror Baldwin whom he had consistently underestimated and who distrusted and disliked him succeeded. For the first time for more than a decade Beaverbrook found himself on the outside of politics, his contacts with Downing Street cut off. He was left with his newspapers as his only hope of political influence.

This being so, he decided in 1923 that he needed a London evening paper to complete his kingdom. The means by which he acquired one illustrates very well the extent to which newspapers had become at this time counters in the financial dealings of ambitious and avaricious men and the degree to which a good deal of journalism had fallen away from original conceptions of the public interest. Away in Manchester Scott of the *Guardian,* as much a predominant individualist of the press as Northcliffe or Beaverbrook but of a very different character, might declare when asked if he would sell his evening paper, the *Manchester Evening News,* 'There are papers which will never be sold—which would rather suffer extinction. . . . The public has rights. The paper which has grown up in a great community, nourished by its resources, reflecting in a thousand ways its spirit and interests, in a real sense belongs to it. How else except in the permanence of that association can it fulfil its duty or repay the benefits and the confidence it has received.'

But Scott's, if not quite a solitary voice, was increasingly a lonely one. It evoked few echoes in the metropolis.

The paper Beaverbrook had in mind as the most suitable for his purposes was the London *Evening Standard.* It was a paper then as now of some influence in Whitehall, Westminster and the political clubs and was owned by Sir Edward Hulton, the son of a former *Manchester Guardian* compositor who had made a success of a daily racing sheet, the *Sporting Chronicle,* and gone on to establish a chain of newspapers centred mainly in the North. Sir Edward Hulton himself had substantially extended the newspaper interests he had inherited. He had acquired the *Evening Standard* during the war when its parent, the once famous *Morning Standard,* was in difficulties and owned in addition the *Manchester Evening Chronicle,* the *Daily Dispatch,* the *Daily Sketch,* the *Sunday Chronicle* and a couple of lesser known Sunday papers. He was, however, failing in health and although unwilling to dispose of the *Evening Standard* by itself was ready, Beaverbrook heard, to consider an offer for his whole group.

The Financiers Move In

To Beaverbrook Rothermere seemed an obvious buyer. He had lost *The Times* on Northcliffe's death to the gentlemanly Anglo-American figure of Mr J. J. Astor, but under his brother's will had been permitted to acquire the rest of the Northcliffe properties, including control of the *Daily Mail*, the *Daily Mirror*, the London *Evening News*, the *Weekly Dispatch* and the Amalgamated Press which published *Answers* and more than a hundred other periodicals, for the bargain price of £1,600,000. Of this he had recovered £1,440,000 by a public issue of debentures, leaving himself with control of the equity for a mere £160,000. Rothermere, therefore, had plenty of resources. He also had an appetite for expansion. But Hulton disliked him and was unwilling to sell to him. Moreover, there were others interested, notably the Berry brothers.

The Berry brothers were sons of an estate agent in Merthyr Tydfil but early left South Wales for London to make their fortunes. William, later Lord Camrose, came first in 1901 with £100 to start him on his way. He was only twenty-one but already had a shrewd eye for the main chance. He saw the shape of admass to come and used his money to start a weekly magazine, the *Advertising World*, which cashed in on the bursting new trade in selling consumer goods by giving its practitioners their own trade paper. The venture was so successful that he soon sent for his younger brother Gomer, later Lord Kemsley, then aged nineteen, to help him with the business side of things. After the *Advertising World* came *Boxing*, 'The only newspaper in the world,' so it claimed, 'wholly devoted to boxing.' Although themselves 'privately educated', to use the favourite British euphemism for the entries in *Who's Who* of those who have made their way in the world without benefit of a public school education, the Berrys had a great respect for the social cachet given by one of the older universities and they chose to edit their new paper an impecunious but scholarly Cambridge man much devoted to the art of prize fighting, of which he wrote with much wit and many Latin quotations as when he observed of one regrettable National Sporting Club contest that until he saw it he 'had not fully grasped the meaning of *lucus a non lucendo*'. Despite, or perhaps because of this—for at that time proficiency with the gloves was still regarded as an essential attribute of a gentleman's education, improving to the moral character and making for a healthy mind in a healthy body, and even professional fighters retained a fine Corinthian glow—*Boxing* was a great success.

The brothers branched out into other magazines and trade papers until, like other newspaper owners before and after them, they were in a position to advance on stepping stones of their former selves to higher things and buy themselves into the quality market. They acquired the *Sunday Times*, then in decline, at a bargain price and greatly expanded both its circulation and its prestige. After this they went into city journalism in partnership with Sir Edward Iliffe, owner of the *Midland Daily Telegraph*, and bought the *Financial Times*. Most of their lives they were buyers rather than starters of newspapers, representative of the second wave in journalism, commercial developers not pioneers. The *Financial Times* had begun life as the creature of Horatio Bottomley, demagogue and swindler who later served a long prison term for fraud, but under the Berry touch it soon transformed itself into a highly respectable journal much read by stockbrokers and bankers. They were later to buy the *Daily Telegraph* and with William, the editorial brains of the combination, as Editor-in-Chief, bring about an even greater transmutation in that famous but at that time declining newspaper.

Quality, however, was not enough for them. They wanted quantity also and were poised for expansion wherever a chance offered. Hence their interest in the Hulton Press.

To Beaverbrook this situation in which Rothermere wanted the Hulton papers but Hulton did not want him to have them and might prefer to sell to the Berrys, seemed to offer an ideal field for those talents as a go-between he had exercised so successfully in political affairs—but this time with a good chance of getting hold of something tangible for himself as well.

Although it was not then generally known he and Rothermere were already financial partners. It has usually been assumed that it was the Hulton transaction that brought them together. However, two letters written to the present writer by Lord Beaverbrook on 30 October and 12 December 1960 in amplification of some references I had made to him in an essay 'Challenge by the Press Lords' published in *The Baldwin Age*, edited by Mr John Raymond, make it clear that their partnership pre-dated the Hulton negotiations by some nine months and was quite close. It had begun in January 1933. In that month Beaverbrook had found himself in need of funds to develop the *Daily Express* and somewhat surprisingly, in view of the fact that it was the up and coming rival of the *Mail*, had turned to Rothermere. Rothermere thereupon agreed to take over 49 per cent of the shares of the *Daily Express* Publishing Company in return for cash and shares in the Daily Mail Trust, which owned the *Daily Mail, Evening News* and *Weekly Dispatch*. The transaction was kept secret.

Late in 1923 when Beaverbrook first heard that Hulton was thinking of selling his newspaper properties but that Rothermere was a non-starter so far as he was concerned, he approached Rothermere again. The proposition he put before him was that he, Beaverbrook, should make Hulton an offer on Rothermere's behalf but should conceal from Hulton the fact that he was acting as Rothermere's agent. If he pulled it off he should get control of the *Evening Standard* as his commission. Rothermere agreed and he got to work. The Berry Brothers wanted the Hulton group badly. But they could not make up their minds what price to offer. While they were still deliberating they received the news that Beaverbrook had got in ahead of them and bought the whole of the Hulton Press for £4,500,000.

After detaching the *Evening Standard* from the group Beaverbrook then re-sold the rest to Rothermere at his buying price of £4,500,000—thus showing how a clever man with his wits about him could get an evening paper for nothing. However, he saw that he might be in need of more capital to develop it and following the pattern already established with the *Daily Express* offered Rothermere a forty-nine per cent interest in the *Standard* for shares in the Daily Mail Trust. The end result of all these transactions so far as he was concerned was that while keeping control of all his three papers he had in his possession 120,000 Daily Mail Trust shares readily realisable on the Stock Exchange if he should find himself in need of more funds for development. The financial wizardry that had served him well in his Canadian career was still potent.

However, Rothermere did well too. He put the *Glasgow Daily Record*, which he and his brother had bought in 1895 for £7,000 but of which he had later become sole owner, into the Hulton Press packet and sold the lot to the Berry Brothers for £5,500,000. This was a good deal more than they had originally hoped to have to pay for the Hulton Press as a whole, including the *Evening Standard*.

As, however, they then formed a new public company, Allied Newspapers, and sold the papers they had bought for £5,500,000 to it for £7,500,000, financed by a share issue which was rapidly oversubscribed by the public they had nothing to complain about either, especially as they retained voting control of the new company.

Beaverbrook himself was now well content. He believed in concentrating his energies and had no desire for a larger press empire than the compact one provided by a morning, evening and Sunday newspaper. As he was to tell the first Royal Commission on the Press a quarter of a century later, he had gone into newspaper publishing 'purely for the purpose of making propaganda and with no other motive'—although he added sensibly, 'no paper is any good at all for propaganda unless it has a thoroughly good financial position so that we worked very hard to build up a commercial position on that account.'

He was not, like Rothermere and others of their contemporaries, a buyer and seller of newspapers for the profit to be made out of them. What he owned he owned for keeps. Thus when Rothermere whose *Daily Mail* had begun to find the competition of the *Daily Express* increasingly troublesome, offered him the then very high price of £2,500,000 for the remaining fifty-one per cent share interest in the *Daily Express* he wasted no time in making it plain that he was not interested in an offer of any kind. His only interest, in fact, was to accumulate sufficient reserves to buy out Rothermere and get his papers entirely into his own hands. This he was able to do a few years later.

In November 1932 he bought all Rothermere's holding in the *Evening Standard*. Three months later he followed this up with a purchase of 2,371 London Express shares from the *Daily Mirror* which had got them from the Daily Mail Trust. He had to pay a high price, 41*s* per share, but inside another three months evened things up and recovered full independence by buying the whole of what remained of the Daily Mail Trust's holding of ordinary and preferred shares in London Express Newspapers at 30*s* an ordinary share and 22*s* a preferred share. He financed this partly out of accumulated profits and partly from funds set aside from the profitable sale of his Daily Mail Trust shares between 1928 and 1929 before the financial crisis and the Stock Exchange slump.

The interlocking share arrangements between the *Express* and the *Mail* which had so admirably suited his earlier purpose were now done with for good. He was big enough to stand by himself. Subsequently he established two Foundations together owning fifty-one per cent, and with members of the Aitken family seventy-three per cent, of the voting shares in Beaverbrook Newspapers so that even the fact that it had by now become a public company with outside shareholders could not put his control or that of his heirs at risk.

Others were more concerned with the profits to be made out of newspaper deals than with newspapers themselves. While Beaverbrook concentrated his energies on his own three they went in for buying and selling on a massive scale, mimicking the chain developments that had become so popular in American journalism at the turn of the century. The scramble was led by the Berry brothers. With appetites excited by the Hulton deal, they now embarked on a buying spree that brought twenty-six provincial morning and evening papers, as well as the Amalgamated Press group of periodicals, into their net. Rothermere followed. He had got £8,000,000 from the Berry Brothers for the Amalgamated Press and this he now used to out-bid them in the scramble for provincial newspapers. He bought fourteen altogether. As he and the Berry brothers frequently found themselves in a cut-throat fight to drive each other's papers out of business and at the same time make life impossible for any independently owned ones in the same circulation area losses often out-topped profits. Rothermere spent £1,000,000 in Newcastle alone in the effort to establish a newspaper there before he was forced to withdraw. The effect of this war of giants on locally owned newspapers was devastating. Some were bought and sold at fantastically inflated prices, others were forced out of existence without regard for community interests. Neither the costs nor the effect on relations between press and public deterred other eager buyers.

The Westminster Press controlled by an oil and public works millionaire, Lord Cowdray, who had bought the evening *Westminster Gazette* and turned it into a morning paper—perhaps because he found it easier to think of losses in terms of hundreds of thousands of pounds rather than thousands—also joined in. This company finished up with thirteen provincial papers. A fourth group, the Iveresk Paper Company, got nine. Iveresk had as its Chairman an ambitious solicitor named Harrison. He knew little about newspapers but persuaded his board that they were a good investment to safeguard their markets for newsprint. In 1928 he crowned his effort by buying the *Daily Chronicle* which once great paper he managed to kill in two years flat. After that he disappeared from the newspaper scene.

Before the flow of capital was dammed by the financial crisis of 1929 and the buying had to stop, nearly half of all the newspapers published in Britain had fallen into the hands of one or other of these four major groups. Once checked, however, the rush to trustification never recovered its momentum. The Berry brothers had been the pacemakers. They now turned to other newspaper activities and split up. Lord Camrose, the elder and much more able of the two, kept the Amalgamated Press, the *Financial Times* and, what was to him by far the most important part of the package, the *Daily Telegraph*. On this he thereafter concentrated his main attention with remarkable results in circulation and prestige. Lord Kemsley took the group's provincial and Sunday newspapers, including the politically and socially important *Sunday Times*.

No doubt even without the chain makers many provincial dailies—particularly morning ones—would have died during this period. Their day was over. It had been a short one. With the end of the stamp taxes in the middle of the previous century there had been a flowering of provincial journalism almost comparable to that in the United States. But geography and a national rail network was against them as was the domination of the metropolis in politics, finance and the arts, and the rise in newspaper production costs. Provincial evening papers, particularly those sufficiently far from London to escape the competition of the London afternoon papers, were still viable, indeed as the invasion by the Berrys, Rothermere and the others indicated, they offered, or seemed to offer, fine prospects of profit. Even among provincial evening papers, however, there was some fall in number as production costs rose and advertisers concentrated on the circulation leaders in each area.

It was, however, the provincial morning papers that proved most vulnerable. Outside a few great centres few could now hope to meet the competition of national newspapers delivered at the same time as journals locally published.

The Financiers Move In

In the United States distance and political decentralisation favoured the development of strong regional papers. For the British, however, it was natural to look to London for political, intellectual and cultural leadership, excessively so, perhaps. Of course the great American political issues were also at the centre of government in Washington, but apart from issues of the very greatest sort on which the regional press could keep its readers informed through the wire services and the syndicated columnists, the decisions of State legislature were often likely to be of greater importance to Americans than those of the central government. Moreover, many of the basic functions of government—education, health and law enforcement among them—which in Britain were subject to policy decisions at the centre were and are in the United States handled by local governments or agencies subject to local elections and to the pressures of local communities. Lacking local newspapers such communities would have felt themselves denied the means to make local democracy work. In addition the constant pull between State and Federal rights and the vast area of activity which is subject to State decision all gave importance to the regional press.

So, too, did the pattern of advertising. Operating in a more competitive, more consumer-orientated society than the British and one much more inclined to use the techniques of special offers and price cuts to attract custom, local retailers in America looked to local advertising in local newspapers to a much greater extent than did their less competitive, more traditional equivalents in Britain. These tended to expect trade to come to them by word of mouth recommendation and the pull of local reputation rather than to have to go out and gather it in by aggressive advertising of special bargains. Moreover the national audience sought by national advertisers could be reached through national newspapers in Britain, whereas in the States it had to be sought through regional newspapers.

This capacity to reach a national audience through nationally circulated newspapers assumed a new importance for the British popular press in the twenties when an event took place that was later to be described by Lord Beaverbrook as a turning point in newspaper history. This judgment may seem odd when compared with the great political issues that had provided landmarks in the development of a free press. But it was valid enough in practical terms. The great London department stores began to advertise on a national scale. Previously such firms as Harrod's and Whiteley's had been inclined to rely mainly on customer recommendation and family patronage for their trade, although the *Daily Mail* did obtain a certain amount of department store advertising which was much enjoyed by women readers. Now, however, department stores began under the competitive spur of Selfridge's, whose American founder, Gordon Selfridge, had little respect for stick-in-the-mud British selling attitudes, to book full page advertisements in the popular papers. Selfridge and Beaverbrook were old friends and it was Beaverbrook himself who got the first Selfridge full page for the *Daily Express*, thus showing his advertising young men where the future lay.

It turned out to be a future of Klondyke proportions, a rich new vein of gold for popular newspapers, although only for those with circulations giving access to a truly popular market.

As other caterers to this consumer market followed the example of the department stores the prizes for circulation success became steadily more glittering, the penalties for failure more disastrous. In such a market economy a buoyant net sales certificate was the key to fortune.

But its cost was high. More expensive news services, more costly features, bigger pictures, more pages using more newsprint, all these were necessary to keep in the race. Nor were such editorial qualifications sufficient on their own. Ancillary aids had to be employed. By 1928 free insurance offers to registered readers— readers, that is, who were prepared to place a firm order for the newspaper for a definite period of time—had cost the *Daily Mail* alone £1,000,000 and the costs incurred by other newspapers were not much lower.

The *Daily Mail* still had the first place in circulation but it was under increasing pressure from the *Daily Express* which led the field from the *Daily Chronicle*, the *Daily News*, the *Westminster Gazette*, the *Daily Mirror* and the *Daily Graphic*. *The Times*, the *Daily Telegraph* and the *Morning Post* had opted for a different, quality race of their own, in which the *Manchester Guardian* could also be thought of as a contender. As the pace in the popular race grew hotter it proved beyond the capapcity of some. In 1928 the

The Financiers Move In

Westminster Gazette collapsed and was absorbed by the *Daily News*. Two years later despite a circulation of 1,000,000 the *Daily Chronicle* followed it and the *Daily News* became the *News Chronicle*.

By this time a new competitor had joined the race, the Labour *Daily Herald*. The *Daily Herald* had originally come into existence as a small strike sheet during a printers' stoppage in 1911. It had outlived the strike to continue as a fighting bulletin of the political left. During the war it was forced to turn itself into a weekly but was revived in 1919 as a daily: 'The Miracle of Fleet Street' Northcliffe called it. With George Lansbury as its editor, it struggled on, puny in size, permanently in debt, aggressively independent of voice, living by audacity and Lansbury's talents as a fund raiser. Osbert Sitwell wrote leading articles for it. Siegfried Sassoon was its literary editor. H. M. Tomlinson, H. W. Nevinson, Havelock Ellis, E. M. Forster, Walter de la Mare, Edward Garrett, Aldous Huxley, Robert Graves were among its regular contributors Only the *Morning Post* on the far right could rival it in literacy. But advertisers were unimpressed by literacy either on the right or left. The bills mounted. Soon they became too many and too large to handle. In 1922 it was forced to retreat into the safe mediocrity of existence as an official organ of the Labour Movement supported by a regular trade union levy secured by the energy of Ernest Bevin. As such it secured a circulation of around 250,000 and the devoted loyalty of many working class readers but had still practically no success in getting advertisements.

In 1929 it was again transformed, this time by an infusion of commercial blood and capital from Odhams Press which needed a daily paper fully to employ the printing presses of its vastly successful mass circulation Sunday paper, the *People*.

J. S. Elias, later Lord Southwood, the presiding genius of Odhams, was a new kind of newspaper proprietor: a small, premature wave of the future, an early Lord Thomson. Unlike Northcliffe, Beaverbrook, Rothermere or, on a more public spirited level, the Cadbury family who owned the *News Chronicle*, he had no interest in newspapers as vehicles of ideas, neither his own nor anyone else's. He was concerned with them simply as merchandise. A small, kindly, uncultured man much given to public benevolence for its own sake and as a means to a peerage ('We have no party creed or bias. We want a peerage for Elias,' sang the Labour wits of the *Herald* when he took over) he had raised himself from office boy to Managing Director by hard work and strict attention to business and in the process had surmounted such bitter blows as that inflicted on Odhams's reputation by the exposure and arrest for fraud of Horatio Bottomley, founder and editor of *John Bull*, which Odhams printed and later published.

Elias had few pleasures outside business. His only extravagance was to have his shirts made for him by the gross at Sulka's of Bond Street and to order two dozen new suits regularly each year from a tailor in Savile Row, always in the same subdued shades of brown, blue or grey. He entertained rarely and lived a private life of impeccable dullness with a wife of modest tastes to whom he was devoted. Each morning they listened together to *Lift Up Your Hearts* on the B.B.C. before he went off to the office. His political interests were minimal. In so far as they existed he was a garden party Conservative and in his first search for a printing companion for the *People* had thought of buying the *Morning Post* which was later to prove so much above the heads of its readers as to be compelled to merge with the *Daily Telegraph* against which no such charge could be laid. However, closer consideration compelled him to the conclusion that to make the *Morning Post* popular was beyond even his capacity. He turned his attention to the Liberal *Daily Chronicle*, only to find himself a jump behind Mr William Harrison with his doomed dream of newspaper glory. At this stage the *Daily Herald* was brought to his attention and a deal with Ernest Bevin on behalf of the T.U.C. which reserved political policy to the trade unions but gave commercial control to Odhams ended his search. He prepared to turn Labour's voice into a worthy competitor of the *Mail* and the *Express*.

If he had been a different sort of man, bolder, more original, less anxious to stand well with nice people, he might have made the *Herald* the first genuine mass circulation newspaper in Britain. The great base of the social pyramid was still journalistically un-exploited: there was as yet no working class daily paper that talked to the working classes in their own idiom about things that actually interested them, as much of New York daily journalism had done for nearly a hundred years. However, despite the example of *John Bull* in that line and the *People*'s success in catering for the masses at week-ends, when it came to a daily newspaper Elias and his trade union associates could think only of a softer *Daily Express*.

The *Herald*'s Labour politics were a cross Elias had to bear. He was loyal to his agreement with Bevin and the T.U.C., for he was a very honest little man, but he had no taste for radicalism and longed only that politics should be unobtrusive. He could not bear to think of nice Mr Baldwin and nice Mr Chamberlain being insulted. He wanted a newspaper that the guests at the Grand Hotel in Eastbourne, where he went every year with his wife for a holiday, would think well of. But above all he wanted one advertisers would like. He was a merchant and he set about selling the *Herald* as he would have gone about selling any other product for the consumer market. He was a good man, kind to children and charitable to the poor and he meant no harm to anyone but he precipitated one of the most disreputable episodes in British journalism simply by being himself and doing what came naturally to him.

He could not but be aware that he was late at the feast. If the *Herald* was to get its feet under the advertising table it had to get readers quickly. When it went to Odhams it had already lost the trade unions over half a million pounds and its advertising revenue was negligible. This its staff tended to put down to political prejudice on the part of advertising agents and their clients, but Elias, the a-political, could not imagine anyone letting politics stand in the way of making money. Once the *Herald* became a glistening new paper with a big market he felt sure advertisers would come in. What mattered was sales and to get them the *Herald* must be promoted like any other consumer product. Bigger papers, bigger names. A serial story by Edgar Wallace, a series of articles by H. G. Wells, better pictures, star writers bought from the *Daily Express*, better women's features, better sports coverage. All these were necessary. But privately he had no great faith in editorial content as a draw and thought readers must be given some other reason for buying the product.

Helped by a pre-publication campaign during which Ernest Bevin stumped the country appealing for local Labour and trade union support and vast space was taken on the hoardings to advertise the paper's new attractions, the new *Daily Herald* came out on 17 March 1930 with a circulation of just on a million. A few years previously this would have seemed a remarkable total, a sure guarantee of success. Now it proved insufficient to get the steady advertisement revenue needed. At this stage Elias came to the conclusion that the *Herald*'s only hope was to outpace all the others. It must get the largest circulation in the world.

What followed is to journalists an oft told tale. To bribe readers into taking the *Herald* free gifts of fountain pens, pencil sets, cut glass vases and other things were offered to anyone who signed an order form for it for a few weeks. An army of canvassers, many of them ex-naval and army officers axed in an economy wave, was sent from door to door. It was hoped that sympathy for them as well as greed for something free would swell the order books. However, the Newspaper Proprietors' Association stepped in and ruled that such gifts were against its rules. After heated arguments a new agreement totally banning all free gifts was reached. Elias signed with the others, only, however, to come out almost immediately with an offer of 'handsomely bound volumes' of a number of useful publications, including the *Home Doctor*, the *Handyman* and a dictionary at a cost 'far below their real value'. He was accused of breaking his word and retorted with an even more 'magnificent' offer of a complete set of the works of Charles Dickens in 'sixteen handsome volumes bound in imitation leather'. As readers had to send a small postal order these could not, he claimed, come under the ban on free gifts. He could not be accused of breaking the N.P.A. agreement. He had merely bent it. There were angry scenes at a meeting with his fellow proprietors at the Savoy Hotel, but in self-defence the *Mail*, the *Express* and the *News Chronicle* were compelled to follow his example. Soon the country was flooded with hastily printed sets of Dickens, all apparently in much demand from an avid public. Never before had anyone guessed the British public to be so literate.

After Dickens came other standard authors. However, the public appetite for a good read proved exhaustible. These did not go as well as Dickens. Elias was not daunted. He switched from the needs of the mind to more practical satisfactions and in place of books offered mackintoshes, flannel trousers and ladies' underwear at bargain prices. Again the others were compelled to follow. Boots, shoes, tea sets, mincing machines, cutlery, kettles, saucepans, almost everything short of the kitchen sink, were flung into the battle. At its height the total bill reached over £3,000,000 a year.

The Financiers Move In

With less money to spend than the others and an unfashionable Quaker belief in newspapers as newspapers the *News Chronicle* fell behind. It was passed by the *Herald*. Then the *Express* passed the *Mail*, ending that paper's forty year lead. Even second place was denied to the *Mail* for long. Flinging merchandise into the gap with a lavish hand the *Herald* passed it and drew alongside the *Express*. Finally with yet another stupendous new offer of kitchen ware the *Herald* got its nose ahead and became the first newspaper in the world with a circulation of 2,000,000. Elias had achieved his ambition.

It did not do him much good. Having reached the 2,000,000 he found himself compelled to spend £5,000 a week and soon £10,000 a week to hold it. Nor did his lead last. Beaverbrook's policy of reluctant expenditure on tea sets but lavish spending on editorial enterprise while Elias concentrated on bargain basement offers brought its reward. As the *Herald* contined to spend frantically to keep in the same place, the *Express* moved forward under the stimulus of a genuine readership demand. Nor did its 2,000,000 circulation bring the *Herald* the advertising Elias had anticipated. Advertisers were less easily hypnotised by figures than he thought: they were sceptical of the value of net sales certificates won by bribery.

Nor did he get the co-operation from the *Herald* editorial staff he considered he had a right to. They refused to be bright, insisting that they had a responsibility to give serious news its proper weight and made life hard for Elias by telling the public what they believed to be the truth about international affairs. To Elias, the kindly Jew who had become a Christian and asked only for a quiet life in which to make money for Odhams Press and serve his innumerable charities, gloomy reports of Nazi attrocities against Jews and warnings of impending war seemed a betrayal of the interests of Odhams.

The *Daily Express* was cheerful and optimistic. 'Remember in the *Express* every day is a sunny day,' its noted Editor, Arthur Christiansen, instructed his staff and as the cloud over Europe grew bigger it published on its front page a daily genuflexion to optimism over truth: 'There Will Be No War This Year Nor Next Year Either.'

No wonder, complained Elias, striding about his office with all the national newspapers spread on the floor at his feet, for he seldom read them but only looked at their front pages, no wonder advertisers preferred to take space in the *Express*. Its headlines encouraged people to look on the bright side and go out and buy things, those in the *Herald* filled them with gloom and made housewives too depressed to enjoy spending. Life would have been even darker for him but for his other publications. They had no trust deeds that could be made an excuse for not doing what advertisers liked. They were booming—especially a new one called *Woman*. Apart from the *Herald* Elias was, in fact, a most successful publisher, ruthless with the knife when a publication did not pay but generous when it did, anxious only to give the public what would please it and to upset no one. He deserved the memorial service in Westminster Abbey he eventually received.

With a daily newspaper, however, he was completely out of his depth. He had no understanding of public affairs and no understanding of journalism. He degraded newspapers by his sales methods and did not even make them pay. But for the war which gave it a temporary reprieve the *Herald*'s losses might have proved too much even for the resources on which Odhams could draw to feed the white elephant he had brought into its garden.

Yet although a good deal of the circulation bought by the tawdry promotion schemes of the thirties proved fictitious—how fictitious was shown when Beaverbrook in a fit of revulsion temporarily called off his canvassers as a demonstration and lost 250,000 'readers' overnight—some of it stuck. Between 1930 and 1939 the combined sales of popular morning papers rose by over one million and a half and went on rising during and after the war. However distasteful the means, the habit of newspaper reading was permanently affected by the lavish promotion campaigns of the thirties. Elias has his place in newspaper history.

But it was a bad time for the British press in which many of the traditions on which it had been built were tossed aside. The popular papers fought a catch as catch can fight for circulation: anything went that might pull in readers. As for *The Times* under Geoffrey Dawson, intimate of Lord Halifax, member of the Round Table, Secretary-General of the Establishment and Chief-of-Staff to the Appeasement Group in the higher echelons of English political and social life, it committed the worst sin that can befall a journal of opinion. The principles of independence that Barnes and Delane had set for it were abandoned and it became an instrument of government policy, suppressing or amending such dispatches from its correspondents—notably in Berlin—as might conflict with the illusions of Mr Chamberlain and his colleagues and doctoring the reports of its parliamentary reporters when they gave too clear a picture—as in the response to Duff Cooper's resignation speech after the Munich agreement—of the growing Parliamentary distrust of the course the government was taking.

These conditions brought with them a curious return to an earlier mode in journalism, the rise of a number of privately circulated news letters. Of these Claud Cockburn's *The Week* was the most revealing—retailing in Cockburn's astringent iconoclastic style on cyclostyled sheets of a peculiarly hideous appearance the news behind the news gossiped about but not printed in newspaper offices and whispered in political and city clubs and embassies, flavoured with Marxism but not too pungently so—and Stephen King-Hall's *News Letter* the most solid and informative. These and other news letters flourished because much of the press was failing in its duty—or perhaps because it reflected too faithfully the desire of majority opinion, high and middle, to close its eyes to the facts of international life. Only the *Manchester Guardian* and the *News Chronicle* may be said in their separate ways to have remained faithful to the old allegiance. However the rise of the *Daily Telegraph* in these years reflected the respect that straightforward reporting could still win for itself.

In fact, despite the noise made by the circulation battle between the *Express*, the *Herald* and the *Mail*, this did not shape the future pattern of the British press to anything like so large an extent as did the *Telegraph*'s rise as a serious paper for middle class, middle brow readers on the one hand and on the other the flamboyant advance of the *Daily Mirror*, the first British daily newspaper to reach the vast population of the under-privileged at the base of the British social pyramid.

The *Daily Telegraph* had been born with the end of stamp taxes in 1850 and in the seventies and eighties had claimed the largest circulation in the world, just over 300,000 copies a day. This was down to less than 84,000 by the time the Berry brothers bought the paper in 1927. When Lord Camrose acquired sole control of it in the thirties during the property division between the two Berry brothers he proceeded to develop it along lines that ran completely counter to the general journalistic trend of the times. With considerable understanding of the nature of the middle class he made it a serious journal of record, unassuming in make-up, quiet in style, aimed at a mainly Conservative public of business and professional people of the middling rank who found *The Times* and the *Manchester Guardian* too intellectual for their tastes but wanted something less flashy and exhibitionist than the *Express*, less politically sensational than the *Mail* and less liberal than the *News Chronicle*; the *Daily Herald* with its Labour affiliations did not enter into their considerations. They were steady, respectable people and the *Telegraph* was as respectable as a rolled umbrella and a bowler hat. It provided a sound coverage of news rather flatly reported, an excellent financial service, and feature articles which, if they rarely stirred the blood, were sensible, informative and inviolably safe in attitude. Although not so authoritative as the *New York Times* it could be regarded as in some sense a minor British equivalent. It captured a market in between that of *The Times* and the *Daily Mail* which had been ignored until Lord Camrose, in many ways the most professional and least flamboyant as well as the most traditional of the newspaper proprietors of the time, recognised it. Disdaining extraneous circulation aids, the *Telegraph* built on solid merit. By 1939 it had acquired a circulation of 750,000, which was to be nearly doubled in the war and post-war years. Its readers with their safe jobs and respectable positions in society were advertising bait of the very best quality and the newspaper a sedate goldmine.

The *Daily Telegraph* represented a return to traditional journalistic values, if of a good deal less positive and more unadventurous kind than those that had distinguished *The Times* in its great days and still distinguished the *Manchester Guardian*. In this it reflected the character of its owner and Editor-in-Chief, Lord Camrose, a serious-minded, predictable man of strong Conservative leanings who much enjoyed such trappings of wealth as social position and a large yacht but had no desire to thrust his own opinions down the throats of his readers or use his paper to promote his own ambitions as Beaverbrook did. He was content for the most part to pass on to his readers the pure Conservative gospel which was what they wanted, although he did show considerable courage in opposing appeasement—a courage all the more effective coming from one regarded as one of the prefects of the establishment.

There could have been no greater contrast to him than Harry Guy Bartholomew, the maker of the new *Daily Mirror*.

As already recorded the *Daily Mirror* had originally been founded by Northcliffe in one of his less percipient moments as 'The First Daily Newspaper For Gentlewomen': not only for them, indeed, but written by them. Three months later, with circulation falling catastrophically, the gentlewomen were sacked ('It was a horrid experience, like drowning kittens,' said Hamilton Fyfe who was given the job) and the *Daily Mirror* transformed into a halfpenny picture paper tabloid size 'for men and women', the *Daily Illustrated Mirror*—the first daily picture paper in British journalism. The illustrated *Mirror* was made possible by a former editor of *Home Sweet Home*, one of the Harmsworth domestic weeklies, who, bored with concocting sugary meals for family readers, turned in his spare time to the study of photographic reproduction and developed a method of using half tone blocks on high speed rotary presses. With this process the *Daily Illustrated Mirror* was able to abandon woodcuts and line drawings and reproduce news photographs at speed. Hannen Swaffer, later to become a great name in popular journalism as reporter, gossip writer and theatre critic, was made Picture Editor, with a youth from the engraving department of the *Illustrated Sunday Mail* to help him at a wage of 30s a week. This was Bartholomew.

The reorganised *Mirror* was an almost immediate success. As a paper for gentlewomen its sales had fallen to under 25,000 a day. As a picture paper they rose rapidly to 400,000 and went on climbing. By 1914 it was selling 1,210,000 copies daily. At this point Northcliffe who could never much interest himself in picture journalism and disliked the *Mirror*'s success because it detracted from that of the *Mail* sold his majority interest in it to Rothermere. It remained in Rothermere's control for seventeen years, providing some remarkable picture coverage during the war, but thereafter falling steadily in reputation and circulation as Rothermere made it a propaganda tool in his campaign against what he liked to call squander-mania and used it to shout aloud the virtues of Mussolini and Hitler and their pocket imitator in Britain, Oswald Mosley.

Rothermere was generally credited with being a financial genius. His ambition, which he just failed to fulfil, was to be the richest man in Britain. As a newspaper proprietor he was boorish and dull, a man almost totally without charm and with a belief in his own importance excessive by even the inflated standards of news-paper owners of the time. His touch on any newspaper was like the kiss of death. The *Mirror* would scarcely have survived it but for Bartholomew whom Northcliffe had fortunately made a director before selling the paper to his brother. Through all the desolate, frustrating years of Rothermere's control Bartholomew at least kept it ahead in exploiting pictures.

Fortunately in the end Rothermere's commercial genius over-reached itself. With his provincial adventures turning sour under the impact of economic crisis and his financial position generally badly over-stretched he found it necessary to raise liquid funds by selling his *Daily Mirror* shares on the Stock Exchange. In March 1931 his direct personal control of the paper ended. Some 80,000 shares still remained in the hands of the Daily Mail Trust, but by the end of 1934 these too were sold and all connection between Rothermere and the paper was finished. Instead of a single dominant ownership the ordinary shares were now widely spread among some 10,000 small and medium sized holders with no single block large enough to give actual control, although for practical purposes this rested in the hands of the Sunday Pictorial Company which in its turn was controlled in much the same way by the Daily Mirror Company. For the first time in the *Mirror*'s history the board had no master's voice to tell it what to do.

Freedom struck cold. The Chairman, John Cowley, was a mediocrity whom the Harmsworths had inherited with the *London Evening News* nearly forty years before: a yes-man with no longer anyone to say yes to. The *Mirror* was dying. Its circula-tion was down to 700,000 and was still falling. Its reputation was minimal.

This was Bartholomew's chance. It was impossible to get rid of Cowley, a man well versed by years with Rothermere in keeping his job when all around were losing theirs. But although Cowley remained Chairman, hanging on in that position until he died at

the age of seventy-four in 1944, the real power passed to Bartholomew. He bullied the bemused board into giving him complete
editorial control of the *Mirror*. His title until Cowley died when
he grabbed the name of Chairman as well was Editorial Director.
The title was unimportant. Bartholomew was boss.

He was 51, a man who had come up from the bottom and liked
everyone to know it. By conventional standards he was even less
educated than Elias. But he had what Elias so strikingly lacked,
an instinct for journalistic vulgarity. He realised, as Elias did not
wish to do, that there was a submerged reading public still to be
exploited. He did not need to ask what they wanted. It was what
he wanted himself. He gave it them in earthy prose and the blackest
type, transforming the *Mirror* almost overnight from a sedate
picture paper for the well brought up into a strident caricature of
American yellow journalism at its brashest. Stunts, sensations,
sex, strip cartoons, radical crusades took pride of place in its daily
menu even if it meant leaving out the news everyone else
considered important. He was ready to print anything so
long as it was loud enough or funny enough and would make
people talk.

He went to an advertising agency for advice on the right black-
ness and size of type for maximum impact, had a survey made to
find out how many syllables to a word, how many words to a
sentence his working class readers could take in at one time
without strain. He was the first British publisher to realise that by
the time most people picked up a paper they had already heard
the seven o'clock or eight o'clock radio news and, unless the news was
so big and exciting that they could not have too much of it, wanted
something fresh. He knew instinctively how millions of working
class people would react to any situation and he had a complete
disregard for the proprieties. Not only did he not want to be
thought respectable, he hated the idea that the respectable should
think well of him and he made the *Daily Mirror* the first daily
paper in British newspaper history capable of speaking to and for
the great mass public at the bottom of the social pyramid. There
had been Sunday papers like the *News of the World*, the *People*
and earlier still, *Lloyds Weekly News* to offer them sex and sensation and crime for the weekend, periodicals like Horatio Bottomley's
John Bull to excite with revelations. But there had never before

been a daily newspaper. Much the *Mirror* did was superficial and some of it silly, like the experiment to see if women readers could hatch out a clutch of eggs by nesting cosily on them in bed. It exploited tragedy, broke in on privacy, slopped over motherhood. But its tabloid news was honest and straightforward and it fought against social injustice with sledge hammer indignation whenever it came across it and its record in warning the country against the dangers of appeasement put many more reputable papers to shame—*The Times* not least among them. In the contributions of its columnist Cassandra (William Conner) it brought back to British journalism a voice not heard since William Cobbett and its readers loved him even more than its strip cartoons. No daily newspaper like it had ever been seen in British journalism before but James Gordon Bennett, Charles Anderson Dana, Joseph Pulitzer and the William Randolph Hearst of the *San Francisco Examiner* would have found themselves much at home with a good deal of it. Under Bartholomew it did for British journalism what they had done much earlier for American journalism, not because he consciously copied them, although he and the ebullient group of young men mainly of working class and lower middle class origins he gathered around him did not disdain to pick up a few hints from the New York *Daily News*, but because he and the *Mirror* had a part to play in the British social revolution comparable to the part these others had played in the American one decades before.

Bartholomew himself was in many ways an impossible man, cantankerous, suspicious, dictatorial; a semi-illiterate megalomaniac who got steadily worse in these respects as increasing personal power corrupted him after the years of frustration under Rothermere. But he was also a genuine radical who made the *Daily Mirror* into a genuinely radical paper whose popularity derived as much from its passion for social justice as from its sensationalism. In the end he was too much even for the *Daily Mirror* and was got rid of by a board-room revolution led significantly enough by a Harmsworth—Cecil Harmsworth King, Northcliffe and Rothermere's nephew. Before he went he had brought the *Mirror*'s circulation from the 700,000 to which Rothermere's policies had reduced it to over 4,350,000, the largest circulation of any newspaper in the world. Under his successors it was to reach an even higher circulation. But it was he who first recognised in Britain the existence of a genuinely mass public and while Elias wasted his time trying to buy readers from other papers Bartholomew set out to finish the unfinished newspaper revolution Northcliffe had begun.

CHAPTER SIX

Radio—and the B.B.C.
Misses an Opportunity

Until the arrival of radio broadcasting in the early 1920s the press, and mainly of course the daily press, was the sole medium of mass communication in public affairs—chief protagonist and defender of the public right to know in an expanding urbanised world. Technically the new medium seemed capable of greatly extending the bounds of mass communication. Yet despite its freedom from the restrictions imposed by the nature of the printed word broadcasting proved no more capable than the press of breaking free of the social patterns of the societies in which it operated.

In Britain broadcasting even found for itself a new Barnes of *The Times* in Reith of the B.B.C. Barnes at the age of thirty-two had taken hold of *The Times* newspaper, by then a sound commercial enterprise but not as yet much more, and turned it into a national institution that 'taught, urged and thundered' their duty to the new middle classes. Reith became General Manager of the infant British Broadcasting Company at the age of thirty-four, and turned a commercial company formed by radio manufacturers to promote their products, into a national institution consistutionally recognised as such four years later when it became a Corporation with a Royal Charter and a government authorised monopoly. He, too, taught, urged and thundered their duty to the middle classes, dismissing as craven any suggestion that the B.B.C. should concern itself with mass taste.

As a son of the manse and product of the late Victorian age

Radio—and the B.B.C. Misses an Opportunity

Reith took himself more solemnly than Barnes, a man of the late eighteenth century, would have permitted himself to do: 'I am profoundly thankful to God for his goodness in this matter. It is all His doing,' he wrote in his diary when he got the B.B.C. appointment. But just as Barnes shaped *The Times* into an instrument of the Establishment—albeit an extremely independent minded one—ignoring as beneath a serious man's notice the unprivileged public that William Cobbett spoke for with his *Political Register* or that James Gordon Bennett served and exploited across the other side of the Atlantic, so too in the very different circumstances of the twentieth century did Reith shape the B.B.C.

Britain had travelled a good way since Barnes's day but in many of its assumptions, although less so in its realities, it was still an oligarchical society and it was as a member of an oligarchy of good taste that Reith fashioned the B.B.C. He turned it into an ideal expression of the best of the public school virtues: a national headmaster. Much later he was to confess that the position in life he would most have liked was that of Viceroy of India. It was as a Viceroy—possibly of God, but certainly of high authority—that he conducted himself at the B.B.C., constantly aware that he knew better what was good for the people than they knew themselves. Radio provided the means to cover the entire social spectrum and cater for every layer of the British social pyramid in a way the British press was not yet ready to do even in the twenties. This opportunity was rejected. The masses had to wait even longer for a broadcasting service that would speak to them in their own idiom than they had for a newspaper that would.

The oligarchical function of the B.B.C. fitted Reith's temperament. But even he would scarcely have been able to sustain it if it had not also fitted so well the assumptions of the best people. The B.B.C. embodied the outlook of the educationalists and men of public spirit who although they by no means trusted the people wished to do them good and bring them along in the right way. It was not a medium of release but of order. It opened doors—but only for the purpose of arranging suitably conducted tours to the best places.

Things were different in the United States: as diffierent as

The Right to Know

Bennett's *New York Herald* had been from Barnes's *Times of London*. American society was a commercial society and it was into this society that American broadcasting was integrated. Its commercialism was not of deliberate design. The advertising base that was to become one of the major features of American broadcasting as compared with the public service, licence fee, base of British broadcasting was at first opposed both by the then Secretary of Commerce, Herbert Hoover, and the leaders of the new radio manufacturing industry. At the very first American Radio Conference in 1922, Hoover declared it 'inconceivable that we should allow so great a possibility for service . . . to be drowned in advertising chatter' and David Sarnoff, then Commercial Manager of the Radio Corporation of America, wanted broadcasting to be organised by a Public Service Broadcasting Company.

The American social pattern was too strong for them. In Britain control of the new medium could be canalised, as so much else was, into the still powerful hands of the setters of standards. In the United States no such thing was possible. The American ethic demanded competition. Broadcasting became part of the entertainment industry subject to the same competitive pressures as other entertainers, to the same freedoms but also to the same restrictions, indeed, because of the size of its audience, greater ones.

By the beginning of May 1922 there were already 219 registered radio stations in the United States, by the end of 1924, 530. Despite many drop-outs along the way the total was to go on rising until it reached over 4,000, most of them in direct competition with at least one other station in their area. The early stations broadcast news reports, weather reports, market bulletins, concerts, sports commentaries, prize fights, commentaries on local and national affairs, popular lectures, anything that would fill time and hold attention. Like early newspapers many stations at first were short-lived. Although licences for more than 1,100 had been issued by the end of August 1924, fewer than half found it possible to stay the course. As had happened in journalism chains began to move in. The first network, WEAF, was formed in 1923. In 1926 the first of the giants of national networking, the National Broadcasting Company (NBC) was formed, soon to be followed by a second, Columbia Broadcasting Service (CBS).

Radio—and the B.B.C. Misses an Opportunity

American journalism had built a people's press while British journalism was still concerned with an influential one. The same thing happened in radio. Networks and local stations alike went after a mass public. By Reith's standards at the B.B.C. a good deal of the American radio output was superficial and meretricious. It was the product of an open society, but of one increasingly driven towards conformity by commercial pressures. But although as time went on American broadcasting leaned increasingly on advertising for its moral and social values as well as for money, in its early days it had a vitality British broadcasting lacked and was a good deal more venturesome in exploring the potentialities of radio as a reporter of current events.

In this respect the B.B.C. suffered from its constitution. As a public service monopoly it was at first under strong newspaper pressure to restrict its news coverage to factual bulletins supplied by the news agencies, and even when it managed to break free of this cage and secure agreement that it could run commentaries on events by its own reporters it did very little with its new freedom. It took a man from the *Daily Telegraph*, R. F. Clark, to organise foreign news and a man from the *Guardian*, Kenneth Adam, to organise home news. But although they made a brave fight of it, they could claim few major victories for a long time. It is remarkable, indeed, how little British broadcasting, so admirable in its cultural activities, contributed to the serious reporting of current affairs in what the B.B.C.'s official historian, Professor Asa Briggs, has called 'The Golden Age of Radio'. The only reference to the Spanish Civil War, in Professor Briggs's index, for example, is a complete irrelevancy: the quoted remark by a member of the staff that a 'system of virtual anarchy (rather topical at the time because of the Spanish Civil War) existed in the Talks Department'. Right up to the second world war the B.B.C. was astonishingly unconcerned with radio as journalism; even its reputation for news objectivity was won at second hand. It rested on the transmission of news bulletins composed from material supplied by the news agencies, not by its own reporters.

Over the same period, whatever its shortcomings in other directions, American radio produced a new race of news reporters and commentators bred to the microphone age. Some had previously been newspapermen, others came to the air with no prior initiation, all helped to add a new dimension to journalism. When the B.B.C. was still content with a couple of sub-editors to condense agency tapes, American broadcasting was already beginning to send its reporters across the world. It was soon to have at its command commentators of the calibre of Elmer Davis, Raymond Gram Swing, Eric Sevareid, William L. Shirer, Charles Collingwood and Edward R. Murrow.

This American initiative was partly due to a happy accident of personality. It so happened that there arrived at C.B.S. from a local station on the West Coast a tough, news-hungry fellow built very much to the same pattern as those who had given early American newspaper journalism its zest and *élan*. His name was Paul W. White and he has many claims to be regarded as the unsung and now almost forgotten hero of broadcast news—the progenitor of that brilliant band of reporters who, microphone in hand, were to bring the world to the world. He had a tiny budget and not many of the social graces. But he had a consuming passion for news and a remarkable talent for picking men. He also had the immense advantage, once he managed to get himself put in charge of C.B.S. news, of being left to get on with the job, since it did not spell the sort of money that interested radio executives. With the help of a lean Carolinian, Edward R. Murrow, who lived on his nerves and too many cigarettes and who had been spending his time since leaving Washington State College on university student organisation, White built up a thrusting service of on-the-spot radio news and interpretation that to everyone's amazement soon began to edge many much more costly entertainment programmes out of the top ratings.

With success and a bigger budget White extended the C.B.S. news service until he had at his disposal more full-time foreign correspondents than any American newspaper but the *New York Times*, as well as having on call for domestic news reporters from all the C.B.S. network stations. His foreign correspondents had deadlines for regular news bulletins into which voices from half a dozen or more centres could be fed to produce a composite picture. They were also instructed to get to a microphone without a minute's delay if big news broke and so important and so audience-riveting had White shown news to be that he was given authority to cut into any C.B.S. network programme if he thought a news break warranted it. It was an authority to be used with discretion but one highly significant of the place he acquired for himself and his team in this remarkable chapter of American radio journalism.

Almost all the men he picked proved superb practitioners of a swift, staccato news reporting ideally suited to the new medium. Their lives and style were keyed to a competitive rhythm of which the B.B.C. knew nothing, but they were also encouraged to interpret and comment and to introduce into their news bulletins after the hard news the sort of spoken political essay—a man thinking aloud on the meaning and significance of the events that were his daily life—that the B.B.C. from its established monopoly position was in no position to try or mood to risk.

The B.B.C. got many advantages from its establishment status, particularly the liberty to think of listeners as a public rather than a market. But it also suffered from this status, as when its one serious venture into regular foreign affairs reporting with Vernon Bartlett had to be dropped despite, indeed because of, Bartlett's great popularity with listeners. It was felt to be wrong to put any one man in a position to influence public opinion to this extent. Moreover because of its official status the B.B.C. had a congenital terror of the impromptu that was quite unknown to American radio: one remembers with a nostalgic shudder those high-minded discussions on public affairs presided over by conscientious lady arts graduates from one of the older universities (the B.B.C. took a long time to recognise red brick) which would begin with a cosy talk on the 'ground to be covered', followed by a recording of an appropriately patterned conversation which was then transferred to paper to be edited and scripted with a proper eye to balance, and finally, but only after several rehearsals to get the right intonations, read from the edited script to give an illusion of live and lively debate.

American radio often went to the opposite extreme of seeking to acerbate differences of opinion so as to give serious discussions something of the entertainment quality of a prize fight in a way that seemed excessive to those used to the politer exchanges of the B.B.C. But it moved much more rapidly than the B.B.C. did into the world of current affairs, picking up what it needed to know from journalism as it went along. Only in its sports reporting did

British broadcasting reach the speed and vivacity that American radio brought quite early on to its handling of news as a whole.

In those days American broadcasting seemed likely to take over and extend some of the more essential freedoms of an independent press. It has scarcely done so. The pressures of commercial sponsors excessively concerned with TAM ratings and preoccupied with the listening and viewing tolerance of a market that must not be bored or offended lest it fail to bring home enough advertising cream has dimmed that bright dream. When Fred Friendly, the close associate of Ed Murrow in some of the best of American television's current affairs and documentary broadcasting said, 'What the American people don't know can kill them', he put his finger on the basic weakness of American radio and television, the compulsive search for a mass audience even if it can only be attracted by ignoring a good deal that matters. It was this that led to Friendly's own departure from C.B.S. in protest at his management's insistence on giving viewers a fourth repeat of *I Love Lucy* instead of an important Congressional hearing. It had however thrown its shadow much earlier when Alexander Woolcott's *Town Crier* radio programme was tossed off the air in 1935 because a sponsor complained that Woolcott's criticism of Hitler and Mussolini might offend some listeners.

This is not to say that a good deal of vivid and intelligent news reporting does not find its way on to American radio and television. It does. And so, of course, it does on to British broadcasting, long since freed of the inhibitions that first affected it. But although to some the arrival of radio had seemed to spell the beginning of the end of the press as the greatest force in mass communication, it has not proved so either in America or Britain. Historically, indeed, it is significant that the rise of American radio which seemed to offer what American newspapers for geographical reasons could not, satisfaction of a national audience, actually coincided with the enormous success of a new arm of the press—the national news magazine.

Superficially Henry Luce and his friend from Yale, Briton Hadden, could scarcely have chosen a less opportune moment than 3 March 1923 to launch their new idea in journalism, *Time*. The new medium of radio was well on its way. New stations were opening across the country at the rate of twenty or thirty a month and the public demand for radio sets was so great that customers were crowding the radio supply stores four or five ranks deep. Yet Luce and Hadden were to prove as important innovators in American journalism as many of the press pioneers—and were to reap even larger financial rewards.

The idea for their news magazine came to them when they found themselves exposed for the first time to the ignorance of the ordinary American at Camp Jackson, South Carolina, towards the end of the First World War. Both were privileged products of Ivy League education. They had been together at their private school Hotchkiss, and then at Yale. Having spent his childhood in China, where his parents were Presbyterian missionaries, Luce in particular was short on understanding of what ordinary Americans were like. As student officer instructors to the draftees crowding into the camp both he and Hadden were astounded to find how little most of them knew about the world or even their own country. They talked over the idea of a news magazine to fill the gap.

In 1923 they met again as reporters on the *Baltimore News*. By this time both of them knew more about the American public than they had at Camp Jackson. Hadden had worked on the *New York World*, Luce after a year reading history in Oxford had been on the *Chicago Daily News* as a legman to its noted gossip columnist, Ben Hecht. With increased knowledge their idea still looked good and they put together a typewritten dummy and set off to New York to try to raise capital for it from their friends and relations. Both were twenty-three, young for launching out on their own even in a young man's trade, but they had an infectious confidence and valuable connections among their Yale classmen, most of them the sons of rich and successful fathers, and by the end of a year had promises of $86,000. They had reckoned they needed $100,000, but decided this would do.

Their first issue was very much a scissors and paste affair: the product of intelligent reading of newspaper clippings mostly from the *New York Times* (the venture would not have been possible at all but for a ruling by the Supreme Court in 1918 that news twenty-four hours old was in the public domain) and the synthesis and departmentalisation of what could be gleaned from them. Luce provided the title, *Time*, picked while reading advertisements in a subway, Hadden the style that was to make *Time* famous with its concertina'd adjectives and inverted sentences. They were sufficiently confident of the durability of their magazine to circulate the famous with an offer of a year's subscription at $5 a time. Walter Lippmann was one of their first subscribers.

In many ways their idea was not unlike Northcliffe's when he started the *Daily Mail*; certainly closer to it than to the general pattern of American newspaper journalism at the time. Northcliffe had published the *Daily Mail* as 'The Busy Man's Daily Paper', offering in readable and easily digested form, compartmentalised for quick intake, news and information that it would have taken hours of reading to acquire from the more traditional newspapers of the time. For their new magazine Luce and Hadden made the claim that it was the first publication 'adapted to the time busy men are able to spend in simply keeping informed'. They offered a weekly briefing on events and personalities, political, commercial, cultural, scientific, national and international that would put the ordinary man in the picture, or at least persuade him he was. Both wanted to be editor but agreed to take turn and turn about as editor and business manager in yearly stretches and to toss for who should have the first editorial term. Haddon won and it was his personality and particularly his stylistic innovations that gave *Time* its special character. They worked together in remarkable amity until Hadden died tragically of a streptococcal infection at the age of thirty-one.

By then *Time* was six years old and already well established with a circulation of nearly 120,000. It multiplied this by seven in the next twelve years, branched out into international editions, and became the centre of a great Luce empire of which *Life* and *Fortune* were the other main pillars. It still remained as it had at the start when, relying as it did on press cuttings, it could scarcely be otherwise, indomitably anonymous even although its press cutting days were long past. By now a fast band of senior editors, associate editors, contributing editors, editorial researchers and staff correspondents from all over the world fed weekly into the *Time* machine the raw material that would tell America the background to the news. Their names appeared at its masthead but what they wrote was shaped to a common *Time*-style, each

'Department' the end result of the cutting, checking and reshaping of many thousands of words of material with no man able to lay individual stylistic claim to even a paragraph of the final plastic product.

This anonymity was very different from the traditional anonymity of many famous journals of opinion such as *The Times* of London whose writers wrote their opinions in their own style and jealously guarded the independence of their individual opinions although these opinions assumed—or so it was supposed —greater authority as those of the *Times* correspondent than they would have possessed as the product of mortal man. It broke even more completely with the highly personal by-line journalism of the great American reporters.

Time deliberately submerged the individual in the whole, and dehumanised both the writer and the written about in the process. In this, one suspects, lay much of its success. It matched its period. The old individualistic America was passing, making way for a society in which eighty-seven per cent of all Americans would be on someone else's payroll and less than five per cent of college students would wish to be other than corporation men. Questioned by another Luce publication, *Fortune*, on what business looked for in decision-making, leading executives replied, 'The composite mind.' *Time* was the composite mind in print—and like many composite minds an often shockingly biased and inaccurate one.

At Camp Jackson the news magazine had been conceived of as an answer to the ignorance of the masses. But Hadden and Luce were, as Northcliffe had been, middle class men and they produced, as he did, a publication in their own image. No more than the *Mail* had been was it aimed at the mass public of the original Camp Jackson vision. It was from the first custom-built for professional men and business executives and their satellites who wished to think themselves well informed and to be confirmed in their own prejudices without having to take too much time about it. Nominally it was objective. But portmanteau journalism lends itself easily to the machine imposed view and *Time*'s prejudices went much wider and deeper than those so high-mindedly confessed in its first prospectus: 'Faith in the things which money cannot buy, a respect for the old, particularly in manners, an interest in the new, particularly in ideas'.

The Right to Know

Luce liked to think of himself as a reporter and he had much of that same ceaseless curiosity that had distinguished Northcliffe. But no more than Northcliffe did he disdain power, he clasped it to his bosom, frankly boasting, 'I'm a Jesuit of journalism—a persuader.' His father and mother had been missionaries of God. He was a missionary of American capitalism which he equated with God. They fought evil. He fought Communism which he regarded as the same thing and saw in almost anything that differed from his own rock-like Republicanism. He was as much the apostle of American imperialism as Northcliffe had been of British; the voice of the American century.

In all these ways, no less than in its style of presentation, *Time* reflected themes that were becoming increasingly dominant in American life just as in Britain the free gift silliness of the long weekend during which the English did their best to pretend that their world was not falling apart reflected popular British attitudes. Everywhere one went in the twenties and thirties one could not, indeed, avoid being reminded despite the alleged challenge of the more persuasive, social-frontier-breaking medium of radio, of how true it remained that the state of the press mirrored the state of society.

This was true of France to an even more obvious degree than in Britain and America. In Paris one could find more, and more varied, newspapers than in any other capital in the world; some thirty of them altogether—and scarcely one other than *Le Temps*, and not always that, that one could trust. Of the most highly regarded *Le Petit Parisien* and *Le Journal* in the afternoon were strictly sensational, and the Communist *L'Humanité*, the conservative *La Liberté*, each animated in their several ways by the journalistic thesis once adumbrated by Mr Claud Cockburn is reliving his triumphs of the thirties when he planted on the French press as a factual, sober, yet inspiring piece of war reporting an eye witness account of a completely fictitious anti-Franco revolt in Yetnan, a place he had never visited—that if a cause is worth fighting for it is worth lying for. However, the bias of the principal French newspapers at least was open. One could prepare oneself against it. With most of the rest of the French press it was more difficult without inside knowledge and continuous study. Views went according to paymasters and both might change over night. Some lived on bribes from foreign powers including Nazi Germany and Fascist Italy, others were secretly owned by the steel industry or by other financial and commercial groups. It was common for all but the best known journalists to eke out their small pay by subventions from big business or wealthy individuals. The demoralisation of French society could have had no clearer reflection than the state of the French press in the thirties. Nor could there have been any much clearer indication of what was likely to happen in France in the event of war.

In Germany and Italy, Portugal and Spain the press—always among the first institutions to suffer under dictatorships, left or right—had been forced into a subservience as complete as in Communist countries. Elsewhere in Europe it proceeded on the whole rather quietly on its way, still for the most part an opinion rather than a popular press, mirroring increases in anxiety and tension but still, like governments and peoples, clinging to the illusion that reason could prevail.

Across the world in Japan the newspapers that had so vigorously resisted and outwitted official controls in the first burst of Westernisation had by the 1930s become almost entirely the creatures of the military cabal that had taken over government. By 1936 control of all the press had been put under an official Board of Information and journalists reduced to the status of messenger boys.

However in some parts of the African continent the story was brighter. Press freedom was on the move. An indigenous popular press was at last coming into existence to support and inspire the attempt to win freedom. The *Lagos Daily News,* founded by Herbert Macauley to be the voice of his National Democratic Party, the *Nigerian Daily Times* under the editorship of Ernest Ikoli who had been trained by John Payne Jackson, the *West African Times* under J. B. Danquah, the first West African daily to have both a regular international news service and a woman's column, the *Spectator Daily* which had the West Indian George Padmore—later one of Nkrumah's advisors in Ghana—among its contributors, the *Sierra Leone Daily Mail;* all these and several others combined to make the 1930s, as Miss Rosalynde Ainslie has observed, an exceptionally fertile period for the press in Nigeria and the Gold Coast.

This fertility had a remarkable flowering in 1934 when there arrived in the Gold Coast from America, where he had spent nine years working his way through segregated Negro colleges in the South and had learnt a good deal about popular journalism from the militant Negro press that was beginning to develop there, the most remarkable of modern African journalists Dr Nnamdi Azikiwe, better known as Zik. Zik was to become the first African newspaper tycoon and the creator, in Zik's Press Ltd, of the first successful chain of African owned newspapers. He was at first co-editor of a new Gold Coast paper, the *African Morning Post*, with a Sierra Leonean trade union organiser and Marxist, I. T. A. Wallace-Johnson, who had spent some time in France where he had edited *The Negro Worker*. However he left the Gold Coast for Nigeria in 1937 after a criminal libel suit, and there started the West African *Pilot*.

He had arrived at the right time. Both on the Gold Coast and in Nigeria popular education was spreading and with it political consciousness and the beginning of political organisation. For the first time there was something approaching a mass audience instead of an elite to be tapped. Zik captured this African mass audience, with methods very similar to those that Bartholomew was employing in England at the same time to capture an English mass audience. He learned a good deal in fact from the *Daily Mirror*, copying its large black headlines, its one sentence paragraphs, its radical sensationalism and woman's appeal but combining them with the radical militancy he had learned from the new Negro press in America. Within three years he had achieved what was for the West Coast the unheard of daily circulation of 12,000 and was soon to be in a position to use the *Pilot* as the base for a chain of six daily newspapers covering all three regions of Nigeria and marked out from all other African papers by their professionalism and expertise in popular appeal.

Even in Southern Africa there was enough of a journalistic stir to frighten the big mine owners. Watching the success of such native African newspapers as the *Workers' Herald* started by Clements Kadalie's Industrial and Commercial Union and the Communist *South African Worker* with its vernacular partner *Umsebenzi*, they decided that something must be done to give the natives safer reading matter. The Native Recruiting Corporation of the Chamber of Mines entered the field first with *Umteteli wa Bantu* (the Voice of the People) which sought to woo African support by campaigning against a colour bar while at the same time it looked after white interests by fighting the attempt to form an African Mineworkers' Union to improve workers' conditions. Other commercial groups put up capital for the Bantu Press Publishing Company. This was designed to prevent the 'irresponsible exploitation' of Africans by existing African newspapers. It aimed to merge such newspapers under sound (white) management and to start new ones, and had as its declared objective 'A Bantu paper in every Province from the Cape to the Congo'. After merging three small African papers it launched the *Bantu World* published in English and four African languages. This was followed by the three-language *Bantu Mirror* in Salisbury. Although denounced by African leaders the Bantu Press did what it had set out to do: its competition made it almost impossible for independent African papers to develop in Southern Africa as they were doing at so great a pace in West Africa.

In the Union of South Africa the English language newspapers headed by the *Argus* group and the *Rand Daily Mail* continued on their commercially prosperous way but ran into a foretaste of the trouble they were to be up against with Afrikaner Nationalist Governments in the future when in 1937 Hertzog, the then Prime Minister, called all editors of daily papers together and threatened them with control under a Press Bill already drafted if they did not stop their attacks on the Nazi and Fascist Governments in Germany and Italy. This measure would certainly have been put into effect if the British declaration of war against Germany had not led to Hertzog's fall and his replacement by Smuts. However, the South African shape of things to come was by now beginning to show clearly enough in the rise of an Afrikaans language press which was strongly apartheid and pro-Nazi. *Die Transvaaler* of which Dr Verwoerd was the first editor was the most extreme of these papers, expressing in print the racialist sentiments Verwoerd clothed in executive reality when he became Prime Minister. *Die Transvaaler* and *Die Burger* edited by Dr Malan whose victory over Smuts in 1947 finally set South Africa on its apartheid course were specific weapons of political warfare, financed and launched by the Nationalist Party for that purpose.

The Right to Know

The Afrikaans press never succeeded in matching the English-speaking South African press in popularity and circulation, for there was little genuine demand for daily newspapers among Afrikaners, who for the most part lived in farms and small villages and confined their reading to the Bible and an occasional Afrikaans magazine, while the English-speaking businessmen and mine-workers were concentrated in the cities and had all the urban appetite for newsprint. Nevertheless, its rise in the thirties was as much an indication of the new power balance to which South Africa was moving as the *Argus* group's dependence on the big gold mining interests had been of an earlier power structure, or as the rise of an African press in Nigeria and the Gold Coast was of the new forces at work elsewhere on the African continent.

In none of this stir, be it noted, did the new medium of radio, technically so ideally suited to breaking down the barriers of distance and illiteracy, have much part. In Europe, of course, it provided a new propaganda arm for authoritarian governments, both Communist and Fascist. But even in Russia where it was used to transmit party directives and official news across the vast area of the Soviet Union, it did not, in official eyes, replace the press in significance or reduce the importance of *Pravda* with its numerous provincial editions as the main voice of Soviet domestic and international policy. It was a more potent instrument for the dissemination of Nazi ideas in Germany, whether in news programmes or in the broadcasting of the Führer's speeches at mass party rallies: the People's Receiving Set of which 3,000,000 had been sold by 1939 was specifically designed to receive German stations only and there were penalties of up to five years' imprisonment for passing on 'detrimental news' picked up from a non-German radio station. But although by the end of the thirties Monaco was the only country in Europe without a broadcasting service of its own—some drawing on advertising for their revenue on the American model, although usually much modified and controlled, others run by public corporations on the British model, although often with more direct governmental intervention —nowhere on the European continent did radio replace the press as the main medium of news and public comment or even become a serious competitor in these fields.

This is not to deny its impact in the direct transmission of the speeches of political leaders and in broadcasts of some public events or the extent to which by bringing the voice and tone of Hitler into ordinary English homes it awakened listeners to the threat of Nazism in a way that newspaper reports alone could scarcely have done. But it is to indicate how much slighter the journalistic competition of the new medium was than many had expected. Indeed, so far from supplanting the press, the spread of broadcasting was almost everywhere accompanied by a rising demand for newspapers. Radio had advantages denied to the press. But it lacked both its durability—the quality of being available to be read, and if necessary re-read, at one's own time and pace— and its independence. Except in North America—where the main inhibitions came from advertisers—even when radio did not directly speak for authority it reflected its attitudes, particularly so in public service broadcasting. Because wave lengths and frequencies had to be allotted to take into account the need to avoid interference with other national systems and with inter-national radio communications, most broadcast services tended— particularly in so crowded a continent as Europe—to be either official monopolies or to offer at most two alternatives, one publicly owned, the other commercially supported.

Radio could inform and entertain. It could not compete with the press in variety or, outside the totalitarian states, in freedom. And to a much greater extent than the press, it expressed what a society liked to think itself rather than what it actually was. Thus in Australia in the twenties, the Australian Broadcasting Commis-sion scarcely reflected at all in its attitudes and programmes what Mr Henry Mayer has aptly described as 'an era of general vio-lence just under the surface, of ballot box scandals, corruption in municipal affairs, and political bribery'.

The newspapers could and did. Not only did they do so in their pages which featured sensationalism, sectarianism and the smearing of opponents to an extreme degree, but in their conduct, which, during the worst of the struggles between the Murdoch and Denison newspaper empires, included the use not only of political bribery but actual violence as gangs with bicycle chains for weapons were sent in to stop the distribution of rival news-papers. Broadcasting was a reflection of the respectable side of Australian life: the press a microcosm of the whole society.

This tended also to be the case elsewhere. In developed societies the organisational compulsions of broadcasting made it mostly incapable of fully reflecting the diversities and tensions of national life: in subject territories such broadcasting as there was was firmly under the control of the dominant power. As early as 1924 Reith had urged, first on the India Office and then on the Viceroy, 'the immense potentialities of broadcasting' and 'the unparalleled opportunity for service in India'. But such broadcasting was seen as very much an official matter. The B.B.C.'s own Empire Service, which after many preliminary difficulties of financing began in December 1932 with programmes beamed on short wave to Australia, Canada, India, South Africa and West Africa, was admirable in giving factually unbiased world news along with music and talks. But in terms of what was actually happening in the countries to which it went it was no more than an extension to Empire listeners of Reith's high-minded paternalism at home. As an educational and informative medium it often had considerable value and since education is a necessary prerequisite of change had to this extent its unwitting share in promoting nationalist revolutions. But it offered no true substitute for the vernacular press either in India or West Africa, or for that matter even for the English-speaking press which in such countries could not help but reflect in some measure the stir of anti-imperial ideas and passions even when it denounced them. Reith himself was so out of touch with what was happening to the British Empire that according to the official history of the B.B.C., he actually expressed shocked dismay when he found that 'for all the talk of Empire unity the Dominions always wanted to go their own way and control of broadcasting seemed to be almost a test of national sovereignty'.

Radio brought a new dimension to mass communication in the twenties and thirties. But it failed to provide a substitute for the press—even when, or perhaps especially when, the press was, as in colonial territories, at its most vulnerable.

CHAPTER SEVEN

The Rise and Fall of Cecil King

In most advanced countries the post-war years have brought a steady contraction in the number of newspapers.

Even in Western countries, developments have not, of course, been identical. They differ a good deal in Britain, America, Germany and France. On the whole, however, they have generally been in the direction of greater monopolisation and an increase— not everywhere unchallenged—in commercial pressures and in the drive to maximum profits. Yet it is by no means the case that such developments have inevitably resulted, as many expected they would and as was the case with commercial television, in a weakening of the professional elements in the press or in those public service responsibilities that are, or should be, particularly the concern of the professional journalist. On the contrary they have sometimes produced, either as a reaction or even as a necessary response to large scale organisation, an actual strengthening of them.

British experience in this respect can best be traced in the careers of two very dissimilar men—Mr Cecil Harmsworth King and Lord Thomson of Fleet—and as much in Cecil King's fall as in his rise.

These two do not, of course, represent the whole of the British press. The *Mail* and the *Express*, although diminished in personality, are not fundamentally different from what they were under Northcliffe and Beaverbrook: they are second generation shadows of what were once world champions. The *Daily Telegraph* continues under his sons in the image Lord Camrose made: a good grey paper with many of the virtues of a more famous guardian of such journalistic tradition across the Atlantic; a compact model of the *New York Times* built for the English middle classes and similarly prosperous. And the *Guardian*, although economically vulnerable, continues, as God and C. P. Scott intended it should, a defender of eternal journalistic virtues. So, also, does the *Observer* on Sundays, fortunate to find in the at first sight unlikely figure of David Astor the nearest modern equivalent to a C. P. Scott as editor-publisher. But it is the International Publishing Corporation created by King, and the Thomson Organisation created by Thomson that most clearly represent in Britain the press as big business.

Newspaper publishers come in all shapes and sizes. King is an intellectual *manqué*, a tall, bulky man whose clothes usually seem too tight for him, withdrawn in manner and inhibited in personal relationships by his obvious doubt whether there is anyone worth listening to. He collects eighteenth century furniture, early silver and fine glass. Thomson is short and tubby, a teddy bear of a man —although with a grizzly's hug—as extroverted as a Rotary Club Chairman and as cultured as a fair-ground barker. One made a corner in the mass press while the other has concentrated on the quality press and by an interesting irony the mass man was the intellectual and the quality man the cultural illiterate.

Cecil King, whose career as a newspaper magnate was brought to an abrupt end in May 1968, started life with the advantage of being a nephew of Northcliffe and Rothermere, son of their sister Dot who helped with *Answers* when it and they were young. He did not, however, like his less able cousin Esmond Harmsworth, son of the first Lord Rothermere and now principal owner of the *Daily Mail*, have the advantage of a newspaper inheritance. His father was a member of the Indian Civil Service in the Edwardian autumn of British imperialism and later Professor of Oriental Languages at Trinity College, Dublin. King himself went to that most austere of British public schools, Winchester, and hated it and from there to Christ Church, Oxford, where he got a second in History and fell in love with Agnes Margaret Cooke, daughter of Canon G. A. Cooke, the Regius Professor of Greek, whom he married when he was twenty-two.

None of this would seem to provide a natural background to tabloid journalism. But the Harmsworth blood was stronger than Winchester or Christ Church and when he came down from Oxford with his way to make in the world King was delighted to take a job on Uncle Rothermere's *Glasgow Daily Record* as a reporter. After a year Rothermere, who unlike his brother Northcliffe had no great opinion of reporters, moved him to the advertisement department of the *Daily Mail* which he had acquired on his brother's death. Three years later King was sent to the *Daily Mirror*, then at a low ebb, and after another three years put on its board, rapid progress even for a nephew of the boss although he thought it too slow for his talents. He was thirty when Rothermere pulled out of the *Mirror*. King kept his seat on the board and was one of those who backed Bartholomew in his bid for editorial control. However he had no part in the editorial revolution produced by that rough hewn genius. His talents at that time seemed more akin to Uncle Rothermere's than Uncle Northcliffe's, although it was Northcliffe he admired most, as he still does: the Chairman's suite at the top of the huge new International Publishing Corporation block in Holborn Circus when he occupied it was dominated by a portrait of Northcliffe above the only fireplace in the building: supreme status symbol of a centrally heated age.

It was as Financial and Advertisement Director of the *Mirror* that he first showed he had more than heredity to commend him. But he wanted editorial power too and in 1938 persuaded the board to make him Editorial Director of the *Sunday Pictorial* which had been kept out of Bartholomew's hands by John Cowley and his fellow traditionalists with the result that while the *Mirror* boomed the *Pictorial* drooped.

King was no Bartholomew but he knew that only a revolution comparable to that on the *Mirror* could save the *Pictorial*. He also knew at that time, although he sometimes forgot it later, that although he could administer he could not edit. He asked the twenty-four year old Features Editor of the *Daily Mirror*, Hugh Cudlipp, to join him, thereby earning Bartholomew's animosity for both of them. Cudlipp turned the *Sunday Pictorial* into a spicier version of the *Mirror* and circulation rose. The King-Cudlipp partnership had begun. It was to continue for close on thirty years with only two interruptions—one when Cudlipp edited an army newspaper during the war, the other when Bartholomew sacked him during King's absence abroad and he went to the *Sunday Express* for two years. It was to prove a legendary association during which King, with Cudlipp close by his side, steadily extended the range of his influence —only to find himself at the end deposed in favour of his lieutenant.

With his feet firmly on the ladder of power King found it necessary to get rid of Bartholomew who on Cowley's death had become Chairman of both the *Mirror* and *Pictorial* companies with their maze of interlocking shareholdings. Since Rothermere's withdrawal neither company had had a controlling proprietor: the only large shareholders were institutional investors, among them several insurance companies and the Ellerman interests headed by Sir John Ellerman, a shipping and property millionaire. None of these holdings, however, was sufficient to give control and the rest of the shares were widely distributed among private investors. The two papers were thus unique in Fleet Street in being managed by a board of executives, self-perpetuating in character, who so long as they kept shareholders happy with rising profits were free from either financial or political interference.

Clothed in his immense prestige as the genius who had created a new form of popular journalism and brought the *Mirror* to unexampled success Bartholomew ruled over his board like an oriental potentate surrounded by obedient but often seething courtiers. He was growing old and, never a man of moderate habits, was drinking more and more heavily and showing himself increasingly idiosyncratic in his relationship with his colleagues, although still capable of some of the old flashes of fire. Also he had made the mistake of thinking he could repeat the *Mirror*'s success in Australia where he had bought the *Melbourne Argus*. It lost money heavily and by 1951 had become so much of a financial embarrassment that he decided that he must go to Australia to see what could be done.

His absence provided King with an opportunity for a putsch long contemplated. He persuaded a number of other directors to back him in forcing Bartholomew out. When Bartholomew returned for Christmas (a favourite time for *Mirror* assassinations) it was to discover that instead of discussing the *Argus* his fellow directors proposed to discuss him. He was met when he arrived by his friend, Philip Zec, the *Daily Mirror*'s famous cartoonist, one of whose cartoons had led to the paper being warned— absurdly most people thought—for spreading alarm and despondency during the war.

Zec had for some time been worried by Bartholomew's drinking and had felt that the time had come for him to retire. He now told him that King's campaign against him had gone so far that he would be well advised to resign. Bartholomew fell into a rage and refused. He believed that he could rely on the vote of Sylvester Bolam, the Editor of the *Mirror*, who owed him his professional advancement and was a close personal friend, and that without Bolam's vote King could not get a majority. At this Zec had to tell him that Bolam had already gone over to King's side. For Bartholomew it was the fatal stab. Bolam's defection, which he could at first hardly believe ('Judas, Judas,' he said over and over again) ended his hopes of resistance. Under Zec's guidance he wrote the necessary letter of resignation and on 21 December a public announcement gave the news that the paper he had created no longer wanted him. His resignation, said the notice with the polite hypocrisy he had so often derided 'had been accepted with regret', but had been inspired by his desire 'to promote the advancement of younger men'. This hypothetical desire was soon satisfied. Mr Cecil Harmsworth King, aged 50, stepped into his place as Chairman of both the *Mirror* and *Pictorial* Companies.

Bartholomew found it hard to reconcile himself to his fall. He rang me, and I suppose others, several times to deny the stories which he said King had put about that he had been incoherent at board meetings, and was no longer in a fit state to take important decisions. He was very bitter about King. 'A bloody adding machine that thinks it's Northcliffe,' he said. He was bitter, too, about the frequent comparison made between King as an intellectual and himself as a semi-illiterate and on one occasion brought his wife to the telephone to tell me how knowledgeable he was about music. He was altogether lost without the *Mirror*. And indeed he was its true creator. He had made it the genuine voice of those 'lower orders' of whom the British ruling classes had been so long afraid, the champion of the women who flooded into the factories during the war, and of the men in the ranks of the fighting services; earthy in its patriotism, ribald in its attacks on bureaucratic authority, tenacious in its criticisms of what it regarded as national inefficiency or complacency, delighted in for its frankness, its rough language and its strip cartoons. Of these latter a strip recording the adventures of Jane, a young lady in constant danger of losing her clothes and her virtue who always managed at the last minute to cling to the second however careless she might be of the first, became so much a favourite with the American as well as the British army that advance copies had to be run off to go with the D Day forces so that they could keep their minds on fighting Germans without worrying about what was happening to her while they were away.

Official appreciation of the paper was smaller. Reacting to its attacks much as an eighteenth century Whig would have done Churchill demanded its suppression and it was warned under section 2D of the Defence of the Realm Act by the Home Secretary, Herbert Morrison, who himself had the sensitivity to public criticism of one convinced that he understood the ordinary man better than anyone else. So far from shaking the confidence of its readers the official warning confirmed their belief in it. It was the people's paper. As such, it had a part in the Labour victory of 1945 which although not as decisive as its staff liked to think was nevertheless significant. It was thus riding high both in prestige and circulation when King's boardroom revolution ended Bartholomew's reign.

King's first act was to send for Hugh Cudlipp. Cudlipp had been promised the editorship of the *Sunday Express* in due course if he would stay with Beaverbrook who thought highly of his talents. He preferred to make his way with King. There was only one difficulty when he returned. King wanted him to run the *Mirror*. But the *Mirror* already had an editor—Bolam, and Bolam had cause to expect gratitude. He had served the paper well, including a three months term in prison on a contempt of court charge. Above all his vote had been decisive in enabling King to get rid of Bartholomew. Without his change of sides the palace revolution could not have succeeded. For the moment he was hard to dispose of. However, Cudlipp was privately told that arrangements would be made and was meanwhile sent to Australia to see if he could find any means to make the *Argus* pay. (He could not, it was eventually sold to the Melbourne Herald Company at a loss.) He had been advised that he should plan to be there six months. But King was not one to let I dare not wait upon I will and scarcely three months had passed when Cudlipp, preparing to enjoy Christmas in the Australian sunshine, received an urgent cable. Bolam was out and Cudlipp was required to return immediately to take over as Editorial Director of both the *Mirror* and the *Pictorial*.

Henceforth Cudlipp was to march always at King's shoulder: the indispensable man, never envious, or so it seemed, of the royal authority or likely to challenge 'the man with the last word' as he frequently called King, but complementary to him, possessed above all of what King most notably lacked: a talent for the techniques of tabloid journalism and a natural understanding of the way working class people think. Most journalists live on their youth. Despite middle age, high living and a steady diet of large cigars Cudlipp still draws on his. He may sometimes look and behave more like an actor manager hamming it up on the provincial circuit than a modern newspaper editor, but he understands *Mirror* working class readers because he was born among them in South Wales and worked among them as a junior reporter in Blackpool. He is the self-made man at the top that every mass circulation paper needs to keep in touch. It is impossible to doubt his flair for what makes tabloid journalism succeed although the later translation into a big business executive of one who habitually talks like a *Daily Mirror* leader seemed less natural.

Like any paper that makes an impact on the world the *Daily Mirror* is, of course, more than the product of one or two men. It is the sum of its own tradition. Bartholomew taught it to speak in the language of the masses, but it was the waves of loyalty and affection that came back to it from its readers that made it what it is, turning even the most cynical of its staff into a kind of crusader. I once picked a letter haphazardly from a pile on King's table. It said, 'Dear Editor, My husband of whom we are all very fond has been very ill. But I am glad to say he is now getting better and I thought you would like to know.' It is difficult for a paper with such a relationship with its readers to be other than itself. The

Mirror is the sort of paper it is because of the sort of people who read it. Nevertheless for the next seventeen years the most decisive factor in its continued progress was the partnership of King and Cudlipp. To this partnership Cudlipp contributed the newspaperman's quick reaction to events and the ability to translate them into brash colloquialisms working class readers would like, King the cool financial brain and the long term view.

On the foundations of the *Mirror* they built the largest newspaper, magazine and printing group in the world. The building was mainly King's. But Cudlipp, although more of a journalist than a businessman, was King's closest companion at every stage, deliberately chosen as his second in command in each major new enterprise and learning from him all along the way.

Their empire, like many others, was constructed partly by design, partly by accident and partly in reply to the empire building of rivals. King's first move once he had the *Mirror* firmly in his grasp was to buy 'uncle's old business in Farringdon Street': the Amalgamated Press, home of *Answers*, *Comic Cuts*, *Home Chats* and the rest of the Northcliffe *table d'hôte* for the semi-literate. When he bought it it was in the possession of Lord Camrose and his brother, the Hon Michael Berry, owners of the *Daily Telegraph*, who had inherited it from their father, the first Lord Camrose. The Berrys were, however, much more interested in looking after the *Daily Telegraph* than an indiscriminate hotchpotch of cheap magazines. They were glad to sell, so glad that they took a good deal less for their controlling block of shares than they were worth. King got their shares for the equivalent of 42s a share. He had to pay the remaining shareholders 52s a share.

By this purchase, the *Mirror-Pictorial* group obtained control of forty-two weekly magazines, twenty-three monthlies and twenty annuals of varying merit and profitability and started a chain reaction that set the whole magazine world of Britain rocking. King of the *Mirror* had represented no threat to the great magazine empires of Odham's Press and Newnes. King with the Amalgamated Press (which he renamed Fleetway Press) was a different matter — especially when it became known that he proposed to spend substantial sums on bringing the 1,500,000 circulation *Woman's Weekly* within challenging distance of Odham's first runner, the

3,000,000 circulation *Woman*, and Newnes' *Woman's Own* which was only a little behind *Woman*.

Odhams made the first counter-move. Although bereft by now of its original master builder, J. S. Elias (Lord Southwood), who had died in 1946, the company was still run as he would have wished by men he had trained—indeed its Chairman, Southwood's former chief accountant, A. C. Duncan, who was a keen spiritualist, still consulted him regularly. He reported him worried about the *Daily Herald*, as well he might be, and puzzled about the ban on free gifts, but proud and happy that his old firm had established for itself so dominating a position in the market for popular woman's magazines impeccably a-political in content. Two months after King's successful bid for the Amalgamated Press, Odhams paid £1,800,000 for Hulton Press, controlled by Edward Hulton, son of that Sir Edward whose dislike of Rothermere had given Beaverbrook his chance to get the *Evening Standard*.

Hulton Press had earlier had a great success with *Picture Post*—a *Life*-like weekly with a social conscience which under the editorship of Tom Hopkinson had acquired both substantial circulation and much intellectual and political prestige. However, when Hulton banned the publication of a Korean war dispatch critical of the Americans by *Picture Post*'s brilliant and morally much involved correspondent, James Cameron, Hopkinson and Cameron both resigned leaving a gap it proved impossible to fill—autocratic proprietors seldom prove adequate replacements for intelligent editors and writers. The magazine began to lose both influence and circulation and rather than face a humiliating decline Hulton abruptly ended its life. What was left of the Hulton Press after this was a comparatively small magazine group. But it had one or two woman's papers and a series of successful children's comics, *Eagle*, *Swift*, *Girl* and *Robin*, created for Hulton by a modern-minded clergyman. It thus fitted satisfactorily into the Odhams pattern.

Scarcely was this deal completed, however, than a new enemy entered the field. Activated by King's obvious conviction that big money was to be made in magazines, Sir William Carr, principal owner of the *News of the World*, made a take-over bid for Newnes which had grown from the acorn planted in Manchester when the fancy-goods salesman George Newnes was prodded by his wife into launching *Tit-Bits* into a lush magazine forest second only to Odhams in size.

This take-over bid represented a completely new development for the *News of the World* and one that the existing magazine barons dare not let pass. Concentration on the spicier side of life as disclosed in police court reports of divorces, rapes, violent assaults and carryings-on in public parks, plus lurid confession stories from criminals and other notorious persons, and extensive sports reporting not only of the big spectator games but of pigeon racing, public house darts and bowling matches had given the *News of the World* the largest mass circulation of any Sunday newspaper in the world—more than 8,000,000 at its peak. It had therefore vast financial resources to call on. It was also the owner of one of the largest and most modern photogravure plants in the country, Bemrose of Liverpool. This did a good deal of magazine printing on contract, so that the step to magazine publishing was logical enough. Carr opened his bid with an offer of £5 10s a share to Newnes shareholders. This was the equivalent of £9,700,000 for the whole company. The Newnes directors shuddered and advised their shareholders not to accept. Thereupon Carr raised the offer to £11,000,000.

As Charles Morris, Chairman of Newnes, gloomily contemplated this second offer which he feared he would have difficulty in advising shareholders to reject, he met on the train to London from his house in Cobham, Surrey, a neighbour of his, Charles Shand. Shand had first come into prominence as head of the Odhams book department which had made it possible for Elias to flood Britain with all those copies of the works of Charles Dickens. He was now Joint Managing Director of the Odhams group and he, too, had been thinking of the *News of the World* offer. When the train arrived at Waterloo Station Shand drew Morris aside and as the commuters swirled past them suggested that Odhams, who took no pleasure in the idea of yet another newspaper proprietor grazing in their pasture, might possibly be interested in outbidding Carr if Morris would be willing to consider an approach. To this Morris replied that he would rather a devil he knew than a devil he didn't, and so far as he was concerned anything was preferable to the *News of the World*. However, Odhams would have to act quickly. He could not delay communicating the *News of the World* offer to his shareholders more than a day or two.

Shand jumped into a taxi and drove as rapidly as London traffic allowed to his office. There he at once saw Duncan, his Chairman, Surrey Dane, the Vice-Chairman who had previously been Elias's promotion and publicity chief and the man most closely concerned with him in launching the 'new' *Daily Herald*, and H. L. Gibson, his fellow Joint Managing Director. They decided to outbid the *News of the World* with an offer of just under £13,000,000 in cash and shares. For his part Morris was as good as his nod on Waterloo station. He and his board unanimously recommended the Odhams offer to their shareholders and ninety per cent accepted almost by return of post.

With Newnes as well as Hultons in their possession Odhams were—or thought they were—in an impregnable position to repulse any new attack King might contemplate. Their magazine fortunes secure, they turned their minds to their remaining, and, as it seemed, perpetual, problem—the *Daily Herald*. After reaching an immediate post-war circulation peak of 2,145,000— artificially supported by news-print rationing which kept competition at a minimum—the *Herald*'s circulation was now down to only 1,466,000. Moreover it was still falling, a decline all the more galling in view of the sharp rise of both the *Mirror* and *Daily Express* which between them had taken some ninety per cent of the post-war expansion in newspaper readership. Duncan, Odhams' Chairman, had reached an age when, even with Lord Southwood's encouragement from the other side, he felt he needed a rest. He decided to step down from the Chairmanship and bring in a man more capable of meeting King on equal terms when it came to grappling with newspaper problems.

The man on whom his choice fell was a neighbour and friend of his, Sir Christopher Chancellor, an Etonian who after taking a first in history at Trinity College, Cambridge (King, after all, had only taken a second at Oxford) had joined Reuters and risen to be its highly successful General Manager. Chancellor at once got to work re-organising the *Herald*. The experienced newspaper technician who was then its editor was replaced by one more to Chancellor's mind—a former London editor of the *Manchester Guardian*, John Beavan, who had left journalism for the Nuffield

Trust, but found he liked Fleet Street better than charity. At the same time the T.U.C. was persuaded to relax its demands on the *Herald* as an official journal. This improved the editorial quality of the Herald, but not, as had been hoped, its circulation.

Although possibly good for the *Herald*, Chancellor soon proved unequal to dealing with his fellow historian, Cecil King, in other matters. Instead, he accidentally precipitated a crisis. The two men were well known to each other and at a cocktail party given by King's cousin, the second Lord Rothermere, in December 1960, King, who had come to the conclusion that there were too many women's magazines chasing too little advertising, remarked casually to Chancellor, 'If you stop one of yours, I'll stop one of mine.' They arranged to lunch at the Savoy a few days later. King came on his own, expecting a private chat between equals, but Chancellor was accompanied by the two Joint Managing Directors of Odhams, Shand and Gibson. In the course of a preliminary talk over drinks either Shand or Gibson jokingly remarked that if King was having woman trouble the best thing might be for Odhams to take the whole lot off his hands. Those who joke with King do so at their peril and after an inconclusive lunch during which little progress was made on methods to reduce competition, he returned to his office and wrote to Chancellor that he would be prepared to consider £10,000,000 for Fleetway Press—but there 'must be no fishing'.

Chancellor and his colleagues who had had no serious bid in mind then made a fatal mistake. They wrote to King saying £10,000,000 was too much but, put off by his warning against 'fishing', did not make any counter proposal such as he had expected. Very well, said King in reply, if you won't buy Fleetway Press, what about amalgamating with us? Unused to such high tycoonery and much shaken by it, Chancellor incautiously responded by asking King if he was preparing a take-over—an operation to which, as Odhams directors were well aware, their group might prove highly vulnerable because of its large number of publicly held shares. To this King replied, 'I have not reached that point yet. I am proposing a merger. But I want you to answer quickly.'

At this Chancellor and his board took even greater fright. If King was really after them they had, they decided, better run for cover. Some time earlier Roy Thomson, the Canadian (not yet ennobled) who had recently acquired the *Sunday Times* and the rest of the Kemsley group of newspapers, had met Chancellor at a dinner party and remarked in his genial way that if Odhams ever wanted to sell he was in the market. The suggestion had at the time been treated as a typical Thomson impertinence. But Thomson was known to have a thick skin where money was concerned and it was not thought he would bear malice for past snubs so long as he saw a chance of profit. It was, therefore, agreed that Chancellor should approach him to see if he might still be interested in some sort of a deal more satisfactory to them than a King take-over was likely to be. Thomson announced himself ready to talk and, unwisely as it turned out, Chancellor decided to go to ground while the talks proceeded. When King telephoned to ask if the Odhams board had considered his suggestion for a merger and would like to discuss it he was told that Chancellor was 'not available', a procedure designed to give the greatest possible offence to King and make him all the more determined to have his way. Meanwhile Chancellor was seeing Thomson. They agreed to form a new company, Thomson-Odhams Ltd, with Thomson as Chairman and Chancellor as Vice-Chairman.

All this was done without any word to King. The first he heard of it was when a Press Association message was handed to him at the end of a talk he was giving at a conference of the International Press Institute. He immediately left the meeting and as Chancellor and Thomson, flushed with success, met the press and the television cameras to announce their nuptials, he called his directors and financial advisors together to prepare a counter blow. News of the proposed Thomson-Odhams merger hoisted Odhams shares to 40s on the Stock Exchange. Two days later King made a take-over bid equivalent to 55s 1½d a share.

At this stage the battle moved to another front—the political one. Although the real struggle was about magazines it had by now become clear that the future of the *Daily Herald* was also much involved. And not only did the Trade Union Congress hold forty-nine per cent of the shares in the Daily Herald Company (Odhams holding the remaining fifty-one per cent), but it was the official paper of the Labour party and its only certain voice in the press, despite the *Mirror*'s generally radical line. There were natural anxieties as to what was likely to happen to it as the outcome of financial deals concerned only with securing maximum profitability in magazine publishing. Who could be most trusted to safeguard its political integrity: Thomson or King?

I was at the time in California on a visit to Berkeley as Regents' Professor and was wakened at 6.30 one morning by an urgent telephone call from London. George Brown was on the telephone seeking my views on behalf of himself and Hugh Gaitskell. Gaitskell favoured Thomson, Brown favoured King. They wanted to know what I thought. From such meagre information as had reached California—not a State much interested in the outside world—it looked to me that in any event all was over bar the shouting. But if the future of the *Herald* could be isolated from the magazine sale then I would, I said, marginally prefer Thomson to King. My reasons were that King already had one national daily paper and was known as an editorial interventionist, whereas Thomson had none and was an a-political owner who, on past form, would be more likely to be happy to leave political policy to the editor.

As it turned out all such considerations were by then irrelevant even although wide-spread political anxiety had developed regarding this further move towards monopolisation, especially as the *News Chronicle*, the last of a notable line of Liberal newspapers, had but recently died and buried its remains in the *Daily Mail*.

Leaders of the Labour Party and the Trade Unions were lunched alternately by Thomson-Odhams and the *Mirror* on the basis of 'Codlins the friend not Short' and demands were made in Parliament for an enquiry into the whole condition of the press with a freezing of all press deals until the inquiry was completed. The proposal for an inquiry was accepted and a Royal Commission announced. But Mr Macmillan, the Prime Minister, while agreeing that the Odhams-King-Thomson affair, following as it did so hard on the heels of the *News Chronicle* closure, appeared symptomatic of some general malady in the press, declared himself without power to require the participants in the Odhams fight to hold their hands until the Royal Commission reported. King was free to go ahead.

He comforted Labour fears with a promise inspired by Hugh Cudlipp that the *Herald* would be kept alive for a minimum of seven years whatever might happen, and assuaged such anxieties as Odhams shareholders still had with an improved offer equivalent to 63s 4½d a share as compared with his original offer of 55s 1½d. At this stage Thomson publicly withdrew. 'It's no use just making a bid,' he wrote to me in California. 'You have to live with it.' The Odhams directors continued to oppose the take-over. But there was no fight left in them. Although they would not accept the *Mirror*'s offer for their own shares they felt unable to advise shareholders in general to reject it.

Just three months after King's casual cocktail remark to Chancellor and only a little more than two years after he had bought Amalgamated Press, the four major magazine groups which then existed had been replaced by one giant and King had secured a complete monopoly of popular women's magazines in Britain. In the course of doing so he had, almost against his will, acquired a politically important national daily newspaper, the *Daily Herald* and the second largest mass circulation Sunday newspaper in Britain, the *People*. On the morning the deal was completed four Odhams directors, including Duncan, the former Chairman, Harry Ainsworth, the Editorial Director, and Surrey Dane, all of whom had spent a lifetime in the company's service, found curt notes awaiting them when they arrived informing them their services were no longer required. They left without even a handshake or a letter of appreciation for past services. 'It was like a kick in the teeth,' one of them said to me. Cecil King had no time for unrewarding courtesies.

The creation of the International Publishing Corporation followed the Odhams take-over, if not quite automatically at least predictably. The clumsy arrangement whereby the *Mirror* and the *Pictorial* were owned by separate companies with interlocking shareholdings had been overdue for reform even before first the Amalgamated Press and then Odhams had been bought: with their acquisition it became imperative. The I.P.C., 'a mixture of history and enterprise,' as the thirteenth annual report of the Press Council called it, came into existence as an agglomeration of everything 'from trees to newsagents', constantly extended by new take-overs and mergers.

In addition to the *Daily Mirror* and *Sunday Pictorial* (renamed the *Sunday Mirror*) the I.P.C. owns the *Sun* (into which the *Daily Herald* was transformed shortly after the Odhams take-over), the

People, *Sporting Life*, the *Glasgow Daily Record*, the *Scottish Sunday Mail*, a number of local British weeklies and the *Daily Times* and *Weekly Times* of Nigeria—it formerly owned other newspapers in West Africa and in the West Indies but has disposed of them. It publishes ninety weekly periodicals ranging from women's papers, children's comics, mass circulation 'pulp' weeklies like *Reveille*, and recreational papers like *Popular Gardening* and *Anglers' Mail*, to papers for the huntin' and shootin' classes, like *Country Life* and *Horse and Hound*, and prestige intellectual weeklies like *New Society* and the *New Scientist*, and about one hundred and twenty monthlies and other periodicals. It also controls a great many trade and technical papers not only in Britain, where its possessions include *Flight*, *Motor*, *Autocar*, *Farmers' Weekly*, *Melody Maker*, *New Musical Express*, *Electronics Weekly* and the *Stock Exchange Gazette*, but in the United States, where it bought in 1960 a forty per cent interest in the Cahners group of Boston, and in France, Germany and Italy. It has eight book publishing companies grouped under Paul Hamlyn Holdings and a majority interest in the long playing record company, Music for Pleasure, in which it is associated with Electrical and Musical Industries. It also has a 21·5 per cent interest in Associated Television (A.T.V.), a 15·8 per cent interest in British Relay Wireless, a 28·4 per cent interest in the Reed Paper Group and a $33\frac{1}{8}$ per cent interest in Forbuoys which, after W. H. Smith, is one of the largest chains of newsagents in Britain. Its printing division grouped under International Printers owns nineteen non-newspaper printing works including modern rotary gravure plants and a large new webb-offset plant in London.

The International Publishing Corporation thus presents a conglomeration of linked interests far removed from the original press tradition of the single newspaper owned, and often edited, by a predominant individual, although not all that different from the newspaper and periodical empire King's uncles, Northcliffe and Rothermere, built up some seventy years earlier.

Such political influence as King possessed—and he sought latterly to claim a great deal—derived, however, not from the I.P.C. but from the *Daily Mirror*, which under King's and Cudlipp's control continued the revolution in newspaper readership Bartholomew had begun and showed itself far more responsive than other popular newspapers to changes in public taste. Not only did the King-Cudlipp partnership attract nearly a million more readers, but it did so while progressively making the *Mirror* a more serious newspaper—wedding the tabloid form to the examination of public affairs to an extent that had previously scarcely seemed possible. The decision to do so was taken as a deliberate act of policy based on the conviction that mass readers were becoming steadily more interested in public affairs and anxious to be informed about them. This decision aroused a good deal of derision when first made and was dismissed by many in Fleet Street as a high falutin' notion bound to fail. But it proved brilliantly successful. Nor is the seriousness any the less significant for being inter-mittent, based on the sensible principle that for the *Mirror* to ram run-of-the-mill serious news down its readers' throats day after day would merely bore them, but that to splash a really serious issue all across the front page and perhaps across the whole of the middle pages as well in brash, simple language under large black headlines not only makes them read it but makes them say to them-selves, 'Well by God, if the *Mirror* thinks it's that important it must be.'

Mass circulation newspapers have to go with the prevailing mood. They cannot deflect the waggon of public opinion once it has started to roll, and certainly cannot reverse its course. But they can enormously increase its weight and velocity. Although arro-gance kept breaking in and some of the *Mirror*'s political pro-nouncements while King was there gave the impression that it be-lieved itself specially chosen by God, it also frequently showed itself a highly skilled popular educator in such matters as the case for European economic unity, Britain's future defence role, and the technical and human problems of automation, and did so while fully retaining its hold on a mass public. It has also had a large part in creating a more liberal social climate in British middle and lower middle class society. Barnes of *The Times* would, one feels, have appreciated its purpose and general stategy while being somewhat shaken by its methods—these James Gordon Bennett would have better understood.

The King-Cudlipp flair proved less successful with the *Daily Herald* when it was dumped on them as part of the price they paid for their magazine monopoly. Its circulation continued as tenaciously downwards as it had under Odhams. Nor has the ending of the official trade union link and the decision to turn the *Herald* into a new paper, the *Sun*, had any happier results.

The *Sun* was the King-Cudlipp team's first new creation, a paper born, as its pre-publication publicity excitedly declared, of the age we live in. But although it has won some new readers, younger, better off, less working class than the *Herald*'s were, it has lost more circulation than it has gained. This is the more disappointing to its promoters in that in addition to spending £600,000 on launching it, they invited to its baptism the youngest and, so it was thought, most powerful of all modern fairy godmothers —sociology.

A survey of the probable British newspaper reading public over the next ten years was commissioned from Dr Mark Abrams, Managing Director of Research Services Ltd, and a former President of the World Association for Public Opinion Research. Among the conclusions he offered were that the traditional classification of the British people into social classes was passing and was being replaced by differences related to age and to stages in the family life cycle: 'The middle class teenager probably has more in common with a working class teenager than he has with middle-aged middle class people. Or again, young middle class married people have more in common with young working class married couples than they have with their parents.' It was, Dr Abrams suggested, increasingly the needs, interests, and values of the under thirty-fives —children, teenagers and young parents who by the end of the sixties would make up half the population—that determined the general climate of British society and therefore the mood of newspaper readers. By past British standards a high proportion of this generation had already received, or would receive, education beyond the minimum school-leaving age and have formal academic and technological qualifications. They would neither feel, as their parents were inclined to, that they must accept the station in life into which they were born, nor that they could only succeed 'by acquiring the habits of a body of people described as their social betters'. They would expect—indeed they already did—a high and rising standard of living. They would travel and they would have been given by their schools the capacity to understand and enjoy the arts. Of those who went out to work the great majority in the socially predominant age group would be in white collar jobs, or would be skilled manual workers.

Dr Abrams envisaged, in fact, although he did not specifically say so, a British society increasingly like the American in its concentration on material affluence and in its social ambitions. Within it he foresaw women as enjoying a much higher status than formerly and their activities and interests as the main force in shaping the family's ties with the outside world. Political outlooks, he considered, would be secular and critical rather than ideological. Ideological politics would be displaced by consumer politics and political support given to those who offered the greatest competence in social engineering.

By this somewhat chilling chart of the future the *Sun* set its course. But success did not come. On the contrary after three years of trying hard to do as the sociologists told it, the new paper was losing money at the rate of £1,750,000 a year and had gone back in circulation to where the *Herald* was in 1930.

One reason for this may be that just as newspapers cannot be edited by committees, no more can they be run by reference to market reports. Although the *Sun* has done some things well and is in some ways a better paper than the public response indicates, it has always seemed to lack the impress of a strong editorial personality. Preoccupied, no doubt, with reader appeal, it seems to have forgotten that newspapers must sometimes be prepared to lose readers in order to gain them.

However, there are reasons other than the merits or demerits of the *Sun* itself which help to account for its failure. The British people are more ardent for newspapers than any other people in the world—much more so, man for man and woman for woman, than the Americans, despite the fact that there are some fifteen times more individual newspapers in the United States than in Britain.

Each weekday morning the British buy more than 15,000,000 copies of national morning newspapers and 2,000,000 copies of provincial morning newspapers. Each weekday afternoon they buy another 9,500,000 copies of evening newspapers and each weekend they take in a total of 24,000,000 Sunday newspapers. But the pattern of this reading is changing. From the beginning of the Northcliffe 'revolution' onwards the dominant feature of popular journalism had been the pre-eminence of the middle range text newspapers, among which the *Sun* has sought to establish itself. Not only Northcliffe's *Daily Mail* itself, but the *Daily Express*, the *Daily News*, the *Daily Chronicle*, the *Westminster Gazette* and the *Daily Herald* all fell within this group. Even thirty years ago despite the death of both the *Westminster Gazette* and the *Chronicle*, seventy-two per cent of all national morning newspaper readership was covered by it. The war-time expansion in newspaper reading and the rise of the *Mirror* altered the balance somewhat. But even twenty years ago more than sixty-two per cent of all newspaper readership belonged to this middle range of popular text newspapers. In the subsequent decades total national daily newspaper circulation has remained virtually unchanged, there is no more than 100,000 difference between the figure for 1948 and 1968. But the share of the middle group has fallen from sixty-two per cent to less than half—only just over forty-seven per cent. Moreover, the rate of decline seems to be accelerating. In the second half of 1967 the three papers in the middle group, the *Daily Express*, the *Daily Mail* and the *Sun* between them lost 263,000 readers compared with the second half of the previous year, although the circulations of all other national daily papers rose. Over the last six years they have lost in total more than 1,000,000. Nor has this trend affected only the two most vulnerable, the *Mail* and the *Sun*. The most successful paper of the group—and formerly the most successful of all British newspapers—the *Daily Express*, lost 380,000 readers in these six years.

This middle territory once comfortably supported six newspapers. It is now scarcely able to maintain the three to which its numbers were reduced by the death of the *News Chronicle* in 1960. In seeking to establish itself on this ground, therefore, the *Sun* was trying to build on territory consistently eroded.

There are deflections in two directions: to the quality press at one side, to the tabloid press at the other. Thirty years ago the quality market represented by *The Times*, the *Guardian* and the *Daily Telegraph* accounted for only a little over seven per cent of total newspaper readership. By the end of 1967 this had nearly doubled to 13·5 per cent and was still rising. In the same period the much larger tabloid share, mainly taken up by the *Daily Mirror*, but also including the *Daily Sketch*, had also nearly doubled. From twenty per cent, it had risen to just under forty per cent.

This trend away from the once dominant middle group has been even more marked among Sunday newspapers. In the quality market the *Sunday Times* and *Observer* have both risen remarkably in circulation despite the competition of a new entry, the *Sunday Telegraph*. At the other end of the scale the mass circulation Sundays, the *News of the World*, the *People* and the *Sunday Mirror*, are all flourishing. But no less than five Sunday newspapers in the middle group have died in the last thirteen years: the *Sunday Dispatch*, *Sunday Chronicle*, *Empire News*, *Sunday Graphic* and *Sunday Citizen*. Only one such paper now remains: the *Sunday Express*.

King's calculation was that with even the *Daily Express* unable to hold the position Beaverbrook had given it and with the *Daily Mail* in a highly vulnerable state under a proprietor who, to judge by the number of editors he was going through, was rapidly losing his nerve, it was worth hanging on to the *Sun* as a long term gamble. There was a good chance, he thought, that in the end the *Mail* would go—probably by way of a merger with the *Daily Express*—and if the *Sun* were still around at the time it might be in a position to inherit sufficient *Daily Mail* readers to make it not only economically viable but perhaps able ultimately to challenge the *Daily Express*, which was living, he thought, on the Beaverbrook formula without the Beaverbrook energy. In this game of newspaper poker the jack-pot would fall he considered to whoever could stay in the game longest and with its widely spread interests, I.P.C., he judged, was in the best shape to do just that.

In this King may have miscalculated—even apart from his own disappearance from the scene which he never seems to have thought of as a possibility. A year before the curtain fell for King himself, it was already beginning to look as if he were better at growing than consolidating. He had built the I.P.C. into an organisation of vast potentialities. But few of these potentialities were as yet being realised. It was, in one financial writer's phrase, 'a jam tomorrow company'. The *Daily Mirror* and *Sunday Mirror* could still claim to be the richest newspaper combination in the world, but the corporation as a whole was a long way from the pot of gold at the end of the rainbow. King had brought under one financial roof activities ideally suited, it seemed, to take advantage of some of the richest growth areas in the world of mass communications and leisure pursuits. Intellectually one could not but admire its comprehensive and intricate design. But the fact remained that in practice the larger the amount of capital involved the more the earnings per share fell.

By 1968 not only was the continued drain of the *Sun* on I.P.C. resources making King's poker game a very expensive one indeed, but the women's weekly magazines, for whose sake the *Herald* had been bought and the seven years' survival promise given, had been badly hit by changing tastes and the advertising competition of commercial television—much as the glossy money spinners of American magazine journalism were. Labour disputes over new processes had led to continued stoppages in the printing division and what had been intended as the largest, most profitable printing combination in the world was, despite its technological advances, currently faced with losses of nearly £2,000,000. Nor were the other trading and investment activities of the corporation yielding the rewards anticipated. Also, it was committed to a £5,000,000 investment in computer services which although promising big profits in the future were currently a further very heavy drain on reserves. That there was pie in the sky, and very tasty and nourishing pie at that, could scarcely be doubted. Meanwhile a penny increase in the price of the *Daily Mirror* was still sufficient to cover all the I.P.C.'s trading losses. But an increase had to be delayed from autumn 1967 until spring of 1968 because of the refusal of the Prices and Incomes Board to accept it as justified at the earlier date. It therefore came too late to stave off a substantial dividend cut. Devaluation had meanwhile imposed another £7,000,000 burden on the corporation.

Two things in fact had become plain. One was that the vast structure King had created with Cudlipp, now Deputy Chairman of the group, at his shoulder was—whatever its future potentialities —uncomfortably dependent for the time being on the commercial success of one product, the *Mirror* in its daily and Sunday manifestations. The other was that although King had brought in a number of new working directors of great ability, it was imperative that he himself, as the architect of the whole, should put imperialist ambitions aside, cease expanding, and devote his talents exclusively to the existing managerial and planning problems of I.P.C. if the institutional investors who held some fifty-one per cent of its shares were not to become restive. This, however, was what King was unwilling to do. Less so, indeed, than ever before, for he had meanwhile become preoccupied with national problems and convinced that he had a mission to save the country.

When he had deposed Bartholomew, King had presented himself to the world as a new kind of figure in the British popular press and perhaps an archetype of its future. He was not a press baron as Northcliffe had been and Beaverbrook was, nor a journalistic voice of the masses like Bartholomew, but a business intellectual, a managerial executive talented in running a big organisation and in providing a broader base for newspaper enterprise by skills which might have been equally applicable in any other large commercial enterprise. Like other such men in the second half of the twentieth century, he was not an owner but a paid executive—his personal holding in I.P.C. was at no time more than one per cent of the total shares. But this, too, seemed in keeping with the new pattern and with the end of the era of personal ownership of newspapers by men using them for their own political and social purposes and their substitution by professional managers. King's original partnership with Cudlipp—although it changed with success as did Cudlipp's role also—was the partnership of a professional business administrator and a professional journalist in which the one devoted himself to newspapers as big business while the other looked after them journalistically.

It is a nice irony and perhaps an evidence of the underlying force of the new press trends he originally seemed to represent that King's fall from power finally came because he refused to conform to the pattern his own rise had appeared to initiate. Once he had tasted power and success he found it temperamentally impossible to confine himself to business management. Moved by imperial longings he began to act not only as if the *Mirror* were as much his personal property as the *Mail* had been Northcliffe's, but as if he were living in the Northcliffe era. It had long been his habit to talk of 'my papers' and 'my editors' and even of *Daily Mirror* readers as 'my people', but such egocentricities had been forgiven because his financial and administrative talents, his scientific approach to the problems of commercial planning, and his dominant personality, which was strengthened if anything by his apparent inability to make a close relationship with those with whom he worked—combined, it should be said, with a shrewd eye, as in the case of his partnership with Cudlipp, for those who could supplement his own deficiencies—seemed almost to justify so arrogant an assumption of power. He frequently derided Thomson for his shopkeeper's attitude to his newspapers, was openly contemptuous of most other newspaper publishers for their lack of professionalism and much enjoyed regular forays to the United States to tell the American press how bad it was. With success to justify him there were few in the I.P.C. organisation or outside it who were not ready to take him as his own valuation or regard him as other than immovable so long as he cared to stay. He was so much the biggest personality on the I.P.C. board and it was so much his creation that when he remarked in a television interview that his fellow directors could sack him at a moment's notice if they wished to do so it seemed as good a joke to everyone else as it did to him.

It would probably have remained so if heredity had not proved too strong for him. He had looked so long on the Northcliffe portrait above his mantelpiece that he saw himself in it. And curiously it was Northcliffe's mistakes that he most embraced, forgetting as he did so that Northcliffe at least had the protection of a firm financial base in newspapers he actually owned. Just as Northcliffe had expected high office from Lloyd George as a reward for what he considered to be the *Daily Mail*'s essential support, so King, who was convinced that the return of the Wilson government owed a great deal to the *Mirror* and who had at first been much taken with Harold Wilson's abilities and personality, felt satisfied that he would be called to help save the country in high office. Nor was it, perhaps, so very wild an idea in view of Wilson's own approach to Cabinet making—after all if Frank Cousins of the Transport and General Workers' Union could be made a Cabinet Minister, without any political experience, why not Cecil King of the International Publishing Corporation?

When all that was offered King was a minor role at the Board of Trade under Douglas Jay, the strongest opponent of the European Common Market in the Cabinet whereas King was a dedicated marketeer, he was deeply insulted. The insult rankled and, as the Labour Government's economic difficulties mounted, found expression first in a virulent campaign against Jay and then in increasingly bitter attacks on Wilson himself in the editorial columns of the *Mirror*. Even this and his increasing identification in the public eye with grandiose plans for a businessman's government in which he and Lord Robens, Chairman of the National Coal Board and a strong critic of Wilson, would play major parts might not alone have led to his being deposed. Hugh Cudlipp who was Editor-in-Chief of the *Mirror* as well as Deputy Chairman of I.P.C. seemed as happy to go along politically with King as he had always been: for him King was still 'the man with the last word'. Certainly King saw no reason to expect difficulty from that quarter —any more than Bartholomew had from his friend Bolam. Even in the matter that finally brought things to a head King was given no reason to suspect until the very last that the King-Cudlipp partnership was in danger of dissolution. So long as it lasted he was safe, even if he had had any cause, which he seems not to have had, to suspect that other members of the board, from most of whom he remained rather remote, were turning against him. He was not in any event in a mood to read warning signs or to contemplate that anyone in I.P.C. would have the impertinence to challenge him. He had become convinced that not only was he intellectually right, but that, as he confided in one of the television interviews to which he became increasingly addicted, God was at his side. A man with a self-regard so strong that he had always found it hard to have a good opinion of anyone else, he had a monumental ignorance of the political life—he was one of the few men who found it possible to underestimate both Churchill and Attlee at the same time. He now charged into battle like a blindfolded bison with a grudge turned loose in a liquor store in the dark.

It was with a wholly Northcliffeian attitude to 'his' newspapers and his personal responsibility for political events that he composed in May 1968 an attack on the Prime Minister, Mr Harold Wilson, demanding that he should be driven from office by the Labour Party without delay. He issued instructions that this proclamation should be published prominently under the title 'Enough is Enough' on the front pages of both the *Daily Mirror* and the *Sun* over his signature as Chairman of the I.P.C. He did not trouble to inform the Board of what he was doing: they knew nothing of it until they read it in print. But he did show it to Cudlipp and Cudlipp as Editor-in-Chief raised no objection. In the light of future events, Cudlipp's failure either to raise objections himself or to inform other directors of King's decision to issue such a statement as Chairman of the I.P.C. has a somewhat inimical character. However, it may be that at this stage Cudlipp, who in any event shared King's feelings about Wilson, was still too much under the influence of his thirty-year role as faithful lieutenant to think of seriously challenging his powerful Chairman's right to do whatever he wanted.

Other members of the Board were less inhibited. They had been made increasingly restive for some time by King's preoccupation with politics to the detriment of the real interests of I.P.C. Enough was, indeed, enough so far as they were concerned. Even as a *Mirror* editorial its terms would have seemed violent and excessive. But in that form it could have been accepted as a legitimate, if short-sighted, expression of editorial policy—short-sighted because its terms were such as to produce the exactly opposite effect to what was intended and to bring a sharp Labour Party reaction in Wilson's favour, legitimate because the *Mirror* had always been a paper of strong views. Its publication as a personal statement by King, signed by him as Chairman of I.P.C. and seeming to commit not only the *Mirror* and the *Sun* but the International Publishing Corporation as a company to a personal vendetta against the Prime Minister, was a different matter. It deeply affronted many members of the *Mirror* staff who saw the whole relationship between the *Mirror* and its readers in danger of being undermined and themselves made to look as if they were no more than King's lackeys, required to jump to his bidding whatever it might be. And it finally convinced his fellow directors of I.P.C. that at a time when it was essential that he should apply himself single-mindedly to the Company's business, King was so far gone in personal political arrogance that he was in danger both of ignoring its commercial needs and seriously jeopardising the position of its major product, by making it seem to readers whose intelligent interest it had attempted to foster no more than the personal instrument of a rich man in a rage.

King's pronouncement had also disturbed politicians of all colours, not so much by its content, with which some of them no doubt agreed as did also some, although not all, I.P.C. directors, but because it seemed to represent a definite return to the days of the old press barons and their assumption that control of newspapers gave them the personal right to issue orders to Prime Ministers and governments. What was seen to be at issue politically, indeed, was the same principle that had arisen when Lord Beaverbrook and King's uncle, the first Lord Rothermere, had demanded of Baldwin the right to be consulted on Cabinet appointments in return for their support and had been demolished by Baldwin with the contemptuous phrase, given him by his cousin Rudyard Kipling, that they wanted 'Power without responsibility, the prerogative of the harlot throughout the ages.'

It is a measure of the extent to which King's long exercise of almost dictatorial power in the offices of I.P.C. and the flattery of sycophants had eaten into his judgment that he at no time seems to have realised the damage he was doing not only to the I.P.C. but to the whole image of the press by striking such an attitude. He certainly seems to have been totally unaware of the probable effect of his political posturing upon his fellow directors and upon institutional investors in the I.P.C. who were shocked by the irresponsible way in which the company was being dragged into the centre of a controversy which seemed likely to revive all those public suspicions of the press that it had been hoped belonged to the past—all the more so in that King made use of the status he enjoyed as a director of the Bank of England, to which Wilson had appointed him in more friendly days but from which he now resigned, to back his attack on the Prime Minister with one on the exchange position of the £1. Of none of this was King aware. Insulated by his remarkable egotism he rushed to take part in a television interview where he managed to make an even worse impression than his original pronouncement had done.

Yet even so it was not until nearly a fortnight had passed that his fellow directors summoned the courage to dismiss him. Their decision to do so was preceded by ten days of private discussions in small groups with Cudlipp present at each one. No board meeting was called. At no time was King told formally or informally of his fellow directors' dissatisfaction. He was given no chance to reply to it. When the decision was finally taken it had all the melodramatic trappings of a court plot. King had the habit of conserving his resources by retiring to bed at 9.30 in the evening. His fellow directors waited until he was safely between the sheets in his home in Hampton Court before meeting secretly without informing him at the I.P.C. building in Holborn Circus. There Hugh Cudlipp, as Deputy Chairman, went round the table asking each director in turn to give his opinion of King as Chairman. Every voice was against him. A vote was taken then—although it was not a formally constituted board meeting since if it had been he would have had to be given notice of it—and it was unanimously agreed to ask for his resignation from the Board on the somewhat odd pretext that it had been decided that the Chairman of I.P.C. ought to retire at the age of 65 and as he was already past this age he should go at once. It was agreed to elect Hugh Cudlipp as Chairman in his place. The King-Cudlipp patnership was over at last.

Unanimity was essential for although King could be removed from the Chairmanship by a majority vote, under the Company's articles of association he could only be removed from the Board itself by a unanimous one and no one could contemplate with pleasure the prospect of having him among them to fight back. When the vote was taken several of the directors seem to have been shaken by the enormity of what they had done. At any rate all were frightened by thought of the retaliation he might take if he were given time to collect his forces. Like Macbeth they decided that if it were to be done 'twere well it were done quickly. They gave orders to the Secretary of the I.P.C. to be at King's house in Hampton Court at 8.15 the following morning with a letter requesting his resignation within three hours. Even by *Mirror* standards it was a uniquely callous way of informing a man who had been with the group forty-two years, a director for thirty-nine and Chairman for seventeen, that his fellow directors, most of whom owed their positions to him, wanted no more of him and that his friend and long-time lieutenant Hugh Cudlipp, whom he himself had promoted to Deputy Chairman, was to take his place.

Subsequently Cudlipp sought to persuade shareholders that this abrupt course was not taken because of King's anti-Wilson pronouncement but came simply as the culmination of the Board's feeling over a long period that King's 'increasing preoccupation and intervention in national affairs in a personal sense' was detrimental to the business conduct of I.P.C. He did not however explain why if this was so the ten days scurry of private talks among

directors did not begin until after King's anti-Wilson pronouncement. When he was asked by a shareholder why their anxieties had
never been discussed with King earlier he replied revealingly, 'He
is a very formidable character. Not the sort of boss to whom one
can go and casually mention the possibility of his retirement
sometime.'

King was shaving when the I.P.C. Secretary arrived and nervously
presented him with the ultimatum the directors had lacked the
courage to give him themselves. Without waiting for breakfast he
drove at once to his office. There a deputation of three, headed by
Cudlipp, waited on him, the first and only time he saw any of his
fellow directors during the whole affair. He told them he had no
intention of falling in with their plans by resigning and showed
them the door. They walked along the passage to the Board Room
where the rest of the directors were waiting. Another meeting was
held and it was formally proposed and passed that in view of King's
refusal to resign he should be dismissed. A letter of dismissal was
typed and sent to the Chairman's room for delivery into King's
hands. He opened it, lifted the telephone receiver and asked for
the news desk of Independent Television News. When they were
on the line he said, 'This is Cecil King. I've been sacked. Would
you like an interview?' At first they refused to take him seriously.
When he had persuaded them he rang the B.B.C. This done he left
the building, in the foyer of which a plaque reads, 'This building
was opened by Cecil Harmsworth King, Chairman of the Daily
Mirror Newspapers, 7th March, 1961', and drove off in his black
Rolls Royce with its licence number CHK 44 to spend a busy
afternoon and evening giving television interviews. He was paid
a year's salary in lieu of notice, and Cudlipp moved into his room,
first very sensibly divesting himself of all his direct editorial responsibilities in order that there should be no further confusion
between the functions of Chairman and Editor.

It was a bizarre close to a career of great distinction, not only as
creator of the International Publishing Corporation but as Chairman of the Newspaper Publishers Association (its title was changed
from Newspaper Proprietors Association to accommodate him)
and a leader of the newspaper industry in many ways. He it was
who was mainly responsible for the decision to commission an
independent survey of efficiency in the newspaper industry and

he who later set going a Joint Board of Unions and Managements to tackle its economic problems. It was largely as a result of his efforts, also, that the Press Council, which he had at first derided, was reorganised and a distinguished judge, Lord Devlin, persuaded to become its independent chairman. In many other ways he rendered great service to the British press. He urged it into the second half of the twentieth century with a well placed kick whenever he had a chance. Yes, ironically, his greatest service may in the end lie in the example of his fall. For years he showed a sharper appreciation than anyone else of the economic and structural alterations that were necessary in the press, only to put it all at risk by a political reversion to the past. It was a sad, sideways ending to a career.

CHAPTER EIGHT

Little Guy Grows Big

Cecil Harmsworth King's fall provides in some ways the most appropriate comment on the rise of Roy Thomson, now Lord Thomson of Fleet, who owns a greater number not only of British but also of American and Canadian newspapers than any other man. Like King, Thomson is an expansionist, an unremitting empire builder. But whereas King became increasingly editorially involved in his papers Thomson has remained entirely commercially orientated. Unlike King, Thomson owns his newspapers in the good old-fashioned way—although in the old-fashioned way brought up to date by one of those pyramidical holding company structures that enable a little money (comparatively speaking) to go a long way. No one is in a position to get rid of Thomson as King was got rid of. He and his family own seventy-eight per cent of the ordinary share capital of his British company, the Thomson Organisation, through two holding companies. Thomson Newspapers of Toronto, which controls his North American interests, is similarly in the hands of family trusts.

Chubby, square, rather badly dressed with a natural joviality that masks but scarcely bothers to conceal his basic ruthlessness, a sort of capitalist Khrushchev, Thomson ('Call me Roy') sits at the centre of what is, although not the biggest, certainly the most far-flung publishing empire in history.

He is now 73, an agressive, self-assured tycoon with an unrelenting itch to buy and buy. Yet until he was forty he had never had his hands on anything larger than a run-down agency for automobile spares in North Bay, Ontario, a township with a present population of around 21,000 which was a good deal smaller when he was there. The story of how he was offered an agency for selling radio sets, found that most of his potential farmer customers would not buy because there was nothing for them to listen to, bought a broken-down second-hand transmitter on borrowed money and ran a transmitting station of his own sited in the near-by gold mining town of Timmins and was so successful in getting advertisements for his radio programmes that he bankrupted the local weekly newspaper and bought it for 6,000 dollars, 200 dollars down and 200 dollars a month, had often been told—not least by Roy Thomson himself.

He had found his metier. By the time he was fifty he owned four small dailies in Ontario. By the time he was touching sixty he had twenty-eight dailies and weeklies in Ontario, Quebec, Saskatchewan, Prince Edward Island and British Columbia, and was ceaselessly on the search for new ones. He operated, he once told me, 'on the basis of the fellow who asked every girl he met to go to bed with him; he got a helluva lot of smacks in the face, but he also got a helluva lot of girls'. He made one or two attempts to get into big city journalism but failed. Montreal and Toronto ladies do not go to bed with hicks from the sticks. The great conservative newspaper families of Canada like the Seftons and the Southams to whom newspaper ownership is a prestige occupation for gentlemen thought of him as an uncouth money grabber with an attitude to newspapers derogatory to all the best principles.

But he went on his way regardless, constantly jotting down profit and loss figures on the back of old envelopes, always on the spot when a family business seemed likely to have to come on the market, as quick to smell death as a mortician and as indefatigable in pursuit as a Canadian Mountie. He had early struck up a friendly relationship with several banks ('It's their business to lend money, ain't it? Its my business to borrow it') and was as proud of his credit standing as a Nobel prize winner of the acclaim of his equals. For the most part his newspapers were small and undistinguished. 'Public utilities,' he called them. They were geared to consumer advertising and much disliked by journalists for their low salaries: good papers to get away from. 'Thomson?' said his fellow Canadian, Beaverbrook, when asked about him. 'He's a little guy. Owns a lot of little newspapers.' When I met him at that time I am regretful to say he made no impression on me at all, so little indeed, did I remember our meeting that it had slipped my mind completely until I found it recorded in his biography. He remained a little guy with a lot of little newspapers until mid 1952 when his wife died of cancer, and tired of Canada, he packed his bags and made for Scotland because, he said, 'I'm told it's the toughest place in the world to make money in and I want to see if I'm as good as I think I am.'

Now sixteen years later he owns *The Times*, the *Sunday Times*, the *Scotsman*, nearly forty other daily and weekly newspapers in the United Kingdom, including three new evening papers started by him with computerised setting and webb offset printing in what are probably the most up-to-date printing plants in the world, more than sixty magazines and technical journals in the U.K., including the *Illustrated London News* group, six book publishing companies, including Thomas Nelson, Hamish Hamilton, Michael Joseph and Heron Books, seven exhibition companies, seven educational companies, four travel companies specialising in package tours, an airline with a fleet of Boeing 737's, a miscellaneous collection of other concerns and Scottish Television. In Canada his interests have grown over the same period to forty daily and weekly newspapers and he has moved across the border to the United States where he has built up a chain of thirty-six daily and eleven weekly newspapers. In Australia he owns some twenty-five magazines and trade papers, over twenty magazines in New Zealand, twenty-six magazines in South Africa, seven in Rhodesia; and daily newspapers in Malawi, Thailand and the West Indies. He has three television stations and five radio stations in Canada and one of each in Trinidad. In addition he operates, mainly for governments, fourteen other radio and televison services scattered from Malta to West Australia. There has surely never been a record like it. So obsessive moreover is the Thomson urge to get bigger that any such list as this is likely to fall short of the total before the ink is dry on the paper.

From the ownership of a chain of undistinguished small town newspapers in Canada to dominance of a world-wide communications empire, most of it built up during one's sixties and seventies, and with a seat in the House of Lord for good measure, is a substantial transformation by any standards. Thomson is one of the most remarkable late developers in commercial history. One asks oneself what he was wasting his time at all those years in Canada.

It is as though a man like Churchill had been content to be a small town alderman until he was sixty.

However Thomson's real impact on British newspapers does not flow only from his indiscriminating acquisitiveness. Nor does it even depend on his ability, remarkable though it is, to move so late in life from a small town league where deals were in thousands to a world league where they are in millions: as he once remarked to me, 'It's all money. What difference do a few noughts make?' What has made him a powerful and perhaps a seminal influence on British journalism is something other than this: the attitude he has developed towards newspaper ownership.

He came to Edinburgh in pursuit of a rumour. He had heard a whisper at a Commonwealth Press Conference that its great morning newspaper, the *Scotsman*, was in financial trouble and the family owners might be glad to sell. When he arrived he took a walk through the city, looked at the *Scotsman* on its island site in the middle of Edinburgh, got a copy of its last balance sheet, did some calculations on the back of an envelope, reckoned that the real estate value of the property was at least £1,000,000 and made a starting bid of £600,000 for the seventy-five per cent family owned majority share holding in the *Scotsman*, the *Evening Dispatch*, the *Weekly Scotsman*, and all the company's properties. When he warned the Royal Bank of Canada that he had a new deal on his hands and would need a loan, the Bank President, a Scotsman, exploded, 'He must be mad. No one's going to sell him the *Scotsman*. It's an institution.' But sell they did. He had to go up a little on his first offer but not too much. Then he bought out the rest of the shareholders. For the first time in his life he owned a prestige paper where the editor mattered as much, or more, than the business manager and where editorial copy was not, as he has said of his Canadian papers, 'just something to put around the ads'.

Of Scottish ancestry—one of the first things he did when he arrived in Edinburgh, much to the malicious amusement of the stiff Edinburgh society which liked the thought of him even less than Toronto society had, was to have a tartan of his own designed —he was immensely proud of being owner of the *Scotsman*. He would, he said, be ready to run it at a loss if need be—a remark that caused his eldest daughter to say he must have blown his top. However, to lose money was not an ambition that came natural to him: his simple standard is that if something makes a profit it is good, if it does not, it is not. He bent his mind, therefore, to the problem of marrying prestige and profitability—something that had scarcely been known in Britain since the end of *The Times*'s near monopoly in the mid-nineteenth century since when it had become almost habitual for influential newspapers to run at a loss. Or to need support from a better selling partner.

Most of Edinburgh society had made up its mind that this brash upstart Canadian would cheapen the *Scotsman* beyond repair. In fact, although he drastically overhauled its creaking business organisation he greatly improved the quality of the paper both in content and appearance under a new editor of his own choosing. He made it profitable not by popularising it, but by turning it into a much better serious paper than it had been before.

He was not so successful with the *Evening Dispatch* which he did try to popularise and in the wrong manner. Indeed, in his British career he has consistently proved less successful with popular newspapers than with quality ones. The formula for utility newspapers brought with him from Canada proved capable of repetition in an improved form in many of the British regional papers he later acquired and with the new ones he started. It was capable of being amended and improved almost out of all recognition to embrace the conception of genuine quality national newspapers. It was not capable it would seem of being adapted to meet the needs of popular newspapers where a quite different flair is required.

The *Scotsman* never made him much of a profit. But it put him in the way of a fortune. Because of it he was in a position when commercial television came along to make a bid for the Scottish franchise. He thought that as owner of the *Scotsman* he would be considered seriously but was doubtful whether the Independent Television Authority would give him, as a Canadian, the franchise on his own. He therefore approached almost everyone of any substance in Scottish business and social life with an invitation to join a Scottish consortium. Almost without exception they turned him down. Their canny Scots business sense told them that television was a bit of Sassenach nonsense. If he wanted to lose his money that was all right with them. They had no intention of letting him lose theirs. He tried again. With the undiplomatic honesty that often distinguishes him in money matters he explained that it was their names not their money he wanted and promised to give them their money back plus interest at the end of a year if they wanted to withdraw. They still refused. As a result he had to tender virtually on his own. On his own he got the franchise and with it, as he tactlessly remarked later, 'a licence to print money'.

Within two years Scottish Television made so much money that he was in a position to think of expansion on a scale he had scarcely dreamed of before. Thomson is by nature a dealer and entrepreneur. He has an almost pathological greed for new possessions. His mind is a cash register in perpetual motion. Now he turned his eyes in the direction of the *Glasgow Herald*— Scotland's other great national newspaper. He made an approach to Outrams, its owners, and was contemptuously snubbed by their Chairman, Sir John Muirhead. He therefore began unostentatiously buying Outrams shares on the open market—so unostentatiously in fact that when I heard a whisper of it and published a warning that if it were not careful Scotland might wake up one morning to find the whole of its quality press in the hands of one man even Cecil King, who rarely missed a trick in the newspaper world at that time, wrote to me to say he was sure I was wrong, only to send a second letter a few days later saying his first had been 'somewhat precipitate' and that he had since ascertained that Thomson was, in fact, buying Outram shares although why he could not think, since he was already losing money on the *Scotsman*.

It was Thomson's plan to buy as many Outram shares as he could in the open market and then make a bid for the rest so good that Outram's shareholders would feel unable to refuse it. However, he misjudged the strength of Scottish national feeling. Warned in time, a rival group headed by Sir Hugh Fraser's Scottish and Universal Investments made a rival offer. It was below Thomson's, but was accepted by shareholders in order to keep the *Glasgow Herald* Scottish and independent.

'You spoilt it. You tipped them off too soon,' Thomson said when we next met and for a time made a habit of introducing me as 'My worst enemy'. But he bore no malice. And in the end his defeat turned to his advantage for he found himself needing all his resources for something much bigger which would have been beyond him if he had been engaged on absorbing the *Glasgow Herald*.

Beaverbrook had introduced him to Lord Kemsley and in his usual brash way Thomson had followed up the introduction by asking this rather pompous peer if he had any newspapers to sell—his Aberdeen one for a start. He was heavily snubbed. But when in July 1958 Kemsley suddenly decided to retire from the business altogether it was to Thomson he telephoned. Thomson caught a night train to London with his Managing Director James Coltart, only to find that Kemsley was asking a price far beyond his resources—£6 a share for his own forty per cent holding in Kemsley Newspapers and the same for all other shareholders ready to sell: a total of perhaps as much as £15,000,000.

Under pressure Kemsley agreed to drop his price to £5 a share. Even so this still meant that a total of £12,500,000 might have to be found—£5,000,000 of it in cash for Kemsley himself. Even with his licence to print money it was more than Thomson could manage. However, with Henry Grunfeld of S. G. Warburg, the merchant bankers, whom he called in as his financial advisor, a 'reverse bid' technique, the first of its kind, was evolved. Since Thomson had not the cash to buy Kemsley Newspapers, then, said Grunfeld, let Kemsley Newspapers buy Scottish Television and pay for it with a block of new Kemsley shares sufficient to give Thomson practical control of both the Kemsley and Scottish Television interests once he had Lord Kemsley's personal shares in his hands. With these resources behind him he should have no difficulty in raising sufficient money to pay Lord Kemsley his £5,000,000 in cash while the dividend prospects he could hold out would be sufficiently high to persuade most of the rest of the Kemsley shareholders to hang on.

A subsequent refinement of procedure provided Thomson with the means to an absolute majority of votes instead of only forty per cent. Grunfeld proposed that the capital of the new company should be divided into 2,500,000 preferred ordinary shares with a guaranteed dividend of 30 per cent which should be offered to Kemsley shareholders and would be sufficiently attractive to make most of them hold on. Lord Kemsley would get a million of them. Thomson himself, it was proposed, should get for Scottish Television 2,000,000 second preferred ordinary shares with a guaranteed dividend of only fifteen per cent, but with the same voting rights as the preferred ordinary and a higher share of subsequent profits. Thomson would then only have to buy Lord Kemsley's 1,000,000 preferred ordinary shares for the £5,000,000 in cash that Kemsley felt he needed for comfortable retirement to have in his control 3,000,000 of the 4,500,000 voting shares in the new group —an absolute majority.

This being agreed, Thomson's only problem was to find the £5,000,000. He persuaded Kemsley to take £1,000,000 of it in promissory notes, leaving £4,000,000 in hard cash to be found. Of this he only had £1,000,000 available but it was an article of his business faith that banks would always lend money and he asked The National Commercial Bank of Scotland for £3,000,000. They had lent him money to finance his Scottish Television bid and had done well out of it, and agreed without demur. He was home and dry—chief owner of the *Sunday Times,* two other national Sunday papers (the *Sunday Chronicle* and *Empire News*), two provincial Sunday newspapers, a chain of thirteen provincial dailies and several provincial weeklies. Helped by esoteric finance and a strong nerve the little Canadian guy with a lot of little newspapers had reached the big league.

The Kemsley transaction gave notice to those who had not already noticed it that a major new figure had arrived on the British press scene. Thomson was at this time sixty-five. Age has since then in no way withered his infinite capacity to seize fortune by the forelock. He has continued to expand, winding his way to new triumphs with unshaken financial serenity. His fellow Canadian Beaverbrook hated banks and could not rest until his newspapers were loan free. The basis of Thomson's success has always been his standing with his bankers and their confidence in his ability to pay out of future profits whatever millions he may need to borrow to clinch a deal. As a newspaper entrepreneur Thomson is one of the most remarkable phenomena of our times. He makes being a millionaire look easy. But it is neither the size and number of his deals, nor the money he has made that give him a place in newspaper history, but what seems at first sight his oddly uncharacteristic approach to serious journalism.

Thomson is a Janus-like figure in the press. Most of his Canadian newspapers are still run on a shoestring. They are utility operations, without pride of vocation: chain store journalism. The newspapers he owns in the United States, most of them in towns of up to 100,000 population (he has kept out of the big cities where he might run into political opposition as a non-American owner, as he did, he claims, when he wanted to make a bid for *Newsweek*), are efficient but undistinguished, neutral in personality and chameleon in character, concerned only to fit the prevailing mode in their circulation areas; segregationalist in the South, anti-segregationalist in the North. The chain of regional papers he acquired in his Kemsley deal have been run in much the same commercial spirit so far as he is concerned, although his editorial advisors have sometimes done their best to make it otherwise: given a good deal of local autonomy if they are doing well, closed down if they are not, like the *Manchester Evening Chronicle*.

He would appear to have no particular pride in these papers except in so far as they serve his commercial interests and to have no journalistic feeling for them. Thus he sold the *Sheffield Daily Telegraph* at the very moment when it had done a great service to its community and won great national acclaim by a courageous exposure of corruption in the Sheffield police force. So far as he was concerned what mattered much more was that it was a useful pawn in a deal with another newspaper chain, United Newspapers, which was willing to take it over in exchange for the *Edinburgh Evening News* which Thomson wanted to merge with his own *Edinburgh Evening Dispatch*. When I publicly criticised him for this and said that to have their paper sold over their heads was a shabby recompense for a fine editor and his staff, he was very hurt. 'You were rough with me Francis,' he said. 'I know the timing looked bad but you couldn't expect me to pass up a business deal could you?'

The new evening papers he has started in Reading, Watford and Luton, the first of a series which will eventually ring the metropolis, have been custom built for readers as consumers, not citizens. Their launching was motivated by the belief that the Home Counties are moving into an era of spiralling advertising on the American model by stores that will need local evening papers to help them sell their goods. Reading was chosen to initiate the experiment because detailed field surveys showed that retail sales in the town were well above the national average: £284 per annum per person compared with a national figure of £174 and £883 per annum per household compared with a national figure of £547, while the average annual sales of retail stores were £27,756 compared with a national average for similar outlets of £15,449. In earlier days local newspapers were born in response to local demands for information and for a place where strongly held views could find expression. Under the Thomson formula they are instruments of consumer marketing.

All this fits in well with his Canadian record. What does not fit in with it is that this man of powerful acquisitive instincts but small intellectual pretensions and even smaller journalistic ones should also have become the owner of some of the greatest newspapers of opinion in the world and in each case markedly increased their quality and influence.

By the time he bought Kemsley newspapers he had already shown what he was capable of in this way in his handling of the *Scotsman*. It could be argued however that this was no more than an example of a shrewd businessman walking carefully in a territory he did not know. But he did the same with the *Sunday Times*. It was a successful serious newspaper when he got it. He made it a much better one. But, as with the *Scotsman*, he had to find an editor of his own choosing first.

When he took over the *Sunday Times* he inherited as its editor a man of considerable ability but somewhat academic character, H. V. Hodson, a Balliol man and Fellow of All Souls. Hodson had got on well with the autocratic Kemsley who liked to be considered his own Editor-in-Chief. Kemsley was a good deal of a social and intellectual snob—once when seeking to persuade me to write for him, an invitation he subsequently regretted, he regaled me for two hours with the story of his social triumphs among the people who came to his bridge parties or accepted invitations to stay on his yacht. No doubt he was flattered to have such a man as Hodson in his employ, just as he was to have on his payroll the well-connected, worldly Ian Fleming—not yet the creator of James Bond.

Hodson and Thomson were less compatible. Sensibly realising this, Hodson agreed to end his Kemsley contract with a suitable handshake and departed to become Warden of Ditchley, an institution for promoting Anglo-American relations in a gentlemanly country setting. This was satisfactory. What was even more so was that there was already on the board of Kemsley Newspapers a journalist with exactly the combination of talents that were needed to jerk the *Sunday Times* out of its plush lined rut. This was Denis Hamilton, then thirty-nine. Hamilton had joined one of Kemsley's papers, the *Middlesbrough Evening Gazette*, as a young reporter straight from Middlesbrough High School, and had moved after a year to another Kemsley paper, the *Evening Chronicle*, Newcastle. War was obviously coming, he joined the territorials and was immediately called up when it did come. He rose to Lieut.-Colonel in command of a battalion of the Durham Light Infantry, was decorated and served brilliantly on Montgomery's staff. At the end of the war he returned to the *Newcastle Evening Chronicle* from which Kemsley, flattered by the dashing military career of this young reporter of his, summoned him to London to be his chief editorial assistant, making him Editorial Director with a seat on the board three years later. Despite his rapid advancement, Hamilton, a man of decisive mind, had sometimes found the autocratic Kemsley mode irksome. The new regime and Thomson's readiness to decentralise authority were more agreeable. Thomson for his part recognised in Hamilton a combination of editorial and managerial talent of the sort he most needed.

When Hodson departed for Ditchley Thomson proposed therefore that Hamilton, who had already done the *Sunday Times* much service by securing it the serial rights of the memoirs of his old Chief, Montgomery, should become its Editor as well as being Editorial Director of the rest of the group. Hamilton agreed on condition that he was given a degree of editorial independence such as Kemsley had never been prepared to allow his editors. To Thomson this made sense. So long as an editor possessed, as Hamilton did, an understanding of the paper's economic and business needs as well as its editorial purposes, he was quite prepared for independence.

It proved a highly successful appointment for the *Sunday Times* which under Hamilton flourished greatly in circulation and prestige. But what was in some ways even more important was that it further extended Thomson's education in the qualities required for his new responsibilities in serious quality journalism. Hamilton taught Thomson—and Thomson for his part proved very ready to learn—that his former Canadian habit of hiring journalists on the cheap and treating them as second class citizens of small importance compared with business and advertising managers, would not work in this new context. He showed him that journalistic talent was at least as important as business skill in a newspaper's success and that you would not get it on the scale and of the character required for newspapers of national influence unless you were ready to give those who possessed it both independence and high salaries. For his part Hamilton learned from Thomson the importance of harnessing editorial quality to efficient business administration, and the need for a successful modern editor to be versed in every aspect of a newspaper's operation. He learned, also, to admire a chief proprietor who having made a decision was prepared to see it through with unruffled calm, as when over £900,000 was sunk in the *Sunday Times* colour supplement which lost heavily for eighteen months before it began to pay its way and was at first derided as a flop by most of Fleet Street's opinion formers, including Lord Beaverbrook: I was, I think, the only newspaper commentator who saw any merit in it when it first appeared.

Thomson and Hamilton have been very good for each other. In its own way their partnership has been no less fruitful than King's and Cudlipp's was in the very different field of mass journalism and with none of the strains latterly arising from King's temperament. In Thomson's Canadian days the independence he boasted of giving to his editors was no more than a matter of convenience: it was simple commonsense to leave a community paper to an editor who knew the community and lived with it—but who also knew that he was regarded as one step behind the business manager in the newspaper's hierarchy, and that if he got out of step and lost circulation he would lose his job. Under the pressure of his *Sunday Times* responsibilities and Denis Hamilton's influence, what had been a convenience became a principle and one which not only gave the editor a higher status but recognised that independence sometimes means annoying people. Thomson's own supreme aptitude is for business. Unlike King he has the self-discipline to stick to it and leave editorial policy to those of editorial aptitude and training.

His success with the *Sunday Times* and his reputation for not seeking to turn his newspapers into instruments of his own policy made him the natural rescuer of *The Times* in 1966. *The Times*'s need for such a rescuer was possibly due more to loss of nerve on the part of its management than to serious economic distress. With total assets of £5,700,000 against an issued share capital of £1,055,000 and liquid assets of £590,000 it could almost certainly have raised what finance it needed for development if it had seriously tried to do so. Its circulation was buoyant. Sales had risen by seventeen per cent in the six months between May 1966, when news had for the first time been put on the front page, and October when the chief proprietor, Mr Gavin Astor, decided to sell. It is true that its profits had fallen from £591,000 in 1960 to £203,000 in 1965 due to a period of stagnation in circulation directly attributable to the refusal to put into effect earlier the changes eventually carried out in May 1966, and that by 1966 it faced for the first time an actual loss estimated at between £250,000 and £300,000. But the bulk of this loss could be accounted for by the cost of changes whose long term benefits were not in doubt.

Editorially *The Times* had pulled itself out of the mire into which it had fallen under Geoffrey Dawson who conducted himself more as Secretary General of the Establishment, a journalistic Horace Wilson, than as Editor of a great independent journal of opinion. Sir William Haley, who had left the Director-Generalship of the B.B.C. to go to Printing House Square, had given it a stronger bite and a ring at times of an almost messianic Gladstonian liberalism. He had also made it a more tidy paper with better ordered news display and improved appearance. However, perhaps because he had started out on it long ago in his youth well below the salt as a shorthand telephonist and to return as Editor was a triumph almost too sweet for bearing, he was almost excessively in awe of its traditions. He saw himself as in some measure guardian of the holy grail of British journalism and could not bear to alter the paper as much as it needed—even if the Astors would have let him. He was terrified that in seeking readers it might be popularised into another *Daily Telegraph*—a paper which he rigidly refused to accept as of the true quality. But his anxieties on this score were nothing to the Astors' fear of changes of any sort. They treated the paper as though it were an ancient great house in which they had been allowed to live by the National Trust on condition they did not alter it.

However changes were at last made several years too late and £140,000 was spent on promotion following the belated change in format. The rapid increase in circulation that followed the editorial changes naturally brought with it larger newsprint and other costs which were not at once compensated for—as they scarcely could have been in the time—by higher advertising revenue. This seems to have seriously disturbed the paper's management although the fact that there would inevitably be a time lag between a rise in circulation and an increase in advertising must have been obvious when the changes made in May were decided on. What was in truth much more significant was that the switch to news on the front page had evoked a much larger and more rapid response than anyone had expected, especially from young readers, thus disclosing a potential demand for the paper that was full of hope for its future.

For all these reasons it could not help but seem to those aware of the facts an odd time to decide that *The Times* could no longer live alone. Moreover, although it is sometimes argued that in present circumstances it is no longer practicable for a quality newspaper to be published on its own without some other major source of finance to support it, the success of the *Daily Telegraph* shows the contrary. So also, in a different national situation, does that of the *New York Times*. In truth, *The Times* was in no sense in a serious decline. Its financial position was still healthy, its prospects good. Its troubles rose from a quite other cause, the fact that its owners lacked either the professional skill to take advantage of its opportunities or the nerve to try. It was because Thomson had both that they turned to him. *The Times* suffered, in fact, from the same disease that in 1960 had killed the *News Chronicle*, despite its devoted readership and its circulation of over 1,150,000 —the disease of amateurism.

The *News Chronicle* had other problems to contend with of course. It suffered from being the weakest member of that declining middle group to which I have already referred. But most professional observers would agree, in part at any rate, with the judgment of the Royal Commission on the Press of 1961–1962: 'We cannot escape the conclusion that the failure of the

Little Guy Grows Big

News Chronicle was not entirely the result of an inevitable law of newspaper economics; different and more consistent managerial and editorial policy might have saved this newspaper.'

Ironically enough in view of its own future problems *The Times* summed this up in a leading article with the crisp phrase: 'To put it plainly, the *News Chronicle* died because it was inefficient.' Six years later it faced an end to its own independence for the same reason.

Other British newspapers have of course been inefficient for years. Both the Royal Commission of 1961–1962 and the report of the Economist Intelligence Unit commissioned by the national newspapers themselves in 1966 found that, protected by their nature against foreign competition and subject to restrictive practices which it had been easier to accept than fight during a period of rising demand, all were inefficient, although some were more so than others. The moral to be drawn from the experience of both *The Times* and the *News Chronicle* was however even more fundamental. It was that newspaper publishing was no longer a suitable part-time occupation for gentlemen, but had become a full-time trade for professionals.

Colonel J. J. Astor was a happy alternative to the first Lord Rothermere when Northcliffe died. He provided *The Times* with an assurance of independence and a promise of civilised appreciation of its traditions. But neither he nor his son, Gavin, were, or were interested in becoming, full-time newspaper men in the same way as Gavin's cousin, David Astor, was as Editor of the *Observer*. Similarly, in easier days the Cadbury family gave the *News Chronicle* valuable support by their liberal and Quaker principles: what they could not give it was the expertise required as the trade became more competitive. Recognising this they put it for a time in the hands of Lord Layton. But he was more of an economist than a newspaperman, and was in any event absent on Government service for most of the war. Nor was Laurence Cadbury, who subsequently took over from Layton, in any position to give the paper what it needed. He was head of the family chocolate concern and could, as he wrote to me subsequently, only give the family's newspapers, the *News Chronicle* and the *Star*, a part of his attention—although he did add, with what was a perhaps characteristic indication of the Cadbury sense of what newspaper

The Right to Know

publishing involved, 'I did, however, see the *News Chronicle* leaders personally or had them read over to me every night.' It would perhaps have been better if he had left the leaders to the editor and had a nightly session with the general manager. Not that even this would have been much use. Newspapers cannot be run by men with their minds on other things. They are allergic to absentee owners. The *News Chronicle* had a devoted readership and a wonderful staff, most of whom refused to leave it even when they knew it was going down. It also had too rapid a succession of editors, including at least a couple of brilliant ones, and no real managerial coherence. Possibly its fortunes would have been different but for a motor cycling accident in France in 1950. It had been intended that Laurence Cadbury's eldest son, Julian, should take over the family chocolate interests and his brother, Adrian, look after the newspapers. But Julian was killed and Adrian had to turn to chocolate. Lacking a strong and wholly committed hand at the helm the *News Chronicle* drifted on to the rocks despite Laurence Cadbury's best intentions and genuine concern. It took with it the *Star*, for which Cadbury had mistakenly, as he ruefully agreed in a letter to me, turned down a good offer from the *Mirror* group some seven years before.

Of the Astors and *The Times* it can at least be said that they were wiser than the Cadburys were with the *News Chronicle*. Lacking managerial expertise and unwilling to take the risk of spending money on trying to find it, they at least gave up gracefully in time. To Thomson the invitation to buy *The Times* was an accolade far exceeding even the peerage he had been chasing for years. Its real importance however lies in the fact that it marked the culmination of a significant trend in journalism of which Thomson had become the most potent, if somewhat unexpected, instrument—the development of an appropriate balance between the professional and business elements in the press.

The press has become a great industry commanding, and needing to command, vast resources of capital. In Britain at any rate much of it seems likely to become concentrated in large multi-publication units with widely dispersed interests on the model of the International Publishing Corporation and the Thomson Organisation, although the *Daily Telegraph* and Beaverbrook Newspapers still stand against the tide, as also still do, although they are economically more vulnerable in their independence, the *Guardian* and the *Observer*. A similar trend to the managerial corporation is also, as we shall see, at work in the United States although the *New York Times* in the hands of the remarkable Ochs-Sulzberger dynasty stands unchallenged, and it would seem unchallengeable, by all movements towards newspaper industrialisation.

Where the press does become a great industry, the owners of enterprises involving large capital resources cannot be expected to hand over their commercial future to men whose professional training and aptitude require, as a journalist's should, non-involvement in commercial interests and concentration instead on the public interest. Editorial independence as it existed in the opinion press of an earlier period is no longer possible. Yet if the professional element in the press becomes wholly subordinated to the interests of the press as big business, newspapers cannot adequately carry out their public service functions. Nor is a situation such as existed in the first half of this century when newspapers were the personal vehicles of rich, autocratic publishers any longer acceptable in the more educated societies of today —as King's dismissal by his more modern-minded fellow directors demonstrated and as the much less positive political role played by Beaverbrook's and Rothermere's successors also shows.

Thomson's achievement has been to reconcile, at first perhaps by accident but latterly by design, the business and professional elements in the press. His practice at any rate in Britain with his major papers has been better than his philosophy. While constantly boasting, perhaps perfectly truthfully in respect of his smaller newspapers, that he is in the business only for the money, he has learned, with help from Hamilton and others, to recognise the importance of editorial quality in his principal newspapers and has made them efficient business units not by subordinating the professional element in them to the commercial one but by providing a framework of order and profitability in which editorial responsibilities can be carried out successfully.

This he had already done with the *Scotsman* and *Sunday Times* and to some extent, despite his cavalier treatment of the *Sheffield Daily Telegraph*, with the best of his regional papers like the *Western Mail* before the opportunity to acquire *The Times* came.

It was his reputation in this respect that made the Astors turn to him. They were very conscious—perhaps too conscious for its health—of *The Times* as a national institution. They wanted to make sure that it would be treated as such by whoever they passed it on to. Particularly they were anxious that the tradition of editorial independence started under the Walter family and restored by them after the Northcliffe interregnum should be maintained. This Thomson was very ready to promise.

He had, however, to convince an even more critical body before the business could go through.

As it happened the *Times*-Thomson deal was the first to come before the Monopolies Commission under a new section of the Monopolies and Mergers Act which required that newspaper mergers above a certain size should be investigated by the Commission to see whether they were or were not likely to operate against the public interest if they were approved by the President of the Board of Trade. This followed a recommendation by the 1961–62 Royal Commission on the Press which had been appointed, as already mentioned, as a result of the public anxiety following the closure of the *News Chronicle* and the take-over of Odhams and the *Daily Herald* by the Mirror group. In its report, the Commission pointed out that in 1949 a previous Royal Commission had declared itself seriously concerned that 'any further decrease in the number of national newspapers would be a matter for anxiety and a decrease in the provincial morning newspapers would be a serious loss'. Yet, since then no fewer than seventeen daily and Sunday newspapers had ceased publication in London and the provinces and the ownership of those which remained had become concentrated in fewer hands. For this reason the second Royal Commission urged that there should be legislation to check, or at least control, further concentration even though this should involve treating the newspaper industry differently from industry in general. 'The answer to that,' it said, 'is that the public interest in relation to the newspaper industry is different. The discrimination is based on the proposition that freedom and variety in the expression of opinion and presentation of news is an element which does not enter into the conduct of other competitive industries and that it is a paramount public interest.'

This new legislation had been denounced by Thomson as the

first example in British history of 'Government interference with the operations of the press' (he has never been very strong on history—or on distinguishing between editorial and commercial freedom) and as 'a danger to freedom of thought and expression'. But it received the support of all parties in both Houses of Parliament and Thomson found himself being judged according to it.

It had been anticipated that the new regulations would operate first in the field of the provincial press where a brisk take-over business was being done. Just before the Monopolies and Mergers Act became law Thomson himself had added another sixteen to the number of his small town newspapers by buying up six existing companies. Sir William Carr of the *News of the World* had added another nine to his provincial group. The Cowdray family, owners of the *Financial Times* and the Westminster Press, had added five to theirs bringing their score up to fifty. And a group headed by Mr H. C. Drayton, controller of some twenty investment trusts and many other enterprises from tea plantations to transport, had bought another eight. However, as it turned out it was none of the provincial newspaper take-overs that came first into the net but the prestigious *Times*.

For the purposes of the investigation the Monopolies Commission under the Chairmanship of A. W. Roskill, Q.C. (now Sir Ashton Roskill), a most able and pertinacious lawyer, was given three additional members, Lord Annan, Provost of University College, London, Donald Tyerman, former Editor of the *Economist*, and myself. It sat for three months and interviewed a great many people. Lord Thomson and his associates were before it for many hours, an experience which Thomson on the whole accepted with exemplary patience, while not hiding his feelings that the whole procedure was an interference with the divine right of businessmen to do as they liked.

The Commission was from the first in little doubt of Thomson's ability to give *The Times* the financial and commercial expertise and the large development resources the Astors felt unable to provide. But it wanted other assurances. The form these assurances took marks a significant step towards a clearer definition of the balance between commercial and professional responsibilities in newspapers—especially those of serious information and opinion. That they were given without quibble by Thomson is an indication not only of his anxiety to have *The Times,* but also of the difference between his philosophy of newspaper ownership and that of the newspaper barons of earlier days—or of Cecil King.

Traditionally editors of *The Times* had been given great independence: the pattern established in the days of Barnes and John Walter II and Delane and John Walter III has been accepted as a necessary part of its texture, although Northcliffe, protagonist of proprietorial absolutism, kicked against it and sought to change it. But it had been independence by favour not by right. Contrary to general belief there was nothing in the *Times*'s constitution that safeguarded the editor's position. Nor did The Times Committee, set up as an evidence of noble intention when J. J. Astor bought the paper from the Northcliffe estate, with its galaxy of eminent members, including the Lord Chief Justice, the Warden of All Souls' College, Oxford, and the Governor of the Bank of England, do so. The Committee had only one function: to be called together when a transfer of controlling ordinary shares was envisaged and to rule whether the transfer would be in keeping with 'the best traditions and political independence' of *The Times* and eliminate 'so far as reasonably possible questions of personal ambition or commercial profit'.

This Committee had never met. It did not meet now, although members were informed individually of what was afoot as a matter of courtesy. For although questions of personal ambition and commercial profit might reasonably have been held to arise in the proposed merger of the *Sunday Times* and *The Times* this merger did not technically involve any transfer of controlling ordinary shares. The Times Committee was a paper tiger without even a roar.

It had never had any control over editorial policy. This was vested solely in the Chief Proprietors, Colonel (later Lord) Astor and a remaining member of the Walter family. They appointed the editor and they had complete liberty to tell him what to say— although in practice they did not often exercise it.

The Commission felt, however, that although ultimately whoever paid the piper would no doubt call the tune, it was important at this stage to strengthen the editor's position. It was concerned, also, that *The Times* and *Sunday Times* should both retain their separate identities and saw some danger on both counts when Thomson disclosed his intention to appoint a Chief Executive who would also be named Editor-in-Chief in charge of both papers. It considered that unless some protection were given the appointment of an editor-in-chief must, both in appearance and fact, diminish the independent status of the individual editors and this the Commission thought it important to avoid. Its anxieties would have been much greater had it not been that Thomson's nominee for this post was Denis Hamilton whose record of independence as editor of the *Sunday Times* was well known to members of the Commission and whose ability and integrity had been much praised by all the professional witnesses examined. Sir William Haley, the then editor of *The Times* who had been active in the negotiations and who it was planned should be Chairman of the new company for a period of three years in order to ease the transition—he actually remained only for a year before leaving to become Editor-in-Chief of the *Encyclopaedia Britannica*, saying that he was satisfied that the traditions of *The Times* were in good hands, and was succeeded by Thomson's son Kenneth—also declared himself happy with the arrangement.

Nevertheless, the Commission felt it important from the standpoint of the public interest to define as closely as possible the proper balance of authority between management and editor. Although advised that it was intended to appoint four so-called public figures to the board—two nominated by Mr Gavin Astor, two by the Thomson Organisation—out of a total of twelve directors it felt that this was no more than window dressing and would not in itself do anything to safeguard the editor's position or for that matter the paper's.

It therefore asked Thomson to define his attitude towards editorial independence. He replied with an interesting description of his relationship with Denis Hamilton as editor of the *Sunday Times*. 'We frequently,' he said, 'talk together, I have views on various questions and I make sure that he knows them but I never see them appear in the paper unless he agrees with them. We discuss things and he knows that on certain matters I am very concerned in my mind that this is the thing and so on, but he is the Editor and nothing of my views goes in the paper unless they are also his views. No newspaper today, and I think we must recognise this, can operate with an Editor in isolation. A newspaper is a very big business proposition. Someone has to decide "How much money can we afford to spend?" on an editorial department or any other department of the business. ... These are matters which have to be defined on a high level basis.' Regarding Denis Hamilton's appointment as Chief Executive and Editor-in-Chief of Times Newspapers Ltd, Thomson said that he was satisfied that Hamilton would have been the best Editor for *The Times*, but that it was too big a job for one man to be editor of both papers: 'There must be an Editor of *The Times* and there must be an Editor of the *Sunday Times* and I think they must both make their own decisions.' He conceived, however, that these separate editors would on occasion seek advice from Hamilton as Hamilton did on occasion from Thomson himself, although 'he does not observe it unless he sees fit to carry it out'.

As a result of these and other discussions with both Lord Thomson and Denis Hamilton the Commission secured assurances of some general importance in establishing the balance of managerial and professional interests that should properly operate in the running of great newspapers of opinion which are also great business enterprises.

In its conclusions it reported, 'We accept the argument of Lord Thomson and his associates that co-ordination of the editorial resources available to both newspapers would be necessary if they were to be used economically and that such co-ordination could be to the advantage of both *The Times* and the *Sunday Times*. We agree also that it would be desirable, if not essential, that one man should be charged with the responsibility for planning in this field and should have the executive authority to allocate resources between the two newspapers and to develop such common services as are necessary.'

It expressed, however, its concern 'that the centralisation of administrative power in this respect should not affect the identities of *The Times* and the *Sunday Times* as separate newspapers or diminish the independence of the separate Editors in the expression of opinion on matters of public policy', and in view of this concern had sought and received specific assurances from both

Little Guy Grows Big

Lord Thomson and Mr Hamilton. These assurances were set out in these words: 'We were assured by Lord Thomson (speaking also on behalf of his son) and by Mr Hamilton, the designated Editor-in-Chief, that they wished to maintain the separate identities of the two newspapers and that it was not intended that the office of Editor-in-Chief should infringe in any way either the independent responsibility of the two Editors for editorial opinion or their direct authority over their editorial staff. In particular Mr Hamilton informed us that although in the natural course of things the Editor of either paper might consult him on particular matters of public policy it would in each instance be for the Editor himself to determine the attitude of the paper and if there should be disagreement between Editor and Editor-in-Chief it was intended that the final decision on all such matters should rest solely with the Editor. Mr Hamilton undertook that this would be made quite clear to each Editor on appointment and that the Editor's independent authority would be made plain to all senior staff members.'

Later these personal assurances were formally confirmed to the President of the Board of Trade by the Thomson Organisation before permission for the merger to go forward was given.

Having got what it wanted, and a further promise that in order to make the position quite clear the board of the new company would be asked to change the title from Editor-in-Chief to Editorial Director if and when Mr Hamilton vacated it (the title the Commission would have preferred from the start if Mr Hamilton's prospective appointment as Editor-in-Chief had not already been announced), the merger was allowed to go forward. For £1,000,000 in cash, another £1,000,000 on a ten year promissory note and additional payments according to future profits which could bring the total up to £3,300,000 Thomson took over at Printing House Square, holding through the Thomson Organisation an eighty-five per cent interest in the new company, Times Newspapers Ltd, which controls both *The Times* and the *Sunday Times*.

By the end of 1970 he will have spent out of *Sunday Times* profits and other resources at least another £5,000,000 on developing *The Times*, and its sales will, it is hoped, have risen to half a million a day with a commensurate increase in advertising revenue.

The Right to Know

The Times's circulation has already gone up considerably since the Thomson Organisation took over and Denis Hamilton moved in as Chief Executive and Editor-in-Chief—a position somewhat analogous to that of executive publisher in American newspaper nomenclature. Its editorial services and foreign news coverage have been improved and a daily business section and weekly arts and entertainments section added (both perhaps designed as much with an eye to advertisers as to readers). It has become both more professional—and also more 'with it' than sometimes seems quite decent to its older readers. Instead of the old anonymity it now flings by-lines about with an almost excessive largesse. It not only reports events but delves into the background of events, deploying news teams with commando precision. There are still gaps in its coverage, but it will fill these as more prosperous times enable it to increase in size.

In all this one can see the touch of Denis Hamilton and his adroit combination of managerial and editorial techniques. But the assurances on the independence and authority of the editor given to the Monopolies Commission have been faithfully kept. It is William Rees-Mogg, as editor, who decides the attitude of *The Times* on all public issues and so far from being blunted, the paper's cutting edge is sharper. Nor has there been any loss of *Sunday Times* identity under its new editor, Harold Evans, formerly a notably crusading editor of the *Northern Echo*. *The Times* and *Sunday Times* speak on many things with notably separate voices and both speak vigorously.

Thomson and Hamilton have altered *The Times*. They have made it a modern-minded paper with a consciousness of the need for economic viability instead of a public institution with its head in the clouds. Some regret the change, and it has, indeed, brought with it some elements of popularisation which the sensitive may find unsympathetic. But although the modern *Times* is not and could not be *The Times* of Barnes and Delane neither is it likely to be again *The Times* of Dawson which under the mask of being a public institution became an instrument of the establishment and the mouthpiece of the most disastrous British Government of modern times. It stands on its journalistic merits. And under its most commercially minded proprietor it possesses them in large measure.

Little Guy Grows Big

They are different from those of the *Guardian*. *The Times* does not have the *Guardian*'s special quality of absolute editorial primacy, of exclusive devotion to editorial purposes and damn the consequences, that makes that fine paper a peculiar delight to its readers even although these qualities depend on its more commercially minded partner, the *Manchester Evening News*, being ready and able to foot the bill if need be. Nevertheless the editorial qualities of *The Times* are great and are getting greater. More than most, Thomson has come to terms with the modern world. He has accepted the fact that however much newspapers may become a part of big business they can only succeed if journalists run them and against all his original instincts has come to acknowledge the supreme importance of the professional element in the press.

CHAPTER NINE

Monopoly in America

A good many years have passed since Henry James Raymond with the help of a small machine gun and Winston Churchill's maternal grandfather persuaded an angry group of *New York Times* readers that they would be unwise to smash up its editorial furniture because the paper supported Lincoln's military draft laws. One can hardly imagine a mob of any sort attacking the *New York Times* today in any circumstances whatever. It would be a kind of blasphemy. The London *Times* nearly died of remaining a public institution too long. The *New York Times* thrives on being one.

Bankruptcy stalks the New York newspaper scene as a plague might. In 1960 there were eight major daily newspapers in the city. A generation ago there were a dozen. By 1968 there were three—one mass circulation morning tabloid, one afternoon tabloid—and the *New York Times*. And the *New York Times* was more prosperous than it had ever been.

More fortunate than the London *Times* the *New York Times* has remained in the hands of the same family for more than seventy years, ever since Adolph Ochs, then publisher of the *Chattanooga Times*, bought it for $75,000 in 1896, twenty-seven years after Raymond's death.

It has escaped the grasp of the great corporations, except in so far as it has itself become one, but unlike too much of the British quality press in the past it has also escaped amateurism. It is not typical of the American press, yet in its way it is a peculiarly American phenomenon. Although it is read by a small number of the influential in most States in the Union and by many more in Washington—the White House alone takes fifty copies daily—

it is a New York daily not a national one. When an attempt was made to turn it into more of a national paper a few years ago by publishing a West Coast edition it failed. Only the *Wall Street Journal* among American newspapers can claim with a string of publishing centres across the country a national readership. Money is the same wherever you live and although the *Wall Street Journal* publishes an excellent general news survey its main commodity is news of money and what makes or loses money. It does not, therefore, need to compete with local newspapers in covering local news (and getting local advertising) as the *Times* would need to do if it sought a national market in earnest.

Possibly the *New York Times* may try for such a market again as methods of facsimile transmission to local publishing centres, such as are already employed in Britain by the *Daily Mirror* for its Belfast edition, further develop. But it is unlikely to do so unless it can afford to be so big that local newspages can be added without in any way reducing its spacious national and international news coverage.

Most journalists live for the day. They leave posterity to the creative writers. Not so those who work for the *New York Times*. Their eyes are on history. 'Our primary responsibility,' observed James Reston, now its Executive Editor, when head of its Washington Bureau, 'is not, perhaps unfortunately, to the commuter reading the paper on his way down from Westchester. Our primary responsibility is to the historian of fifty years from now. Unique among newspapers the *Times* is source material and we must never poison the stream of history.' It is a paper of record without peer in the world. It not only publishes, as Adolph Ochs claimed for it, 'all the news that's fit to print', but frequently prints it several times over in the reports of several different reporters, and always, if an official statement or public document is involved, verbatim.

To provide the newsprint for its date with history 4,500,000 trees are felled each year, most of them from its own forests in Canada and processed in its own papermills. More than 1,600,000 words come into its head office each day, handled by a news and editorial staff of 1,000. It has forty-five full-time and 150 part-time foreign correspondents in every part of the world and thirty in Washington. It also subscribes to fifteen news agencies. On most days the end product is an eighty page newspaper, half of it advertising. On Sundays it may run to several hundred pages and weigh five pounds.

This immense operation is paid for by advertising, which accounts for four-fifths of the total newspaper revenue, by income from subsidiary enterprises, including a radio station, a world news service sold to 175 papers and news agencies in twenty-five countries, and an educational publishing business, and by the ten cents a copy paid for it daily by some 800,000 readers and the thirty to forty cents a copy (it costs more the further you get from New York) paid by 1,250,000 readers on Sundays.

The *New York Times* is big business. But contrary to the trend elsewhere it is big business concentrated solely on the publication of one great newspaper and held firmly by one family. Adolph Ochs ruled for thirty-nine years. When he died he was succeeded as publisher by his son-in-law, Arthur Hays Sulzberger, who ruled for twenty-six, and when Sulzberger retired from active publishing in 1961 he was succeeded by *his* son-in-law, Orvil Dryfoos. When Dryfoos died unexpectedly at the age of fifty in 1963 another Sulzberger took over—Arthur Hays Sulzberger's son, Arthur Ochs Sulzberger, who still reigns. Sixty per cent of the common stock of the company is owned by the Sulzberger family.

Ochs thought of the paper, as Raymond its founder had, as primarily one of information rather than opinion. With the help of a newsman of genius, Carr van Anda, as Managing Editor, he made it the most reliable source of news in the country and perhaps in the world—a good grey paper keeping away from extremes. It remains so. The comprehensiveness of its news coverage is one of the wonders of mankind. Its opinions, carefully insulated from the pressure of events in a separate, near autonomous editorial department—a pattern common to North American and also Australian newspapers but strange by British ideas—are for the most part safe, predictable and dull. Sometimes its consciousness of its position as a public institution gets in the way of its duty as a newspaper. It had advance information of the abortive Bay of Pigs invasion of Cuba in 1961, but its then publisher, Orvil Dryfoos, ruled that to print it would be contrary to the national interest. This later brought from President Kennedy the anguished admission: 'If you had printed more about the operation you would have saved us from a colossal mistake.' However it does not often fail in this way and has been disliked by many Presidents, including Franklin Roosevelt, because of their inability to influence it. It is a sovereign state, a monarchy within a republic, whose hereditary rulers are guardians of a tradition with a pecking order that requires of those who serve it the nicest awareness of protocol; young reporters have been much set back in their careers by innocently taking a seat in the wrong chair at the wrong desk in the wrong place and those who would reach the top in its organisation need not only ability but a sensitive awareness of the right people to be in with at any one time and of how the struggle for power inside the organisation stands at the moment.

The *New York Times* has always been a publisher's paper rather than an editor's paper like the London *Times*. To it the British Monopoly Commission's insistence on the independent authority of the editor would have seemed both irrelevant and dangerous. Indeed, until 1963 when the thirty-seven year old Arthur Ochs Sulzberger, until then no more than an amiable young man about the place known to his friends as Punch because his sister was Judy, became publisher and carried through a palace revolution, it had never even had one editorial figure in sole administrative charge. The managing editor had been at most *primus inter pares*, with the Sunday department and the Washington bureau conducting themselves as independent baronies. As part of his revolution, Arthur Ochs Sulzberger made his long-time friend and mentor Turner Catledge, the sixty-three year old Managing Editor, his Grand Vizier with the title of Executive Editor, the first such in the history of the paper.

Under God, who for *New York Times* purposes is the publisher, Catledge was given dominance over everything—except of course, odd as it may sound to British ears, the editorial page. As his Managing Editor he appointed Clifton Daniels formerly of the London bureau, where he was a much sought-after socialite as well as a brilliant correspondent, who had married Margaret Truman in 1956. Like Catledge whose chief lieutenant he became, Daniels believed in a concentration of power.

The change upset many, including at the time James Reston

who had ruled the Washington office for ten years as well as adding continuous lustre to the paper by his long record of news exclusives and by the lucidity and wisdom of his regular personal column. Lester Markel, the Sunday Editor, who almost single-handed had built the Sunday edition into the mighty power it had become and was the moving spirit behind the formation of the highly valued International Press Institute, was even more put out. Markel, however, was seventy and not in much of a position to fight when he found himself promoted to Associate Editor, an honorific, but purely advisory post, so that Catledge could keep his hand on the Sunday edition under a younger, less prestigious subordinate. Reston was in more of a position to fight and when the first rumour that the *Times* was to have an executive editor fell on shocked ears in Washington, was urged by many to go to New York and advance his own claims to the job.

But although he had been very close to the former publisher, Orvil Dryfoos, he had unlike Catledge failed to recognise Punch Sulzberger as a coming power and was not well placed to challenge his new broom. For a time he thought of joining his close friend, Katherine Graham, on the *Washington Post* which would have been happy to give him a substantial stock holding as well as a larger salary. However, although he could not bring himself to continue running the Washington bureau with Catledge on top of him, neither, when it came to it, could he bring himself to sever his relationship with the *Times*. He opted, therefore, for an Associate Editorship (advisory like Markel's) and patience—meanwhile continuing his widely read and very influential personal column on the editorial page which was outside Catledge's provenance. Patience paid off. It had fairly generally been assumed that Clifton Daniels was being groomed as Catledge's successor. But, in fact, when Catledge did retire at the age of sixty-eight in May, 1968 it was Reston not Daniels who got the job of Executive Editor—plus his own thrice weekly personal column. Distinction plus loyalty had had its reward.

With his immense reputation as a political writer Reston is a much better known public figure than his predecessor, especially in the field of policy making and discussion, and is much closer in stature to the British conception of an Editor than any previous *New York Times* figure. Yet even so, such is the *Times*'s conviction that it is dangerous for views to be on speaking terms with news, although Reston controls all the other editorial departments of the paper and the whole of its immense news service at home and abroad he is allowed no direct influence over what would be one of the principal concerns of a British editor—the paper's opinions. These remain a matter for the editor of the editorial page, John Oakes, a nephew of Adolph Ochs (his father Anglicised his name in the first world war), who has twelve leader writers to help him. Oakes reports only to the publisher, his cousin. Neither Executive nor Managing Editor can say yea or nay to him.

Because of this dichotomy not only do the paper's public opinions have nothing to do with the Executive Editor, but the editorial page is in a position, if it feels like it, to offer a haven to those on whom for some reason or another the displeasure of other departments has fallen—like Herbert Mathews, whom I knew as a member of the London bureau, who appears never to have been forgiven for speaking favourably of Fidel Castro when he was still fighting in the hills and was not as yet, so Mathews who was there with him affirmed and still affirms, a Communist.

Traditionally the *Times* is terrified of anyone suspected of being less 'objective' than its mythology demands. It does not believe in commitment. Nor much, for that matter, in good writing. Although it has many fine reporters it has few good writers: it is Reston's peculiar triumph to have risen to the top as well as writing well. Generally speaking writers are suspect. Like A. J. Liebling, whom the *New York Times* found it necessary to dispense with many years ago, they are thought vulnerable to the temptation to become individualists, carried away by ideas, or even, appalling thought, emotion, instead of being content to be members of the most superb fact reporting machine on earth.

Yet whatever ambivalent feeling some of those who serve it may sometimes find themselves possessed of in the dark hours, the *New York Times* remains a truly remarkable newspaper: a good deed in a naughty press world, dedicated wholly to the proposition that nothing must take precedence over the obligation to tell an informed democracy what it needs to know.

It is satisfactory to note that this dedication has served the *New York Times* so well. It accounts for its present commercial prosperity as compared with the decline and sad death of its one-time close rival, that attractive and often better written newspaper the *New York Herald Tribune*. The *Times* and the *Herald Tribune* had approximately the same circulation when the last war began. Both were faced with a major decision by wartime newsprint restrictions: should they cash in on a sellers' market by piling up advertising revenue from space-hungry clients or should they ration advertising and devote an even higher percentage of their space to news? The *Herald Tribune* opted for higher revenue and opened its pages wide to advertisers. The *Times* in pursuit of its dedication opted for news. It was this decision that put the *Times* in an unassailable position by the time the war ended, giving it a lead over the *Herald Tribune* that paper could never reduce. By prejudicing its soul the *Herald Tribune* also lost the world. The *Times* saved both.

The *Herald Tribune* however had also fallen prey to that disease most fatal to newspapers but from which the *New York Times* has always been immune—amateurism. It had brilliant men and women on its staff, talented foreign correspondents, even more talented columnists, including the greatest of all living political commentators, Walter Lippmann, whose influence has shone on American life like a benevolent sun for more than forty years. It had style and *élan*. Its qualities in some ways resembled those of the London *News Chronicle*. But as with the *News Chronicle* they were not enough. Lacking intelligent—and above all, committed—management, it died.

When the war ended it was still owned by descendants of that Whitelaw Reid who had been one of James Gordon Bennett's war reporters on the *New York Herald* in the Civil War and who had bought the *Tribune* after Greeley's death. Whitelaw Reid's son, Ogden Mills Reid, turned the *Tribune* into the *Herald Tribune* by buying James Gordon Bennett's old paper, the *New York Herald* from the great consolidator, Frank Munsey. In the twenties he made it not only the voice but the conscience, a civilised liberal conscience, of the Republican Party. By the end of the war however he had ceased, or so one could not help but feel when one met him, to give it much beyond general benevolence. He was a pleasant host and boon companion but had retired from intellectual exercise. He left concern for public affairs to his wife, the attractive and formidable Helen Rogers Reid: a lady with many of the qualities of Clare Booth Luce. Tireless in her enjoyment of the political scene, ruthless in her questioning of politicians, Mrs Reid gave the *Herald Tribune* a temporary dash that seemed to hold out the hope that it might recover from its disastrous war-time decision on newsprint. But her husband's death took control out of her hands and deposited it in the less able ones of her sons. The Reid strain had less stamina than that of the Ochs and the Sulzbergers. The new generation was inadequate to the task. Once it had been possible to speak of the *Herald Tribune* as one of America's great newspapers in the same breath, or almost so, as the *Times*. It soon became impossible to do so without a deprecatory stutter. In 1958 the Reids sold out. John Hay Witney took over. He put money, imagination and much ambition into it. But only from a distance. He was busy being American Ambassador in London and newspapers run by absentee owners rarely prosper.

When he bought it it had seemed a useful springboard for political influence when he returned home. By the time he got back the springboard had lost its resilience. A once great and always attractive newspaper had become not much more than an interesting example of how to go into newspapers and lose $5,000,000 a year. Briefly a policy of modernising make-up and concentrating on features rather than news raised circulation. It was a flash in the pan, soon to be fatally doused by a New York newspaper strike of 114 days. There followed a bizarre three-legged partnership with the Hearst-owned *Journal American* and the Scripps-Howard *World Telegram and Sun* under the clumsy portmanteau title of the *New York World Journal Tribune*.

Conceived on 21 March 1966, but not born until 12 September after a bout of severe labour pains resulting from management-union disputes over severance pay for 2,600 redundant staff (the final bill was $7,000,000) the first copy of this homogenised monster had eighty pages, thirty-eight columnists and a ringing declaration that 'This is a new newspaper. It combines the talents, the traditions and many of the features of three publications.' Neither size, talent, nor ancestry sufficed to save it. On 5 May 1967 after losing more than $10,000,000 in the struggle to keep alive it died and left the New York newspaper scene to one liberal-minded afternoon tabloid, the 165 year old *New York Post*, generally believed to be keeping its head just under water by swimming hard, one sensational morning tabloid, the 2,000,000 circulation *Daily News* owned by the *Chicago Tribune*—and the good grey *Times*.

New York thus became the world metropolis with the fewest newspapers—and with only the *Times* to sustain its former international glory. It is a strange and sad ending to the long rumbustious history of New York journalism from Benjamin Day, James Gordon Bennett and Horace Greeley onwards and it too reflects, like so much else in the press, social changes. With the development of the commuter age many former readers of metropolitan dailies have turned instead to new papers in the suburbs like *Newsday*, launched with a Long Island circulation of 11,000 during the war and now with sales of well over 400,000 but content, as most such suburban papers are, to depend for most of its national and world news on agency reports. Some New Yorkers it would seem have stopped reading newspapers altogether. To a newspaperman one of the most depressing of experiences was to be in New York during one of its prolonged newspaper strikes and to find how many people confessed to not missing their daily newspaper at all. The habit once broken many saw little reason to renew it—unless, of course, they were *New York Times* readers.

The *New York Times* is the Everest of the American press: a remarkable example of what is possible when one continuing family ownership concentrates all its intellectual and financial resources on producing one good newspaper. It seems unlikely to be affected by any foreseeable change in the general newspaper situation or to be touched by any of the economic or journalist ills that have shaken so many others. But although it out-tops all others in its dedication to the public interest it is fortunately not alone among American newspapers in such a dedication. The *Washington Post* owned by Mrs Francis Graham provides a similar example of journalism conducted as a public service. It is not so comprehensive a paper of record as the *Times* and pays more attention to its local community than the *New York Times* until recently did. But although its need for a local circulation spread compels it, as Mrs Graham has remarked, to 'appeal to both chairmen and charwomen', the fact that its home town is the political capital of the world gives it both a unique constituency and great influence.

There are others of more restricted scope but not less admirable singleness of mind, among them the *Milwaukee Journal*, on which the present publisher of the *New York Times* served his apprenticeship and which is owned by its staff under a singularly successful employee-partnership scheme carried through by a far-seeing publisher, Harry J. Grant, after the death of its founder, Lucius W. Nieman. And there are the *Louisville Courier-Journal*; the *Baltimore Sun*; the *Minneapolis Tribune*; and the *St Louis Post Dispatch*, all daily newspaper enterprises concentrating their resources exclusively on one newspaper or on a combination of one morning and one afternoon paper and all economically highly viable. A number of less influential but highly successful newspapers of large circulation similarly demonstrate the advantages of single ownership even in these days of large corporations—the *Los Angeles Times*, much improved under a new generation, among them. And there are still, of course, smaller newspapers in which the tradition of single, non-commercialised control still flourishes, as in that great liberal voice in the illiberal South, the *Atlanta Constitution*, or the crusading *Capital Times* of Madison, Wisconsin, whose founder, William T. Eujue, friend and disciple of Robert M. La Follette, remains still at well over eighty Publisher and Editor of his newspaper although he now leaves the hard slogging to his equally crusading Executive Publisher, Miles McMillin.

Nor should it be forgotten that there still remain a considerable number of small local papers under independent ownership. At a time when most of the big city press was handling Senator Joseph McCarthy with kid gloves, it was one such in his own State, the *Sauk-Prairie Star*, that struck the first real blow against him with a petition for a recall election in which the sole issue should be his fitness to continue in office. The *Sauk-Prairie Star* did not get the recall election it called for, but it got 400,000 signatures—more people than had ever before been affixed to a notarised petition in the nation's history. Despite every attempt to intimidate its editor by legal and illegal means it dealt a massive blow to the myth of McCarthy's invincibility when many with larger public voices were fleeing for cover. Such independent small town daily and weekly newspapers are among the glories of American journalism.

It is, however, a shrinking glory. By 1967 more than forty-nine per cent of American daily papers were in the hands of chains and just on sixty-two per cent of the total daily newspaper circulation was chain-controlled compared with forty-six per cent in 1960. Seven out of ten of the morning newspapers bought by American men and women each day were chain-owned. In *The First Freedom* Professor Bryce W. Rucker of Southern Illinois University estimates that unless this trend is reversed independent daily newspapers will virtually have disappeared from the American scene within twenty years and independent Sunday papers within thirteen. This may be a somewhat extreme prophecy but it is probably not much out. Some of the 165 chains are, of course, small and regional—although often all the more timorous and the more oppressive of editorial initiative for that reason. But the number of large chains increases. Already there are nineteen which own ten or more newspapers each—among them that of the ever expansive Thomson who by the middle of 1968 outranked all other American publishers in the number of newspapers owned. He had thirty-six American dailies as well as eleven weeklies in his hands. More than thirty of these dailies had been bought during the previous five years. They included the Brush-Moore chain of thirteen spread over five States which he bought at the end of 1967 for $72,000,000—the largest deal in American newspaper history, involving almost as much money as his purchase of Kemsley Newspapers in Britain eight years before. He is still looking for more. So far he has kept out of the big cities for political reasons and will probably continue to do so. For this reason although he ranks first in the number of newspapers owned he comes only sixth in terms of circulation controlled, with Cowles Publications, Ridder Publications, Gannet Newspapers, Scripps-Howard and Newhouse Newspapers ahead of him in ascending order.

Newhouse Newspapers owned by Samuel I. Newhouse (the initial I is there merely for effect, it stands for nothing) is top of the heap and also the most aggressively expansionist. By mid-1968 it controlled twenty-two newspapers with a combined circulation of well over 3,000,000 and had an outright monopoly in at least six considerable cities, among them New Orleans, Portland (Oregon), Jersey City and Syracuse.

Like Thomson, Newhouse is in newspapers for the money they make. It is not them but their balance sheets he wants to read. Indeed, he exceeds even Thomson in his disinterest in what is, and has been since newspapers began, the main purpose of a free press: the guiding and informing of public opinion. He is prepared to serve any prejudice that pays. Thus although he is personally, he says, in favour of racial integration, the *Birmingham News* of Birmingham, Alabama, which he has owned for thirteen years and which has a circulation of over 178,000, more than double that of the only other newspaper serving the area, is rabidly segregationalist—because that is the way the profit comes. Not for it the courage of the independently owned *Atlanta Constitution* which, no less dependent on a Southern readership, has fought consistently against racialism and succeeded in carrying much of its own community with it, or of the tiny *Lexington* (Mississipi) *Advertiser*, whose Publisher and Editor, Hazel Braunon Smith, has for years fought magnificently for Negro rights in a hate-ridden state: her only reward three national journalism awards and several local advertising boycotts.

A neat, small, anonymous man, only 5 ft 3 ins in height, with meticulous manners and a deceptive diffidence, Newhouse is the son of poor Jewish-Russian immigrants. He started work at thirteen as an office boy to a small time lawyer in Bayonne, New Jersey, who later became a local Judge. At seventy-three, Newhouse is even more than Thomson the embodiment of the commercial principle in newspapers. 'All he's interested in,' said one publisher with whom he tried to do business, 'is the cash register. He doesn't give a damn about newspapers. He just treats them like so many hardware stores.' Like Thomson he owes his success to the realisation that most newspapers are among the most inefficiently run businesses on earth and that you usually only need to apply ordinary commercial common sense to their operations to turn a loss into a profit or make a small profit into a big one—provided, of course, you have a flair for commercial surgery. He has also built up an extensive intelligence service to alert him to any signs of financial distress that might provide an opportunity for a bid. But whereas Thomson appears to have made the jump from the front office to the editorial floor, at least, to the extent that he now has a regard for the editorial quality of his bigger newspapers, Newhouse remains dedicated solely to his newspapers' balance sheets.

He originally came into the newspaper business by accident when Hyman Lazarus, the Bayonne lawyer who employed him, found himself landed with a fifty-one per cent interest in the *Bayonne Times*, a declining property with only 3,000 subscribers, as payment on a bad debt and suggested that Newhouse who had just finished his law studies at night school should look into it for him. Newhouse asked for a cut of any profits he managed to make. A wizard with accounts he soon had the paper so strongly on its feet that he was drawing $20,000 a year out of it. Not unnaturally he decided that newspapers were something a smart man could hardly fail to do well out of. He bought his first newspaper, the *Staten Island Advance*, for $98,000 when he was twenty-seven with the help of a $49,000 loan from Lazarus and a whip round among his relations. He has gone on buying ever since, a newspaper on average every three or four years, small at first, then bigger and bigger. In 1962 he shook the U.S. press world by paying $42,000,000 for the *New Orleans Times-Picayune* and its evening companion, the *States-Item*. This was then the largest amount ever paid in America in a single newspaper transaction. He out-ranked it in 1967 when he paid $53,400,000 for the *Cleveland Plain Dealer*. His total press empire is now conservatively valued at well over $300,000,000. It includes in addition to his newspapers a sixty-six per cent interest in the Condé Nast magazine group, publishers of *Vogue* which he bought for $5,000,000 from the International Publishing Corporation, as a 35th wedding anniversary present for his wife, Mitzi, who, unlike him, is a socialite much interested in high fashion. He also owns nine radio and seven television stations.

He rarely reads any of the newspapers he owns. Of him one Chicago publisher said, 'For any publisher you can respect, any of those who love journalism, Sam Newhouse would be the last person to sell a paper to.' When he buys a new paper he leaves it to be run editorially just as before. If it was good when he bought it, it probably stays good. If it was bad, it stays bad. It is to the advertising, circulation, production and accounts departments that he applies his mind, quick to spot even the smallest way in which money can be saved or advertising made more saleable. Most Monday mornings he leaves his Park Avenue apartment in New York sharp at 7.45, bulging brief case under his arm, to begin his rota of visits to his 'properties'. Those in the New York area, where he likes to claim he sells more than the *New York Times*, are visited by Cadillac and usually take up most of Monday and Tuesday. On Tuesday night he goes by overnight train to Syracuse, where he turned a loss into a profit by merging the two papers he had bought there and offering advertisers a bargain rate. He spends Wednesday in Syracuse which is the nearest thing to a base he has and on Thursday and Friday takes to the air to visit the more distant outposts of his empire following a schedule planned to ensure that none is left alone for long. He is careful of his diet but perhaps because he lives so peripatetic a life he sleeps badly. 'I just toss about in the dark,' he once said, 'and wonder what paper I'll buy tomorrow.'

Unlike Thomson, Newhouse has no international ambitions. He once had a chance to buy the *Jerusalem Post* but turned it down because he could not fit it into his visiting schedule. Since he first began to attract national attention with his purchase of the *Portland Oregonian* for $5,600,000 in 1950 he has employed a public relations firm to look after his public image. Possibly under its influence he donated $15,000,000 to Syracuse University in 1960 to establish a Newhouse Communications Centre, the first part of which, a Journalism Building, was opened by President Johnson in August 1964. A plaque at the entrance, written by, or perhaps for, Newhouse, reads, 'A free press must be fortified with greater knowledge of the world and skill in the arts of expression.' This is a statement irreproachable in sentiment but not something Newhouse has much concerned himself about in his own activities.

Although in some ways strictly a human cash register, Newhouse has a strong Jewish family feeling and was reputed at one time to have no fewer than sixty Newhouses and Newhouse-in-laws scattered about his various properties. They all had good business noses, however, and were well trained as loyal agents in the field. His two sons, Donald and Samuel, aged forty and thirty-eight respectively, are alumni of Syracuse University. They will succeed him in control of the Newhouse properties, but without any chance to turn them into cash. Their control will come from ownership of five voting shares each in a charitable foundation Newhouse established more than twenty years ago to preserve his empire against the inroads of estate taxes or filial temptations to sell out. Although as one of his brothers once said, 'It could just as easily have been shoe factories', he is proud of his newspaper collection and determined that what he has built shall stay. 'I'm hardboiled about the boys,' he once remarked. 'I've built this thing up and I'm not going to let it go to pieces.' There are several grandsons to carry on after them.

Newhouse makes few public speeches and gives few interviews. In this he is unlike Thomson who is endlessly garrulous. However, at the dedication dinner of the Syracuse Newhouse Communications Centre attended by his wife, his sons, his brothers and sisters and as many grandchildren as were old enough to stay up late, as well as Faculty Members, civic dignitaries and publishers, Newhouse did make an attempt to justify his way with newspapers. Whether the speech was his own or part of a public relations service he did so rather well. He looked on his newspapers, he told an audience in no mood to criticise a benefactor, as members of his family—a sentiment which has not prevented him from having a number of bitter disputes with employees hurt by his methods: his *Portland Oregon* papers were picketed by the Typographical Union for five and a half years. Each new paper bought, he said, was like 'the acquisition of another child'. Warming to his theme he went on, 'Although each is flesh of our flesh and ink of our ink each develops in its own way, with its own looks, its own views, its own independent spirit—the way children do. They speak differently too—for they are the voices of all America. Their accents are from the far Northwest, the East and the South—accents from all the regions of our land. But despite the differences in accents they are united in one common aim: the newspapers' dedication to the truth.'

It is possible that he sincerely believes this and that, as seems to have happened with Thomson, the disassociation from editorial policy that began as a commercial convenience has, over the years, been sublimated into a genuine respect for variety and a belief in business efficiency as a supporter of editorial independence. However, since he seldom shows much interest in the editorial content of these properties of his it is hard to be sure. Nevertheless it seemed tactless of the *Editor and Publisher* to describe the presentation to him of a gold medal for 'distinguished service to journalism' as a surprise. What was undoubtedly genuine was Newhouse's emotion when he spoke of the 'dramatic contrast between this occasion and the first time his name appeared on any record. 'The first time it appeared anywhere' he told his audience 'was on a birth certificate written in a New York City tenement where I was born. I am proud of that. Tomorrow I will see my name inscribed on the wall of what is perhaps the most modern School of Communications in the world. I am proud of that, too.' His career has, indeed, been a remarkable success story. Whether American journalism with its tradition of regional independence can stand many other such successes is another matter.

Nor is it only the advance of Newhouse and his fellow exponents of the commercial principle in journalism that is altering the face of much of the American press. Competition has gone out of fashion, monopoly become the usual habit. In seventeen States there are now no longer any competing dailies whatever and in the whole of the 1,470 American cities in which daily newspapers are published there is direct face to face competition between competing morning or competing afternoon papers in only fourteen, competition even between separately owned morning and afternoon papers in only about fifty of the rest. More than nine out of every ten newspapers read across America are monopolies.

Nor is this only a matter of small cities finding it economically impossible any longer to support more than one newspaper. There are newspaper monopolies in ninety cities with populations of between 100,000 and 600,000—sixty-six of them monopolies controlled by newspaper chains large or small. From the readers' point of view this monopoly is the more complete because, unlike Britain, where any newspaper reader can take his pick among seven competing national dailies in addition to whatever provincial daily serves his area, for American readers in monopoly towns there is usually no choice open. Nor do more than a few of such newspapers employ correspondents outside their own areas. Their news of the nation and the world comes almost exclusively from the two wire agencies, Associated Press and United Press International and this is as true of the lush advertisement-crammed suburban dailies like *Newsday* and the scores of others which now ring the large cities and have become a major new development in American journalism as it is of a small town daily in North Dakota or Tennessee. On reports from these agencies the vast majority of American newspaper readers depend for most of their information of what is happening outside their own towns or cities—only about sixteen per cent of all American daily newspapers receive world news from other than these two sources and those that do are mostly large city dailies.

In the main A.P. and U.P.I. staff reporters are no doubt as objective as nature permits. But the wire services depend for a large part of their domestic news not on their own staff correspondents but on their member newspapers. What is transmitted is the news not as an independent news agency sees it but as it is seen and reported by hundreds of local newspapers often chiefly concerned to report nothing that will reflect badly on the sacred cows of their own communities. Nor is bias always absent in international news. Both agencies tend to be over-tender to the presumptions and prejudices of their customers. Thus Robert H. Sollon pointed out in the *Editor and Publisher* in July 1961 that irrespective of their nature foreign news developments tended to be reported by the wire services as either pro or anti-American and to be seen entirely in the context of the cold war.

No doubt the agencies provide the news coverage their customers want. But because of the absence of other independent reports the fact remains that the vast majority of Americans are denied the essential corrective of variety in news reporting. This is especially so where it is most needed—in areas of public concern where few have direct knowledge or experience to set against what they read in the newspapers. They have, of course, local radio and television to turn to. But these may be under the same monopoly control as the newspapers. There are eighty-five cities where the only daily newspaper owns an interest in the only A.M. radio station, twenty-seven where there are newspaper-television monopolies. In any event the local radio and television stations are serviced by the same wire agencies as the newspapers, although fortunately the networks with the Huntley and Brinkley and

Monopoly in America

Walter Cronkite programmes and the news commentaries of Ed Newman and others help to correct the balance.

Lacking the stimulation of competition many local dailies do not even bother to cover the doings of their own state governments with reporters of their own. According to one recent estimate by Ben H. Bagdikian more than half the newspapers published in state capitals take their statehouse news from agencies instead of having their own men on the job. Indeed, where competition no longer exists the temptation to publish what is made easily available without independent report or investigation seems for many to be overwhelming. Professor Scott Cutlipp of the University of Wisconsin, one of the leading academic authorities in the States on the spread and organisation of public relations in both its good and bad aspects, estimates that on average one third of the news content of all American newspapers is now inspired by public relations agencies.

However, whether one likes it or not monopoly is clearly here to stay: the product of economic circumstances that cannot be denied. The biggest task of American journalism is to learn how best to live with it.

Barry Bingham, Editor and Publisher of the *Louisville Courier Journal* whose own newspaper is a shining example of how to be good even when alone, took up this point in response to some observations I made on the responsibilities of the mass media, as an invited speaker to the tenth anniversary celebrations in New York of the Fund for the Republic a few years ago. When it was half its present size his own city of Louisville had, he said, nine competing newspapers. Now there are two newspapers—both owned by his own company. The same was, he added, true of most of the rest of the twenty-two American cities in the same population class as Louisville, cities, that is, of between 300,000 and 500,000 population. All of them used to have several competing newspapers. Now there are only six in which there is competition. Nor can anyone say how long it will last even in these cities.

But, said Mr Bingham, it was not all loss. 'In my own city readers are constantly crying "monopoly" at us. Whenever they see something in the newspapers that they do not like they immediately say, "This town should have another newspaper." I suggest these phrases are shibboleths and that they replace intelligent thought. . . . Monopoly is less a threat to press excellence than monotony. There are highly individualistic newspapers that are flourishing in solus ownership situations. At the same time there are newspapers dropping from the presses all over the United States that are as alike as sausages.' Although monopoly had its dangers there were also, he pointed out, grave dangers in cut and thrust competition 'which is the kind of competition which flourished when there were additional ownerships and that still flourishes in some metropolitan areas.' (This was before the New York holocaust.) Monopoly, indeed, could, he argued 'have certain limited virtues'. It relieved the pressure of advertisers on the owner. 'They cannot be effective in pressurising one newspaper.' It also reduced the temptation of ownership to sensationalise the news. 'In my town again, which is typical,' said Mr Bingham, 'ninety-five per cent of our circulation is by home subscription and only five per cent is by street sales. It can easily be seen how that reduces the temptation for big headlines and for sensationalised news to sell against your competition. A responsible owner of a solus newspaper can give his readers more serious news and can give them bolder and livelier opinions than the man who is running in hot and deadly competition with a rival.'

This is to some extent true. But it is only the opinions that particular editor or publisher likes being bold and lively about that are likely to get an airing. He does not have to think, as the man with competition has to think, that others may decide to explore subjects he would prefer to leave alone or may have opinions different from his which for that reason he dare not ignore.

However, as Mr Bingham said, monopoly is here and must be lived with, It brings its own responsibilities. In indicating those responsiblities he preached a doctrine contrary to much of the current commercial principle in journalism. 'What the press and other communications media need,' he said, 'is more owners of papers and stations who regard their ownership as a public trust, more owners who consider service first and profits second. As a newspaper owner I admit, of course, that newspapers must sell to live, but I would maintain to my dying breath that we must not live to sell. We need more owners with the peculiar passion for communicating thought and not just communicating a welter of facts.'

Such principles are admirable. Mr Bingham and a handful of

other editors and publishers of like dedication preserve them nobly in practice as well as words. But over most of the American newspaper scene their weight is small. It is the maximisation of profits that counts. Outside New York and some other metropolitan areas of press shrinkage, San Francisco among the most recent of them, the American press is today extraordinarily profitable. According to figures published by the *Editor and Publisher* in April 1966 the 'average medium city newspaper showed in the previous year a net profit before taxes of twenty-three per cent.' Since then profits have probably climbed further. But it is in many instance a profitability made possible by an almost total abdication of many of the responsibilities that once animated American journalism and of which Barry Bingham spoke. With seventy-five per cent or more of their revenue drawn from advertising many daily papers have become little more than bill boards of local events in which editorial matter is to be found only in sparse oases amidst vast deserts of advertising. Advertising has, of course, its important place in any sound newspaper system. Although the dangerous dependence of newspapers upon advertisements has often been the theme of newspaper reformers—usually from outside the press—without them daily journalism would never have survived as an independent public force. Moreover advertising commands great popular interest and serves—especially in a consumer society—a social purpose of the highest validity. One hundred and seventy years ago Stuart, the Editor and Publisher of the London *Morning Post* declared, 'Advertisements act and re-act. They attract readers, promote circulation and circulation attracts advertisements.' This is as true today as it was then. Yet a healthy press performing a genuine public service depends on a proper balance between advertising and news. In much of the once vigorous and vocal American local press this balance has ceased to exist.

In the last twenty-five years the average size of American daily newspapers has risen from twenty-seven pages to fifty. But of these additional pages twenty have gone to advertising, only three to editorial and when larger display and the greater use of syndicated features are taken into account the average space devoted to news and locally initiated editorial features and editorials is actually less than it was a quarter of a century ago. In the last ten years advances in educational standards have brought an increase of one hundred per cent in book sales. Sales of books dealing with social and economic matters, the very marrow of public service journalism, have increased by more than six times. Yet newspaper sales per family have dropped by eighteen per cent since the war and on average only thirty people in every hundred buy a newspaper compared with almost fifty in Britain.

Seduced by easy revenue and cushioned by local monopoly far too many American daily newspapers have failed to keep in line with public demand—surely a commercial as well as a journalistic sin. They lack the perception of changing times that paid off so handsomely, for example, in the case of the London *Daily Mirror* when it deliberately adjusted its editorial policies to meet what it recognised as a demand for more serious treatment of news on the part even of a mass public. Yet all the evidence indicates that although as things are at present a great many mediocre newspapers can coast along without much trouble in a non-competitive situation where advertising is easy to get, it is the better papers like the *Baltimore Sun*, the *Milwaukee Journal*, the *Louisville Courier Journal* and others that use monopoly as a spur to public service instead of as a feather bed to relax on that earn the highest profits. This, too, has been the experience of the *Los Angeles Times* since it was made over and improved by a younger publishing generation a few years ago. Contrariwise the collapse of its competitor, the *Los Angeles Mirror* and other Hearst papers, including the founding father of them all, the *San Francisco Examiner*, shows what happens when publishers fail in their respect for the editorial function.

It would seem to be the case, indeed, that so far from Gresham's Law of the worst driving out the best applying in journalism almost the reverse is true—wherever the best is given a chance. The supreme example is the towering success of the *New York Times* amidst the crashing of so many of its contemporaries. But there are other examples in less likely places—as, for instance, in the fate of one of the first members of the Thomson American chain, the *Independent* of St Petersburg, Florida. The *Independent*, run by the balance sheet, was conservative and segregationalist in a conservative, segregationalist, ingrown and insular community. It was left that way after Thomson bought it. It did everything it thought its readers expected of it, supported them in their views, however prejudiced, and did not trouble them with much national or international news since their tastes were not thought to run in that direction—and anyway it was cheaper that way. By the book it should have been a great money spinner. However, it had up against it a quite different kind of paper, the *St Petersburg Times*, edited and published by Nelson Poynter whose ideas of a good local newspaper were as unlike those of Thomson's organisation as they could possibly be. The *St Petersburg Times* was and is a liberal crusading, anti-segregationalist paper in an illiberal community. It carries national as well as local news and insists on making its readers constantly aware of the outside world. It is an investigatory paper, quick to uncover injustice or corruption and not afraid to back up its exploration of serious economic and social issues with graphs and other solid material where such seems useful. It puts journalistic and human values well ahead of commercial ones and above all is dedicated to the principle that it is news that makes a good newspaper.

By Thomson's book—or at least the book he uses for his small local newspapers—it should have been a failure. Instead Thomson's *Independent* made big losses, Poynter's *Times* big profits. So profitable and successful was the *Times*, in fact, that in the end Thomson cut his losses, sold out to Poynter and retired from St Petersburg. Other newspapers differing as widely in politics, social philosophy and the nature of their publics as, say, the *Washington Post* and the *Chicago Tribune* have similarly demonstrated that it is possible to make more profits by running a journalistically good paper than a bad one and by recognising as the *Chicago Tribune*, despite its other vagaries, has consistently done—that it is news and editorial content that matter and that it is worth spending money and talent on them. You might think their example worth noting even by those exclusively devoted to commercial principles. Few however seem to think so.

In this situation the success of such news magazines as *Time* and *Newsweek* is understandable. They repair some of the deficiences of the daily press, bringing to readers who would otherwise feel starved of news a sharp picture of the world as seen through the corporate eye of a team of good Americans. News magazines sell most where there are poor newpapers. *Time's per capita* circulation is, for example, twice as high in San Francisco as in Louisville.

The Right to Know

Apart from the special position of the news magazines in a country where national daily newspapers are geographically impossible—such magazines have never succeeded in Britain because of the existence of a national daily press—general interest magazines as a whole have always had a larger place in the United States than in Britain. However, the increasing dominance of the commercial principle is now playing havoc with them too. Heavily dependent on large advertising they have been badly hit by commercial television. The principle of 'minimum offence' has reduced their editorial quality and their journalistic independence has been eroded by a considerable extension of group ownership, some of it from outside the industry. Simon Norton, head of Hunt Foods and Industries Incorporated, bought control of *McCall's* in 1956 and by spending millions on it toppled the traditional leader in the woman's field, the *Ladies' Home Journal*, from first place. Now the *Ladies' Home Journal* runs only fourth, with two grocery chain distributed magazines, *Family Circle* and *Woman's Day*, second and third, a situation that would have seemed inconceivable even a few years ago.

In 1930 there were twenty-four general magazines with circulations of over 1,000,000. Fourteen have since died, some like *Colliers* and *Coronet* with circulations much larger. *Colliers* was killed off with a 3,750,000 circulation in 1957 because it could not pull in advertising at the rate its situation required. *Coronet* was closed down with 3,200,000 circulation in 1961. Both were casualties of sales promotion schemes that had long since lost touch with common sense. Under them sales were boosted to such a degree and at such a speed by cut price subscription offers that each copy involved so heavy a production loss that the gap could not possibly be filled from advertising fixed at rates based on much lower sales totals. Even if the selling price of a newspaper or magazine remains constant too rapid a rise in circulation before there is time for advertising demand to catch up at rates appropriate to the new sales figure can, because of the peculiar economics of the industry, involve substantial losses. This, indeed, was one of the principal factors leading to the sale of the London *Times* to Thomson. Where in addition each new copy is sold at a cut rate so that the gap to be covered by advertising is extended at both ends, there is no quicker road to bankruptcy. Yet where the commercial principle rules unchecked such is the urge for ever higher circulation as a means to market 'leadership' and ultimately more advertising at higher rates, that circulation promotion by cut price subscription offers backed by an avalanche of importuning literature mounting in hysteria with each mail has become the most characteristic feature of the big magazine trade. In the early sixties well over ninety per cent of *Reader's Digest* subscribers were obtained by such methods, between sixty and eighty per cent of those of *Life*, *Look* and several others. And the drive is still on. Those with vast financial resources can take the strain. Those without die.

Under such commercial stresses and in an atmosphere where editorial quality has come to be thought less and less important in selling to readers battered in judgment by never ending bargain offers, many of the most famous names in American magazine history have disappeared beneath the waters: *Colliers*, *Scribners*, *Liberty*, *Literary Digest*, the *Reporter*—a flagship of intelligent weekly journalism—among them. Even the *Saturday Evening Post*, the granddaddy of them all, has gone after first trying to cut its circulation to a third to save money.

In all this no doubt the American magazine industry reflects the nature of its society. Currently the most dazzling success story in American magazines is *Playboy*, child of the clubs and the Bunnies and the cornucopia of deodorised sex. It is a faithful symbol of admass civilisation. Yet at the same time in reaction to this civilisation an 'underground' magazine press has developed at a spanking pace and a small maverick independent, *Ramparts*, has made itself the most talked of magazine of the sixties by doing what the big magazines no longer dare to do, as in its disclosure of C.I.A. penetration of student organisations which made headlines right across the country in 1967.

The forces making for commercialisation and group domination of the press are now particularly strong in North America. That they can sometimes be thwarted or even hammered to fit non-commercial ends has, however, been admirably demonstrated across the border in Canada. Although most Canadian small town dailies are as flat and tasteless as the twenty-six in the Thomson chain—or as their cousins across the border—an important group of the more important quality newspapers have come together to strengthen their editorial independence, not to lose it.

The Right to Know

This movement may be said to have taken its first important turn in 1959 when the influential *Ottawa Journal*, Conservative in its political policies, was sold to Mr Victor Sifton, publisher of the Liberal *Winnipeg Free Press* and his associates—a transaction which on the face of its seemed at first to carry ominous implications for the future of independent journalism in Canada. It was, however, a sale very different from the usual run of commercial transactions. So far from involving a threat to the *Journal*'s identity the paper's complete editorial independence under its Associate Editors, M. Grattan O'Leary and I. Norman Smith, President and Vice-President of the Journal Company, was written into the contract. There was a further contractual undertaking that when Mr O'Leary came to retire the exclusive control and direction of the *Journal*'s editorial policies would pass to Norman Smith as Editor-in-Chief so that the paper's position as an independent Conservative newspaper with the editorial and news traditions given it by O'Leary and Smith and by their predecessor, P. D. Ross, should be preserved for the foreseeable future.

Writing to me at the time about this link between the Conservative *Ottawa Journal* and the most famous Liberal newspaper in Canada—but one with a long tradition of editorial freedom from proprietorial control—Norman Smith assured me that the sole purpose of the transaction, an economic precaution rather than an economic necessity, had been to bring behind the *Journal* larger resources than it could command on its own and thus prevent any possible lowering of standards by reason of mounting costs and increasingly severe competition from new communication media. He was, he said, completely satisfied that editorial control by O'Leary and himself would remain firm, they would not have gone in under any other conditions. The *Journal* would continue as it had always been, pro-Conservative in an independent sort of way, with no diminution in either editorial or news standards as a result of its membership of a larger group. So it has proved. Group ownership on this model has proved not a threat to journalistic and political independence, but a strong buttress of both. With the title F.P. (Free Press) Publications the group itself has extended considerably since 1959, its last recruit, early in 1968, being the *Toronto Globe and Mail*, the nearest thing to a national daily paper in Canada with an influence extending far beyond its immediate circulation area. F. P. Publications is now in terms of circulation much the largest group in Canadian journalism. Under John Sifton, son of Victor Sifton, as President it links in one powerful commercial organisation the most famous and influential quality daily newspapers in Canada from the *Toronto Globe and Mail* and the *Ottawa Journal* in the east to the *Winnipeg Free Press* and the *Albertan of Calgary* in the central wheat and prairie lands and the *Vancouver Sun* and the *Victoria Times and Colonist* in the far west. But although linked commercially and supported by common resources each retains its separate identity and editorial independence and speaks with its own political voice.

In spite of the mediocrity of much of its small town press Canada has thus presented to its greater neighbour one excellent example of how to turn the tables on the chain store monopolies by using their methods for genuine journalistic purposes.

CHAPTER TEN

Monopoly in Europe

It is not only in Britain and North America that monopoly and group ownership are on the march. When mobs of German students tried to prevent the distribution of newspapers controlled by the Springer group in early 1968 they were protesting, amongst other things, against the greatest single concentration of newspaper ownership in any country in the world. The Springer group is in German terms almost the equivalent of the International Publishing Corporation and the Thomson Organisation put together: it is as though Thomson had the *Mirror* as well as *The Times*, or, across the Atlantic, Newhouse had by some disastrous miracle added both the *New York Times* and the *New York Daily News* to his chain. The Springer newspaper empire does not, as Axel Springer is quick to point out, have a monopoly in Western Germany. But it is much the largest national group and in West Berlin has the nearest thing to a monopoly in any major capital in the world. It is a text book example of the German habit of going too far.

Axel Caesar Springer is a handsome, elegant man of fifty-eight with something of the well-preserved looks and smooth charm of Governor Ronald Reagan. He has had four wives and is generally regarded by envious contemporaries as irresistible to women. He collects houses, one splendid one in Berlin, two large and almost equally splendid ones in Hamburg, a house in Mayfair, London, which once belonged to General Gordon, two villas on the North Sea island of Sylt and a chalet in Klosters, gathering place of the international rich in the Swiss Alps. His Berlin house is decorated with Flemish frescoes originally acquired for the Federal German President, one of his Hamburg mansions with ancient Chinese wall decorations, and he is a knowledgeable buyer of English

Regency and Georgian furniture. He much admires the style of the English upper classes, has his clothes built in Savile Row and owns a considerable racing stable. He is strongly political and extremely right wing but to his credit is a firm opponent of anti-semitism and a generous supporter of all measures for German-Jewish reconciliation.

His father owned a small weekly in the suburbs of Hamburg, the *Altona News*, and he was apprenticed to the printing trade. He managed to keep out of the Nazi Party without being in any way involved in active opposition to it and escaped being called to the armed forces partly because of bad health, partly because his father's printing shop, to which he had returned after working as a news agency reporter, was on important war work—it had an army contract to print romantic novels and light literature to keep up the spirits of soldiers in the field.

When the war ended there was nothing in his record to stand in the way of getting a printing licence from the occupying power—in Hamburg, the British. But the queue was long and delays interminable. Each applicant had to be interviewed and approved by a member of the Control Commission and Commission members had begun to grow a little weary of a succession of stories of Nazi oppression and political innocence. When Axel Springer arrived with a request to be allowed to publish a radio magazine he was greeted coldly by the British major behind the desk. 'And who,' asked the major sourly, 'has been persecuting you?' 'Only women,' said Springer and was smartly given a licence by an officer glad to meet someone with a roving eye instead of a grievance.

His radio magazine prospered. So did his relations with the British. They liked him, he says, because he liked horses. By 1953 his first small radio periodical had been transformed into *Hör Zu* (Listen), which now sells close on 4,000,000 a week and he was also publishing a local afternoon paper in Hamburg, *Abendblatt*. In that year the British decided that the time had come to hand over to a German publisher the prestige morning newspaper, *Die Welt*, which had been founded by the Control Commission, originally as a bi-weekly but later as a daily, in order to fill the journalistic vacuum left by the Nazis and provide a working model of how a quality newspaper ought to be run in a democracy. Axel Springer bought control.

The Right to Know

Die Welt lifted Springer out of Hamburg into national journalism. It was already a highly regarded and very profitable journal with a national circulation among the commercial, professional and intellectual classes—a substitute, although by no means a complete one, for such famous pre-war journals of opinion as the *Frankfurter Zeitung* and the *Berliner Tageblatt* which had been crushed by the Nazis. It had a circulation of 130,000 a day.

Springer has more than doubled this circulation without reducing the quality of the paper. It is one of the only two quality newspapers with a national circulation, the other being the *Frankfurter Allgemeine*. It has three publishing centres, Hamburg, Essen and Berlin, and is read by almost everyone of importance in politics and commerce throughout Western Germany and by a large number of school teachers and others of the professional classes. It still carries traces of its British journalistic parentage in a make-up and news presentation a good deal lighter and typographically more pleasing than that of most serious German newspapers, which tend to be close printed and solid in appearance. It also has a wider news coverage than any other German daily and employs full time correspondents in sixteen countries. In politics it is strongly conservative but with a reasonable liberal approach to social problems. Its Sunday edition, *Welt am Sontag*, has a circulation of over 480,000 and it also publishes each Thursday a literary supplement closely modelled on *The Times Literary Supplement*.

It was not, however, Axel Springer, owner of *Die Welt*, that the German students were demonstrating against, but Axel Springer, owner of *Bild-Zeitung*, the Federal German Republic's only mass circulation tabloid daily. *Bild-Zeitung* owes something to the London *Daily Mirror* under Bartholomew and something also to the *New York Daily News* under Patterson, but it has out-paced both in extreme sensationalism: 'Mind you shake the blood out,' say the newsvendors when you buy it, and violence and sex are major factors in its massive popularity. All this is allied to a right wing policy far more reactionary than that of *Die Welt*. It is an ugly paper to look at, but with a massive impact. Springer himself sometimes calls it an 'optical' newspaper meaning by this, presumably, that it appeals to the eye rather than the intellect and should not be judged by normal newspaper standards. It aims to identify with every reader's prejudices and to stimulate any they do not have and to this end uses a combination of lavish picture display, sledge hammer headlines and emotionally charged leading articles written in words of one or two syllables to ram home views that sound as though they had crawled out from behind the woodwork of a psychopath's unconscious. It has a circulation of over 4,600,000 and despite the existence of a large regional press is the only newspaper a good many Germans read.

Springer is the only German newspaper owner to have set out deliberately, as Bartholomew did earlier in Britain, to reach the masses with a newspaper in their own idiom. Significantly the idiom was right wing, not as in Britain, radical. *Bild-Zeitung* is credited with hounding several Ministers out of office and was, it is claimed, largely instrumental in toppling Dr Erhardt and bringing in a 'grand coalition'. Herr Springer himself likes to refer to it as his *Kettenhund*—his dog on a chain—and few politicians are ready to risk seeing the chain slipped for a pounce at their throats. It is published simultaneously in Hamburg, West Berlin, Essen, Frankfurt and Munich. With *Bild Zeitung* for the masses and *Die Welt* for the serious minded Springer owns two out of the only three national daily papers in the Federal German Republic. He also owns the only two national Sunday newspapers, *Welt am Sontag* and *Bild am Sontag*—the second with a circulation of 2,700,000. Nor is this by any means all. His *Hamburger Abendblatt* is now the largest afternoon paper in West Germany. It is also the only one to carry a page of comic strips. He also owns the *Berliner Morgenpost* which has the highest circulation of any Berlin paper. Altogether he commands seventy per cent of the total daily newspaper readership in West Berlin.

In West Germany as a whole his share of total circulation is smaller because of the grip of regional daily newspapers. Most of these are small and purely local in news and influence, but some twenty-six have circulations above 100,000. Despite the hold of the regional press Springer papers account for forty per cent of the total circulation of daily newspapers in Western Germany.

At the time of the student riots he also owned a rich stable of glossy weeklies, among them *Bravo* for teenagers, *Twen* for those in the twenties, *Jasmin* for newly weds and *Eltern* for parents. He disposed of these in June 1968, mainly, it was generally believed, because of the report of a government-appointed commission warning of the danger of press monopoly. However, although Springer felt it politic to make some gesture, he did nothing to meet the main burden of the Commission's findings which were concerned not with magazines, but with daily newspapers of political influence and which argued that press freedom was in some danger if twenty per cent of newspaper sales were in one control and that if forty per cent was, then a serious encroachment of press freedom existed. Springer obviously qualifies under both headings in West Germany as a whole and very much more so in West Berlin.

Springer has publishing centres in Hamburg, Munich, Essen, Frankfurt and Darmstadt but the true heart of his empire is now a vast new steel, concrete and glass skyscraper, the Axel Springer Publishing House, built at a cost of twenty-five million dollars beside the Berlin wall, 200 yards from Checkpoint Charlie. His office overlooks both West Berlin and East Berlin and his mission in life, he declares, is their reunification. His violent anti-Communism, frequently expressed in the most primitive terms—he tends to see Communists under every printing press but his own—is generally believed to spring from his cold reception when he visited Khrushchev in 1958 in the hope of promoting this. The Axel Springer Publishing House was opened by the Federal President, Heinrich Lübke, and Mayor Willy Brandt in October 1966, and was the occasion for an emotional speech from Springer himself. This had as its climax this verse from a favourite song:

> I devote myself to you,
> With heart and hand,
> Land full of love and life,
> My German fatherland.

Springer likes to quote, as he did on this occasion, the remark, 'The papers of the Springer House are not loyal to the Government—they are loyal to the Republic', and it is as a counter-power to government that he sees his newspapers. Not for him the managerial pre-occupations of Thomson or Newhouse, or the objectivity of Sulzberger. He is a newspaper owner on the model of Hearst or Northcliffe or Beaverbrook. This is why the extreme concentration of German press power in his hands is regarded by many of his fellow publishers and—privately—by many German politicians who applaud him publicly as so dangerous. He tends to disclaim direct editorial interference—a disclaimer sceptically received by insiders—but argues that a publisher must be responsible for the basic postures of his newspapers. Beaverbrook explained to the first British Royal Commission on the Press that he did not need to issue orders to his staff: 'They follow my teaching.' Springer editorial staffs are in the same position. They are trained to ask themselves, 'What would Herr Springer do?' If they hope to succeed they come up with the correct answer.

Springer's power would be greater but for the fact that his dominant influence in the German daily press is countered in the periodical field by the news magazine *Der Spiegel*, by the illustrated weekly, *Stern*, which with a circulation of over 1,850,000 runs neck and neck with *Paris-Match* for the title of the largest selling weekly picture magazine in Europe, and by the comparatively small but highly courageous liberal weekly *Die Zeit*. Of these *Der Spiegel* has the biggest influence.

Like Springer's *Die Welt*, *Der Spiegel* was the foster child of the British Control Commission, although Luce's *Time* must be suspected of being its true parent. It was started by a major in the British Military Government, John Chaloner, with the help of a sergeant in the press section, Harry Boliver. What post-war Germany needed to fill the gaps left by an inadequate and still cowed daily press was, they decided, an independent news weekly. They got permission to start one under the title of *Diese Woche*. However, it proved too independent. Its first number contained a vehement attack by Victor Gollancz on the British Government, which was, he declared, 'more and more shameless' in its policies towards Germany. The weekly continued as it had begun: each new number demonstrated the meaning of independence by including several sharp slaps at authority. The British Military Government was tolerant, admirably so. However, by the time the fifth number had been published it came to the conculsion that although no doubt criticism of authority was healthy and what the bruised German ego needed, it would come more appropriately from a less official publication. *Diese Woche* was granted a paper licence sufficient to allow for a circulation of 15,000 copies a week and transferred to German hands, with the new title of *Der Spiegel*. Modelled closely on *Time* in appearance and style it soon proved so successful that only the readiness of the British to look the other way and not ask questions about where its paper supplies came from when circulation shot far beyond the 15,000 for which a licence had been given enabled it to meet readership demand.

Since then, under its Publisher and Chief Editor, Rudolf Augstein it has made for itself a unique place in German journalism as an organ of dissent and investigation and as an independent source of national and international news. According to its executive editor, William Busse, it operates on the assumption 'that there are human beings and human traits behind activities which do not, superficially, seem to justify this assumption—such as politics'. Its declared intention is 'to bring into relief from behind the curtain of the public statements the men responsible for actual policy'. It has been remarkably successful in doing so. It now has a circulation of close on 1,000,000 and an editorial staff of sixty backed by a research staff of the same size. Like *Time* most of its reports are the product of a combined effort and appear anonymously, but it has a number of distinguished signed columns and has made a speciality of disclosing what German governments would prefer not to be known.

It had its finest hour during the *Spiegel* Affair of October 1962 when officers of the security services raided its offices and occupied them for four weeks, arresting its publisher, editor and five members of its staff on charges of treason and of being in possession of secret State documents. This was because an article on NATO manoeuvres highly critical of German military preparedness had been published by its defence correspondent, Conrad Ahlers. The paper was able to show that the article had been cleared for security by a member of the Information Section of the *Abwehr* (the German Secret Service), Colonel Wicht, but to this the official response was not to drop the charges but to arrest Colonel Wicht. Indeed, so great was the anger of the ageing Chancellor, Dr Adenauer, that at one stage he ordered his Minister of Justice to arrest not only Wicht but his superior, General Gehlen, Head of the *Abwehr*, as well. *Der Spiegel*'s offices had been ransacked for incriminating documents without success, therefore, shouted the enraged Chancellor, General Gehlen must have given them advance warning to destroy the evidence. However, the Minister of Justice sensibly refused to make the arrest without more to go on than Dr Adenauer's inflamed imagination.

Monopoly in Europe

When Adenauer, whose old man's ego was by now completely out of control, made a speech in Parliament branding *Der Spiegel*'s publisher and editorial staffs as traitors without troubling himself to await the result of their trial there were strong protests from Deputies, and students of eleven universities took to the streets with banners proclaiming, 'Strike at *Der Spiegel* and you strike at democracy.' So strong, indeed, was the public reaction that despite Adenauer's objections the police were compelled to vacate *Der Spiegel*'s offices and release all the arrested men pending trial. It was a trial that never took place. After the most desperate attempts to make the charges stick the Security authorities had to confess to the Supreme Court that they had no case. The proceedings were dropped.

Several things flowed from this affair. The Minister of Justice was forced to resign and Chancellor Adenauer was compelled to give a definite date for his own retirement before he could obtain support from a reconstructed Government. New and more liberal press laws were adopted by nearly all the *Länder* of the West German Republic, the rights of arrested persons under the Federal Law were extended and the treason laws were reviewed. As for *Der Spiegel* itself, it acquired a place in the sentiments of German progressive and student groups that vastly extended its already substantial influence and greatly strengthened its investigatory role in German life.

In the past *Der Spiegel* has been one of the Springer Group's most dedicated opponents. However, economic needs make strange bedfellows and to the dismay of many of his supporters Rudolph Augstein signed in mid 1967 a contract for the printing of *Der Spiegel* on the ultra-modern printing presses of Springer's new publishing centre. It is a business arrangement only and does not, of course, give Springer any editorial influence in *Der Spiegel*. But the more suspicious see in it the beginning of a truce between the two and claim that already *Der Spiegel* has become more establishment minded. Indeed the paper has lately found itself in the unusual position of being criticised instead of praised by the student organisations that were formerly among its most fervent supporters. Even those less apt than students commonly are to sniff betrayal in the air fear that some of *Der Spiegel*'s bite may go.

If this should prove to be the case—and there is no firm evidence of it yet—German press power will be in danger of becoming even more monolithic than it already is. Variety still exists in the regional press. But there, as in the United States, monopoly is now moving in. There have been more than a hundred mergers in the past ten years. If Axel Springer is right in his much publicised calculation that it will soon be impossible for any city with a population below half a million to support competing newspapers, there will be many more. There are some eighty-five local dailies with circulations of 5,000 or less and it is difficult to see how most of these, or indeed a good many in the middle group with circulations up to 100,000, can hope to survive in a situation where local consumer advertising on the American scale is not to hand. Neither Springer nor anyone else is likely wholly to supplant the powerful local press of Essen, Dortmund, Düsseldorf, Cologne and other great cities and there are plenty of middle range newspapers with well entrenched civic loyalties to rely on. But some changes in the traditional regional pattern of the German press are already taking place and any change is likely to be to Springer's advantage.

As in Britain, falling advertising revenues due to the competition of television and to economic recession are making the strong relatively stronger and the weak weaker. Few outside the Springer group have the financial resources to meet the costs of re-equipment even of a conventional kind, fewer still to face the capital investment involved in a switch to modern printing methods of the sort Springer is using in his new publishing centre. No other post-war German newspaper publisher has shown evidence of Springer's business genius, none except him has shown any interest in developing a mass market. He is a new phenomenon in the German press, a Northcliffe with the Northcliffe publishing flair but also something of the Northcliffe messianic attitude half a century out of date and he is immune from a boardroom revolt of the kind that toppled King because he is an absolute owner. His prudent decision to divest himself of some of his magazines in no way diminished his grasp on the daily press. However, it did indicate awareness of his vulnerability to public criticism and suggests that he may feel it wise to abandon his plans for extending further into the provinces.

There has been no comparable concentration of press ownership elsewhere in Europe. Traditional citadels of press influence like the *Neue Zürcher Zeitung* in Zurich, *Dagens Nyheter* in Stockholm (exceeded now in circulation but not in reputation by the tabloid *Expressen*), *Berlingske Tidende* in Copenhagen and *Aftenposten* in Oslo still hold their place and life still goes on much as it used to do. But the trend to fewer newspapers is common in most countries. It has gone farthest in France where the traditionally strong regional press fell in numbers by twenty-five per cent between 1958 and 1967, despite an overall increase in regional newspaper readership as compared with that of Paris dailies.

France has so far escaped a Springer but the trend to large multi-interest units found in Britain in the Thomson Organisation and the International Publishing Corporation can plainly be seen in the Hachette group. This controls *France-Soir*, France's largest selling daily with a circulation of a million plus, the smaller *Paris-Presse* and a string of some thirty other publications, including *France-Dimanche* with a weekly circulation of over 1,000,000, the influential *Journal du Dimanche*, particularly strong on economic affairs, *Réalités*, which covers the cultural scene and *Elle*, a successful woman's paper. It has a complex of other interests, including a monopoly of newspaper distribution through the *Nouvelles Messageries de la Presse Parisienne* and the railway station news-stands. Nor is it alone in its concentration of press power. Jean Prouvost, the textile manufacturer who founded *Paris-Soir* before the war, controls *Paris-Match*, Europe's biggest and best picture weekly, *Marie-Claire* and *Télésept Jours* and owns, with Ferdinand Beghin, a sugar and paper industrialist, ninety-seven per cent of the shares of the most influential of conservative Paris morning papers, *Le Figaro*. Emilien Amaury, the owner of *Le Parisien Libéré* which has a mass circulation second only to *France-Soir*, owns also two provincial dailies and a leading sports daily, *L'Equipe*, four weeklies and two magazines. Cino del Duca, who owns a mass appeal daily, *Paris-Tour*, also controls most of what is called the sweetheart press and several successful general magazines. Marcel Boussac has *L'Aurore*, *Paris-Turf* and *Sports-Complet* as well as big publishing interests.

Yet although in France as elsewhere the movement towards greater press trustification has gone some distance along the British, American and German roads and there has been a sharp trend to fewer newspapers, the most significant development in many ways has been a counter-reaction to all this in the form of an increasing emphasis both on the importance of the professional element in the press and on its public responsiblity. Much of the credit for this belongs to *Le Monde* which is by any standard one of the most remarkable newspapers in the world. But it has also spread elsewhere, erupting often in the most unlikely places. It has done so, moreover, in circumstances which according to British and American press precepts are entirely antagonistic to independence.

French newspapers are the most heavily state subsidised in the world outside Communist countries. According to the traditional principles of freedom of the press they ought, as a result, to be, at the best, so enervated and, at the worst, so cowed by this fact as to be incapable of fully serving the public interest. In total the French press receives more than £100,000,000 a year in state subsidies, approximately half its total revenue. These subsidies come to it in the form of subsidised newsprint, subsidised printing ink, subsidised rail freight charges, subsidised postal and telephone rates and other similar concessions.

In Britain and the United States, in Canada, Australia and in most other parts of the world where independent newspapers have been long established it is held that however dire the economic position of the press it must not take a penny from the State because to do so is to put its freedom in jeopardy. This has not happened in France. Before the war the French press was the most corrupt and the most tied in the world. Today it is among the most responsible and independent. French television is the creature of the government. It has been wholly dominated for more than a decade by the requirement to report only what the government of the day agrees it should and to make no comment that will embarrass the administration. For twenty years, with or without de Gaulle, it has been entirely a tool of the government of the day in its public service broadcasting. Not so the subsidised press which has retained complete freedom to bite the hand that feeds it and has often done so. Some ninety per cent of newspapers both in Paris and the provinces were, for example, openly anti-Gaullist well before the student and workers' protests of mid-1968.

One reason for this independence from government influence despite large subsidies would seem to be that when all newspapers are subsidised as of right, as French newspapers have been since the Liberation when this seemed the only means of restoring a press shattered and demoralised by Nazi occupation, none is vulnerable. The element of political blackmail that exists where individual newspapers are subsidised, either by governments or by other powerful political or industrial interests, disappears. Certainly despite the copy book maxims and in spite also of the fact that Clause 16 of the constitution of the Fifth Republic gives the head of state the right to take any action he feels necessary regarding the press, including suspension, today's subsidised press is a good deal more independent than the French press has ever been previously. It is far more so than it was before the war when economic weakness made most French papers vulnerable to pressure.

Not only has the French press become politically independent, it has also, despite the trend to trustification already noted, become more conscious of the need for editorial independence from commercial pressure and in several instances remarkably successful in establishing the paramountcy of the editor. For this a good deal of the credit must, as already stated, go to *Le Monde* for the example it has set. It has demonstrated in a fashion worthy of note elsewhere the rewards of a strict regard for editorial integrity.

Le Monde owes its existence to de Gaulle—a fact that must at times have had a peculiarly bitter taste for the General, for it has never been sparing in its criticism of him. It was born of his wish at the end of the war to restore the tarnished reputation of even the best of the French press by establishing a newspaper which would embody the traditions of the pre-war *Le Temps* without that paper's uncomfortable financial dependence on French heavy industry. *Le Temps*'s plant was available and he offered Hubert Beuve-Méry, formerly a distinguished member of *Le Temps*'s foreign staff who had resigned in disgust at its support for the Munich agreement, the use of this plant to produce a new paper. *Le Monde* was born in December 1944, three months after the liberation of Paris, with a minute share capital, initially obtained from a group of respected but politically uncommitted public men, and an editorial staff of twenty-six, all of whom like Beuve-Méry himself were convinced of the importance of responsible journalism to the future of France and prepared to work for negligible financial reward to achieve it. De Gaulle had conceived of *Le*

Monde as a mouthpiece for his policies and his ally in the restoration of the glory of France. In choosing Beuve-Méry, however, he caught a tiger by the tail. Beuve-Méry admired de Gaulle, but he had no intention of being anyone's mouthpiece. From the beginning he followed his own wholly independent line. In recent years this has brought him increasingly in opposition to de Gaulle, especially so in defence of what he considers to be the intellectual and spiritual values most necessary to the dignity of man—high among them freedom of expression.

In most countries even the most serious quality newspapers have been compelled to consider their appearance and make some concessions in make-up to popular taste. *Le Monde* has refused to do so. Its print is tiny and unattractive. It uses no pictures. It is written impeccably—but only for those willing to read. Its editorial staff has now risen to ninety and it has eight foreign correspondents carefully chosen and sited, but it operates on a budget any comparable English or American newspaper would regard as laughable. And although these days it is offered plenty of advertising it restricts it to a level which will involve no danger of the paper coming to depend on it too greatly economically. It prefers the support of readers to the support of advertisers.

What it holds out to its readers is the intelligent examination of serious affairs and the firm promise of independence and integrity in dealing with them. Against every expectation by which most modern journalism steers its course it has been rewarded not only with immense prestige but with a circulation that has risen continuously and consistently. It went up by seventy-five per cent between 1957 and 1968 to 350,000, a substantial figure anywhere for a quality newspaper as austere as *Le Monde*, and especially so in France where the total number of newspaper readers is less than half what it is in Britain with a somewhat similar population. During the disturbances of 1968 its circulation rose to over 800,000 because readers felt it was one paper on whose objectivity and integrity they could absolutely rely and subsequently settled at over 600,000—a figure the London *Times* is spending millions to try to attain. What is perhaps even more significant is that it has a higher proportion of youthful readers than any French newspaper and is one of the very few that could economically survive even if the newsprint and other subsidies were withdrawn.

There have been several governmental threats to suspend it when its intellectual integrity has proved inconvenient politically. When it insisted on publishing the report of a commision of inquiry into allegations of torture in Algeria which the government would have preferred to suppress its offices were ringed by police awaiting the order to move in and take over. The order did not come. The government's nerve broke before Beuve-Méry's did and the report was issued officially. Moreover, it is significant that when in 1951 Beuve-Méry was faced with an ultimatum from two of his directors and felt compelled to resign on an issue of policy, the entire editorial staff not only refused to continue with the paper unless the ultimatum was withdrawn and he was restored to full authority, but in a short sharp engagement compelled the board to agree that in future twenty-eight per cent of the share capital of the paper should be vested in the editorial staff, so that never again should one or two major shareholders be in a position to infringe the independence of the editor. Since then the predominance of the editor has been both complete and accepted.

The *Le Monde* example, and particularly its staff's insistence on their superior right to say who should edit a paper which owed so much to their energy and talents has since been copied elsewhere. In 1965 Pierre Brisson, Editor of the *Le Figaro*, died. As the largest shareholder Jean Prouvost assumed the right to appoint his successor. The editorial staff rejected his choice and compelled him instead to accept an editor of their choosing in whom they had confidence. They have since secured a general voice in management. Nor has *Le Figaro*'s staff been alone in so doing. When the Editor of France's largest provincial paper, *Ouest-France*, a former M.R.P. deputy and substantial shareholder in the paper, resigned he sought to put his two sons in editorial control along with the son of the paper's original founder. The staff refused to accept them. They insisted instead on the appointment as Editor-in-Chief of a journalist of their own choosing whose competence and integrity they knew. They won their fight, plus an allocation of shares to the staff and a voice in management. A similar demand for a voice in management by editorial staffs has been made on several other French newspapers, among them the sports daily *L'Equipe* and *La Croix*, the principal Catholic daily, where the staff has secured the establishment of a publishing committee consisting of two representatives of management, two senior editors, and four representatives of the general editorial staff.

One way and another there has thus been a remarkable break with the past in the French press: the past of Nazi occupation, which left France almost denuded of daily papers it could trust, of course, but also with the pre-war past when the French press was commonly regarded as the most corrupt in Europe and, with the exception of a few outstanding individuals like Pertinax and Madame Tabouis, most journalists were badly paid, ill considered and expected to do whatever their paymasters told them. The French press is still much less of an information press and more of an opinion press than the British or American, as is indeed the Continental press generally, but it is far less politically committed than it once was. And despite some trustification and the emergence of four major press groups centring respectively around *France-Soir*, *Le Figaro*, *L'Aurore* and *Le Parisien Libéré* (balanced in part by the growing strength and readership of provincial newspapers) and despite, also, a degree of official subsidisation which in Britain and the United States would be regarded as an intolerable threat to press freedom, the most remarkable feature in this new situation is the extent of editorial independence from either commercial or political pressures and the strong and increasing emphasis on the status of the professional element in the press. This is not, perhaps, exactly what de Gaulle was looking for as a contribution to the glory of France when he asked a restored press to reflect his ambitions after Liberation, but it is a significant one nevertheless.

There has been no such radical change in Italy. On the contrary, not only has the number of daily newspapers fallen sharply—twenty-one disappeared between 1955 and 1962—but two-thirds of those of any size, meaning in Italy with a circulation above 100,000 are now controlled by large industrial companies, including in the case of *Il Giorno* of Milan, Italy's nearest approximation to a *Daily Express*, E.N.I. the State oil trust. Most of the rest, among them a substantial Communist press led by *L'Unità* of Rome, are the official or unofficial organs of political parties, like *Il Popolo*, the Christian Democrat paper in Rome, and the Left Socialist journal, *Avanti*, in Milan, or of the Catholic Church. Only two Italian dailies, apart from *L'Osservatore Romano*, the official

Monopoly in Europe

Vatican daily, have much claim to national or international influence: *La Stampa* of Turin, owned by the Fiat group but given a large degree of independence for some twenty years under the editorship of one of the most outstanding of Italian journalists, Dr Giulia De Benedetti, and *Corriere della Sera* of Milan, with the largest circulation of any Italian newspaper, just over 400,000 and better foreign coverage than most, although *Il Tempo* of Rome speaks for the far right over an area much wider than Rome itself. South of Rome illiteracy and poverty still effectively rule out much newspaper circulation or influence.

Italy as a whole, indeed, remains not much of a newspaper reading country. Less than half the men over sixteen and less than a quarter of the women read a daily newspaper. It is the magazine press and particularly the women's magazines, bought, according to a recent survey, by well over 50 per cent of Italian homes, and the illustrated magazines, chief among them *Oggi*, that make the real journalistic impact. *Oggi*'s success story is comparable to that of *Der Spiegel* in Germany, although of a different character.

Born less than three months after the end of the war its first leading article, 'The Dead Want To Die', was an appeal to forget the past and start rebuilding national unity. It has had a success quite unequalled in Italian press history. Within three years of its foundation it had reached a circulation of 400,000—and that at a time and in a society where a readership of 150,000 was regarded as remarkable. By the early 1950s this had been increased to 700,000 and by 1960 to 1,000,000. It has stayed around that level despite a general fall in both newspaper and magazine circulation and despite, also, the rise of more sensational magazines with much more lurid disclosures to make.

Oggi's ambition from the beginning has been to be a magazine of the Italian bourgeois. It is against scandal, pornography and Communism, but for exclusive revelations of a kind to excite but not disturb its middle class readers. Over the years it has had a good many of them, beginning with an interview with the much hunted but never apprehended Sicilian bandit, Salvatore Giuliano, which led to a court action against it by the Minister of the Interior for 'supporting an outlaw'. It went on from this to the exclusive news that Pope Pius XII had received a miraculous vision of Jesus Christ during a brief illness, and from that to Mussolini's widow's own story, the memoirs of Porfirio Rubirosa and a 'secret' biography of Jacqueline Kennedy. No doubt its remarkable success reflects as much as does the regionalism of the daily press or the scarcity of newspapers south of Rome the nature of Italian society beneath the iridescent bubbles of its international reputation in film and fashion.

Similarly the remarkable post-war development of the Japanese press at the other side of the world reflects both in technological achievement and in content the nature of its very different society. With a total of 157 daily newspapers with a combined circulation of over 45,000,000 and a newspaper readership of just on 440 copies per thousand population, second only to Britain which has 523 and way ahead of the United States with 314, Japan has gone further than any country in the world in developing new printing and publishing techniques. In some ways, indeed, its press may be said to represent the culmination of many of the tendencies at work in the press of the West: the development of large technologically advanced units but also the attempt to satisfy all tastes in one package by a bland smoothing down of economic and intellectual conflicts and an insistence on the newspaper's role as a universal compendium.

This was not so in the immediate post-war period. Then, in reaction against the subservience to the pre-war military clique and in a frenzy of introspection following defeat, the Japanese press seemed for a time determined, in spite of some censorship by the MacArthur regime, to return to the radical vigour that had distinguished it from 1890 until the late 1920s. It harried a succession of weak conservative governments, championed democracy at all levels, attacked militarism and nationalism and supported, and to some extent incited, the street demonstrations that followed the ratification of the United States Security Treaty by the Diet— only to back down hurriedly when violence temporarily seemed to be taking over. In response to this violence a joint statement came from all the leading newspapers that freedom of comment had gone too far and that henceforth moderation would be the rule. Since then the daily press has largely retreated into caution and inoffensiveness—produced with remarkable efficiency and a high gloss.

This change of character cannot, however, be put down entirely to a sudden rush of political responsiblity to the head. It has other roots of much interest to the press in other countries—chief among them the achievement of, and dependence on, an immense amorphous readership no section of which must be offended lest the careful balance of appeal on which circulation and revenue depend should be upset. Japanese newspapers have reached the ideal of the well stocked department store with something on its shelves to satisfy all tastes enunciated by Hippolyte de Villesmessant of *Le Figaro* nearly a century and a quarter ago to a degree undreamed of by its enunciator.

Three national newspapers, *Asahi Shimbun*, *Yomiuri Shimbun* and *Mainichi Shimbun*, each have morning editions with circulations between four and five millions, swollen by another two to three millions by afternoon editions sold to subscribers as part of a 'set'. They cover the country by the use of high speed wireless photo-facsimile combined with offset printing to enable simultaneous publication in five major centres, including cities as wide apart as Tokyo and Osaka. In this, as also in the use of colour printing, they are far ahead of the rest of the world. They have, moreover, completely overcome the specific handicap formerly imposed by the Japanese ideographic script which forced newspapers to use handsetting. In 1959 ideographic tele-typesetting, based on a Chinese system perfected in Taiwan in 1958 but never used there because of cost, was developed and used in conjunction with automatic Monotype machines.

Technologically the present Japanese press reflects in high degree the exceptional technical talent of the Japanese people. Facsimile transmission of whole pages from a central point combined with web-offset printing to permit simultaneous publication in widely separated centres, pioneered by *Yomiuri Shimbun* and later developed by all the major Japanese national dailies, has since been copied in Britain by the International Publishing Corporation for the Belfast editions of the *Daily Mirror* and *Sunday Mirror* and in Australia by the Robert Murdoch group in its project for the first all Australian national daily paper, *The Australian*, which will ultimately, it is hoped, be published simultaneously in every State.

But although the Japanese press has led the world technologically and achieved huge circulation by skilful distribution and marketing something has gone out of journalism in the process.

Thus *Asahi Shimbun*, the circulation leader which was founded some ninety years ago to 'teach social justice' and was for years an advocate of radical policies and an opponent of the military caste, and after the war the strongest opponent, also, of governments which were thought to be too subservient to America, has now become a superb amalgam of news and features for all tastes but with little editorial bite and a cautious approach to political issues: a paper dedicated, it would seem to the proposition that to succeed it is necessary to be inoffensive. It likes to describe its readership as a 'mass elite', but it is, in fact, as near as possible a cross-section of Japanese society brought together by a great variety of news and features specifically tailored to attract differing tastes and interests: serious news and interpretation for politicians, businessmen and members of the professions; special features for industrial and rural workers; home pages for housewives; a serialised novel for the romantically inclined, something, in fact, for everyone, whether they want the erudite or the popular. It is a great department store of a newspaper which offers what otherwise could only be found in several newspapers and avoids only the sensational and the controversial. *Asahi* has news bureaus in fourteen foreign cities, an editorial staff of over 2,000 and a total staff of nearly 8,000. Of these 500 sleep on the premises in dormitories every night to be ready for any emergency. It has a long waiting list of university graduates applying for jobs: they are sifted by a stiff house entrance examination which on average only one in eighty passes. Some fifty-four per cent of its revenue comes from advertising, it charges the equivalent of around £12,000 for a full page in all morning editions, and it earns about £4,000,000 a year altogether, although when its high costs, which include the upkeep of a fleet of planes and helicopters for news gathering and newspaper distribution, are taken into account this leaves only a fairly modest profit on the newspaper itself. Like each of the other national newspapers—all of which follow much the same policy of offering something for everybody and annoying nobody—it is supported by a maze of other commercial and industrial interests, including a general store, a theatre and an hotel and large television holdings. Its closest rival, *Yomiuri Shimbun*, even owns a baseball team as well as being a major operator in real estate.

The Japanese press, in fact, exemplifies and underlines—as

does, also, much of the rest of Japanese industry—what might seem to be the logical conclusion of trends generally at work in the urbanised, industrialised world. Those who own and operate this press are, in the main, men more interested in it as business than as an editorial force: Lord Thomson and Mr Newhouse would be completely at home with them. They provide an admirable informational public service, fulfilling to a high degree Lord Thomson's somewhat chilly dictum that newspapers are common carriers and should be operated like public utilities, but they leave out much that earlier newspapers, including those of Japan itself, once thought vital to good journalism and the public interest. And despite the queues of university graduates clamouring for admission to the practice of journalism, and the technical excellence of much journalism training in Japan, there is not as yet much sign of that insistence on the importance of the professional element in the press as a counter balance to the necessarily powerful commercial element in the higher direction of newspaper enterprises which has been so striking a feature in post-war France and to some extent, also, although in a different manner, in Britain. One must hope that this will come. Meanwhile, industrially and technologically the Japanese press has outpaced most of its Western models.

CHAPTER ELEVEN

The Press
in the New Nations

It is simple enough to trace the course of the press in developed political democracies; remarkable how consistent the pattern is despite some natural differences from country to country. In the still developing countries it is a different matter. For many of them this pattern has no relevance or, in so far as it has, it is for the future.

Every stage of society, observed Wilbur Schramm in his UNESCO study, *Mass Media and National Development*, has its appropriate stage of communication. The sophisticated communications systems of a sophisticated society are useless in an unsophisticated one. Nor could they exist, for they depend upon a level of industrial and educational development that itself does not exist. Seeking an adequate definition of developed and undeveloped countries Schramm decided that the only distinction universally applicable was that between states which had experienced the Industrial Revolution, or their version of it, and those that had either not experienced this revolution at all or had done so only in a limited way or only in limited sections of their population. He also pointed out that if it were possible to gather all the peoples of earth together and split them into two groups those from undeveloped countries with an average per-capita income of $300 of less per annum on one side, those from developed countries with average per capita incomes per annum above this on the other, then even with an income level as low as this as the determinant those on the undeveloped side of the line would be twice those on the developed side. They would be drawn from the whole of Africa except for the Union of South Africa, all South Asia except Singapore, all East Asia except Japan, all Central Asia except Soviet Asia, a large part of Latin America, most of the Middle East and, in Europe, Albania, Bulgaria, Portugal and Yugoslavia. There are, of course, pockets of development in all the undeveloped areas. The industrial revolution has its footholds in most: in India, for example, it has some substantial ones. The $300 is an average. A minority—considerable in some, tiny in others—is well above it in all undeveloped countries; in some cases, where extreme poverty looks across at extreme wealth, enormously so. But the majority are below and very many far below even this wretched figure.

For the majority of this vast constituency of two-thirds of the world's population, the press as a mature medium of communication has no meaning. Nor has freedom of the press. This, however, is unlikely long to remain so. For the first time in world history this vast constituency of the under-privileged is on the move; especially so in the ex-colonial territories. All over Africa and Asia what were undeveloped colonial societies have become independent developing ones. They are in no mood to remain underprivileged. They are in a hurry, or at least the educated and politically active among them, the leaders, are. Their hurry is understandable for they have to try to do in a few decades what elsewhere has taken centuries.

This makes the role of the press of vast importance and also subject to the prospect of rapid transformation. The nature of communications in a society depends on the general level of development it has reached. But there is a powerful interaction between the two. Just as developments in society affect communications so new developments in communications have an effect both on the capacity of a society to develop and on the course its development will take.

In this situation of rapid movement in which the struggle of the have-nots to become haves has broken out of its old national contexts into an international one, the press may take one of two courses. It may seek to learn from the press of the West from whose traditions it often borrowed heavily in colonial times— sometimes with the assent and under the guidance of the colonial power, sometimes in revolt against it, turning its own weapons against it—and try to compress a Western press experience of nearly two centuries into a matter of a few years, leaping over some stages of development, telescoping others. Or it may turn to another model, the model of the Communist press as the servant and instrument of government and seek to copy that.

The strength of the appeal of the Communist example or some modification of it should not be underestimated. To governments in a hurry seeking to merge differing groups and interests into one nation, conscious that the press as an instrument of criticism can undermine their authority and satisfied, as it is in the nature of popular leaders to be, that they themselves are the true and natural bearers of the torch of national revolution, it has obvious attractions. This may well be so whether they themselves are Marxists or not: indeed, it may be just as strong if they regard themselves rather as the inheritors of colonial authority as if they think of themselves as revolutionary socialists. It is sometimes forgotten that although colonialism may sometimes have done a certain amount to improve the material conditions of its subject people and to bring order and law among them, and although its administrators on the spot may sometimes, if they were honest and dedicated men as they often were, have done even more, yet there is one thing it could not teach its wards: democracy—for democracy is contrary to colonial rule itself. Even when democratic institutions were promoted and self-government at some levels encouraged, the ultimate freedom was—and could not help but be —withheld. In the last resort it was in the hands of the Governor not the people that power resided.

In British Colonies the Governor sat, of course, as representative of the Crown. But of the Crown long before it had become a constitutional monarchy. The Governor was the local embodiment of the monarch, but of a monarch with an absolute authority —even if only in the last resort of veto—long since discarded at home. It is scarcely surprising that those who acquired their practical knowledge in such a situation should sometimes take to themselves a similar role and see themselves as the embodiment of an equal authority. You cannot insist for generations that even in the most liberal colonial systems democratic authority stops where the Governor sits and be surprised if the President of an ex-colonial territory sometimes decides that the same goes for him.

The built-in political obstacles to a wholly free press are thus considerable even apart from the absence in most cases of the economic and social conditions necessary to its sophisticated development. To those struggling to overcome the obstacles of poverty and illiteracy and conscious, as their colonial past can scarcely have avoided making them, of the interests standing in their way and of the threat of rivals if they should seem to be weak, it is natural that the investigatory and critical functions of a free press should sometimes seem a luxury neither they nor their countries can afford. After all, the rulers of most of the older powers resisted them as long as they could.

On the other hand the informational function of the press has an obvious importance in new societies which need to change as swiftly but also as painlessly as they can and to do so must secure the active participation of many who will be required to abandon traditional habits and modes of thinking if modernisation is to be possible. For this populations must be fed with information, both general and technical, either directly or through local leaders, on a scale far greater than ever before in a form they can understand and to which they will respond with personal or communal action.

It is exactly this that the Communist press is designed to do and it is its ability in this respect that sometimes makes it seem attractive as a model to those with similar problems. In the press systems of Soviet Russia and China developing nations can find methods ideally suited to many of their needs—once they accept the premise that information is necessary but criticism is dangerous and free speech to be abhorred. In both countries the press is still the primary agent of information: an agent wholly committed to the interests of State and Party and all embracing in its penetration of every level of population. In addition to *Pravda* with a daily circulation of 7,500,000 and *Izvestia* with one of 7,700,000 (both made possible by multiple publication in several centres with the help of page matrices delivered by air) Moscow has a dozen other dailies and some 450 regional morning and evening papers are published in twenty-eight different languages in the autonomous Republics and Regions. There are also nearly

7,000 weekly, twice weekly or tri-weekly newspape rsin some fifty-eight different languages ranging from substantial printed publications with circulations of 800,000 or more to wall newspapers and roneo-typed factory sheets. More than sixty reasonably substantial new dailies have been established in the last fifteen years or so and total newspaper circulation has more than doubled in the same period. It is now well over 70,000,000. Add to these some 400 periodicals, including such giants as the weekly *Rabotnitsa* (The Working Woman) with a circulation of over 10,000,000, according to returns published in early 1968, *Zdorov'e* (a popular health journal) with over 8,000,000, *Krestyanka* (The Peasant Woman) with 5,500,000, *Vesyolye Kartinki*, a humorous picture magazine with 5,000,000, the famous satirical weekly *Krokodil* with 4,600,000 and *Nauki i Zhizn'* (Science and Life) which had a circulation of only 150,000 a dozen years ago but has now a current one of 3,600,000 and it will be seen that the Soviet press is a very flourishing affair indeed.

All newspapers and most magazines from the largest to the smallest serve in some measure a dual function under the direction of the agitation and propaganda departments of the various party organs. They explain government and party policy at every level but also provide a channel by which public opinion can make itself felt—on many practical matters at least—by means of contributions from factory and village correspondents and the letters of readers. The volume of these letters can be seen by one instance quoted by a UNESCO publication on world communications where a government report on the reorganisation of machine and tractor stations brought in more than 126,000 letters to newspapers of which 102,941 were published.

Similarly in mainland China the press remains the principal medium of communication, despite an illiteracy rate of over fifty per cent. The circulation figures of the 400 or so daily newspapers, the more than 1,180 other newspapers and the close on 2,000 periodicals does not approach that of the U.S.S.R. The *People's Daily*, as the main national press voice—challenged as such, however, by the *Liberation Army Daily* during the 1967–68 purges—is the apex of a pyramid. This pyramid broadens down to cover every level of Chinese life through dailies in the provincial capitals and districts to weekly or bi-weekly journals in the smaller town and rural areas and wall newspapers in city streets and rural hamlets. All fit into a pattern laid down and closely supervised by the Ministry of Information and all are serviced by that Ministry's news organisation, the *New China News Agency* (N.C.N.A.) which with more than 1,500 sub-offices and well over 70,000 part-time correspondents is no less pervasive in its influence than *Tass* is in the U.S.S.R. Every editor, even those who are no more than part-time editors of wall newspapers, has a direct link with the N.C.N.A. It sends them news and publishing instructions by radio and every editor of a wall newspaper has orders to see to it that not only is the newspaper posted where it can have maximum attention but that it is also read to illiterates. Like the Soviet press, the Chinese press goes to great trouble to encourage readers' letters. Criticisms of the workings of Communist administration at local level is sanctioned and encouraged, only ideology is sacrosanct. This all-pervasive press system can get out of hand as it did, presumably, at the time of the Red Guards who made a good deal of use of wall newspapers, but on the whole it seems to offer an efficient and practical bridge between government and governed and it is not surprising that the leaders of some of the new developing countries in Africa and Asia have seen in a comparable—even if much less well organised—press pattern the answer to their problems.

This, however, is only true of some. Obviously no such monolithic control of the press exists, could exist, or has ever been vaguely thought of in India with its 525 daily newspapers, fifty-six of them English language, 148 Hindi and the rest in Urdu, Bengali, Tamil, Marathi and Gujerati, and its 7,500 or so weeklies and periodicals, although the correct balance between private and public ownership of the press has been much debated. A compromise of sorts was attempted in 1965 with the setting up of a statutory Press Council with terms of reference drawn very largely from those of the British Press Council but objections by the Indian Federation of Working Journalists to Council membership as over-weighted in the proprietorial and governmental interest has so far robbed it of an effective role.

With great papers like the *Hindu* in Madras, the *Statesman* and the *Amrita Bazar Patrika* in Calcutta, and the *Times of India* and the more popularly written *Indian Express* in Bombay (all English language publications) at one end of the scale and a growing number of smaller, mainly Indian language, papers at the other, the Indian daily press, which increased its circulation by twenty-two per cent between 1960 and 1965 and is still rising, will, no doubt, change and develop a good deal in the future as illiteracy is gradually conquered. But unless the whole democratic complexion of Indian government changes, there is little likelihood of it ceasing to be either independent or extremely varied in character.

Across the frontier in Pakistan, however, a Press and Publications Ordinance, although temporarily suspended in favour of a voluntary Court of Honour appointed by newspaper editors, remains as a considerable potential threat to press freedom. Several editors have been arrested—among them the first secretary of the Court of Honour!

In Ceylon more than a dozen attempts to nationalise the press and bring it completely under governmental control were made by the Government of Mrs Bandaranaike, in a succession of parliamentary bills between August 1960 and December 1964. These moves were initially inspired by the conviction, for which there had been some justification in the attitude of newspapers during the election, that the trustification of the Ceylon press under two major newspaper chains, one with three dailies and five weeklies, the other with five dailies and three weeklies, had produced a situation in which the new government, bitterly opposed by both, could expect nothing but denigration and misrepresentation from the press. Later, however, they were a major part of the attempt to establish a one-party Marxist state, as Marxist groups moved closer and closer to the centre of power in the Bandaranaike Government. All these successive attempts to nationalise the Ceylon press failed. They did so, in part at any rate, because the Ceylon press succeeded in mobilising outside support through the International Press Institute, the Commonwealth Press Union and the International Federation of Journalists and thus made the issue into an international *cause célèbre* which stirred Ceylonese public opinion, and in part because the Ceylon newspapers themselves, aware of their vulnerable position, went to much greater pains than formerly to report political developments impartially and gave full expression to the government point of view, thus undermining the Government's case for control. Finally in December 1964 the Bandaranaike Government after being forced to go to the country was defeated in a General Election in which freedom of the press was one of the main issues.

Elsewhere in the undeveloped countries of Asia the press is for the most part under strong governmental control, although this tends to vary in stringency according to current political conditions. In Burma an official Policy Direction Board directs newspapers' policies. The *Daily Guardian*, the largest English language newspaper, has been taken over by the Government. Many journalists languish in prison without trial. In Korea, after a period of licensing under Syngman Rhee and of tight control following the military revolution, the press is now relatively free subject to its adherence to a Press Code of Ethics. In Thailand martial law is supported by severe restraints on the press although here and there a certain spirit of independence manages to break through. Indonesian newspapermen were forced by Sukarno to sign a declaration that 'our publication is duty bound to support and defend the Political Manifesto of the Republic of Indonesia in its entirety', thus implementing his instructions to the Indonesian Journalists' Association: 'In a revolution there should be no press freedom. Only a press supporting the revolution should be allowed to exist; those of the press hostile to the revolution must be eliminated.' Under the new Indonesian regime, however, it is a little more free—although it is still only allowed to operate under licence.

Only in Malaysia and Singapore and in the Philippines is there, apart from India, a free press in the vast and troubled Asiatic world. For the most part, however, its position is closer to that of eighteenth century Britain or Colonial America than to that of China, the U.S.S.R. or other Communist countries. It is not, as there, integrated into the political structure, a carefully controlled but also highly valued instrument of public information, persuasion and education. Instead it exists for the most part on sufferance, as does also most of the press of the Middle East and of Turkey, seizing, guerrilla fashion, whatever freedom it can but liable always to censorship, suppression, imprisonment for its editors and attempted intimidation by the withholding of government advertisements or in other ways. In so far as the activities of the Communist press are duplicated at all in most of these countries, they are performed by officially controlled radio services, not by newspapers.

The Communist conception of the role of the press as an integrated part of government has spread a good deal further in Africa, a continent where freedom of the press exists precariously even in European dominated countries such as the Union of South Africa and Rhodesia. Even before U.D.I. the Smith Government banned the Thomson-owned *Daily News* of Salisbury under the Law and Order (Maintenance) Act because it supported the aims of African nationalism. (It must, incidentally, be recorded to the credit of Lord Thomson that although the closure of his paper cost him a good deal of money he remained loyal to its Editor and has since appointed him Editor of one of his new evening papers in Luton—where fortunately no similiar perils exist.)

In Egypt which has the oldest press in Africa with a long tradition of lively political comment behind it, the press was in effect nationalised in 1960. Since then the ownership of all newspapers has been vested in the Arab Socialist Union, the country's single political party, and their administration placed in the hands of a number of large publishing organisations each governed by a council of seven, three nominated by the Socialist Arab Union and four, including the Chief Editor, appointed by the President of the Republic, from the staff. They are required to keep within the framework of the National Charter, to assist literacy campaigns and to advance public knowledge of government policies, but within the framework of the charter, which excludes any criticism of the aims of the revolution, have a good deal of day to day independence.

The three major national dailies, *Al Ahram* which in 1968 became one of the first national newspapers in the world to be produced by computer, *Al Akhbar* and *Al Gomhouriyah*, exercise independence, such as it is, with a good deal of panache—as the first two do. There is, however, no doubt in the minds of their staff or their readers as to its limits. The National Constitution of the Press declares that 'It is not only the right of the Press to criticise, it is the duty of the Press to do so.' But although the importance of the critical function of the press in Egypt, and also in Communist countries, should not be overlooked, it is always directed to the operations of the bureaucracy and never to major policy. Like *Tass* and the *New China News Agency*, the *Middle East News Agency*, which serves many newspapers throughout the Middle East as well as in Egypt itself, is firmly tied to Egyptian government policy. And like the newspapers it is controlled by the Arab Socialist Union.

Nor are the newspapers of the rest of North Africa much freer of government or single party control. Like those of Egypt they are the products of revolutionary situations, in some ways even more obtrusively so than the Egyptian press, which has greater sophistication and a longer professional tradition.

Until independence, the daily press of Algeria, with the exception of *Alger Républicain*, the organ of the Algerian Communist Party and the only popular newspaper voice in the colony, was almost exclusively a settler press. Moreover it was a press dominated by the settler mentality in its most unmoving and reactionary form. The two largest newspapers were *La Dépêche Quotidienne*, controlled by the landowner and financier, Henri Borgeaud, and *L'Echo d'Alger*, owned by Alain Vicomte de Serigny, an intimate of Jacques Soustelle. It could not be expected that such papers would be allowed to continue after independence. Papers of the F.L.N. charged with wide popular educational functions took their place, to be suppressed in their turn when Ben Bella was deposed by the Revolutionary Council of June 1965. The present newspapers with *El Moudjahid* chief among them are specifically designed to 'stimulate the revolutionary spirit' under the guidance of the Party bureau.

In Morocco, Tunis and Libya ruling party control is less direct, but hardly less complete. Although private ownership of newspapers is permitted, those Moroccan newspapers that offend ruling views are liable to be seized and banned. In Libya they are allowed to operate only under licence and are subject to severe press laws and in Tunisia the commercially owned *La Presse*, after some trouble, now sticks to a non-controversial role and leaves politics to the Neo-Destour party-owned *L'Action* founded by President Bourguiba himself in 1934 and its sister Arabic paper, *El Amal*. However, foreign papers, mainly French, are allowed freely in—

a situation no Communist system permits—and an excellently produced photogravure weekly, *Jeune Afrique*, printed in Rome but edited by a former Tunisian Minister of Information critical of some of Bourguiba's policies, is allowed to circulate freely.

Manifestly freedom from colonial rule is too young, the problems of establishing new nations too great, the consciousness of internal challenges to national unity too strong and the economic basis for an independent press still too remote for the principles of press freedom developed over the centuries in the West to be as yet easily assimilated in these new nations of North Africa. This is even more true of the rest of the continent.

The indigenous press had its part in the African anti-colonialist struggle. It provided a stimulant for revolutionary ideas among the politically active and educated and at times an incitement to action. But it was, for the most part, economically too insecure to put down long roots and it was, of course, primarily a press of protest not of news and information. Its voice was that of the pamphlet, not the newspaper. This indigenous press was more active in British Colonies than French. The British Colonies were more politically advanced and their struggle for independence came earlier. This struggle rested, moreover, on greater organised support by local parties than existed in the French colonial empire where political integration with the metropolitan power tended to blur issues of independence until late in the 1950s and to concentrate such nationalist political energy as there was on activity within the French political parties themselves. In most of French West Africa and in almost the whole of Equatorial Africa there was as a consequence little press of any sort prior to independence apart from one chain owned by a French businessman, Charles de Breteuil, who had originally started newspaper publishing in Tangier and Casablanca and whose papers were in any event aimed almost exclusively at a European readership. The French thus left little journalistic tradition behind them and not much in the way of a press structure to build on. There were only three daily newspapers in the whole of French West and Equatorial Africa—all of them owned by de Breteuil—when between 1960 and 1962 a dozen or so new nations were carved out of the old colonialism. In the Belgian Congo things were superficially better. There were nine daily papers before independence. But all of them were

The Press in the New Nations

Belgian owned, all catered only for Europeans, and all opposed independence.

It was otherwise in some of British Colonial Africa. Both Ghana and Nigeria have a press tradition going back more than a century. Moreover, in this tradition indigenous newspapers, African owned and controlled, have a large part even although most of them lived precarious lives and many died young. However, although historically the press background of Ghana and Nigeria was very similar, independence brought a sharp divergence. In Ghana the press is still tightly controlled—only a little less so, indeed, under the present regime than it was under Kwame Nkrumah. So far as the press was concerned, in fact, the only immediate result of the military coup that deposed Nkrumah in 1966 was that a different set of editors went to gaol, including, I remember, six who had had tea with me at the House of Lords during the Commonwealth Conference a few weeks before to complain that the British press did not understand how truly free the Ghanaian press was.

Nkrumah himself had learned the value of newspapers ten years before independence when he founded the *Accra Evening News* as the organ of the C.P.P. (the Convention People's Party). Despite its deficiencies as a daily newspaper—it was hand set, badly printed on a flat press, short in news and dependent for such as it had on C.P.P. members who tended to be more than a little irregular in sending in reports—it showed itself to be invaluable as a weapon in the fight for independence. However, before long strong competition in its struggle for a larger readership came from an unexpected source; a modern daily launched in Accra under the name of the *Daily Graphic* by the Daily Mirror group in London. At this time Cecil King had a great belief in the potentialities of the African market which must, he thought, with increased literacy and the passing of colonialism, become a rapidly expanding one. Also he liked to think he was perhaps helping to build a new sort of Commonwealth and used to say to me that while Beaverbrook talked a lot about the Empire, he was doing something about it. The *Mirror* had already acquired the *Nigerian Daily Times* in Lagos and learned how to appeal to African readers—who are not after all very different from English ones.

The *Daily Graphic* had everything the *Evening News* had not;

modern equipment, a first class distributive organisation, skilled professional journalists, masses of pictures and plenty of capital. For all its political appeal the *Evening News* had no chance against it when it came to circulation. This fact may have influenced Nkrumah when he later decided that privately owned newspapers were intolerable in a 'socialist' country.

When power was won Nkrumah had no hesitation as to the sort of press he wanted. He established a public corporation, the Guinea Press, put more money behind the *Evening News* and turned it into a kind of *Pravda*, to expound C.P.P. doctrines, founded the *Ghanaian Times* to do a job similar to that of *Izvestia* for the government and followed it up with a new Sunday paper, the *Sunday Spectator*. He then bought out the *Mirror* and placed the *Daily Graphic* under the control of trustees with an executive board appointed by the government, banned the only other independently owned paper in the country, the *Ashanti Pioneer* published in Kumasi by a British mining company, and launched *Spark*, an intellectual weekly for the discussion of African problems against a Marxist background. He also established a government controlled news service, the Ghana News Agency.

Much more than any other African ruler Nkrumah thus set out to establish in his one party state a press deliberately planned like the Soviet or Chinese press for the purpose of informing and educating public opinion along lines approved by party and government. Its status and function were set out by him at an all-African journalists conference in Accra in 1963. 'It is,' he declared, 'an integral part of society, with which its purpose is consonance. Just as in the capitalist countries the press represents and carries out the purpose of capitalism, so in revolutionary Africa our revolutionary African press must represent and carry out our revolutionary purpose. . . . To the true African journalist his newspaper is a collective organiser, a collective instrument of mobilisation and a collective educator. . . .' Nkrumah's successors have changed the personnel of the Ghanaian press. So far they have not much altered its role, although the central direction is, perhaps, less positive than it was and newspapers are shorter on photographs of the Head of the State than they used to be— six photographs of Nkrumah in one issue was fairly common in his day.

The Press in the New Nations

Ghana turned to Communism for a model of what the role of the press could and should be. Not so Nigeria. It kept its eyes on the West—to such an extent, indeed, that both the International Publishing Corporation and the Thomson Group (through Thomson International of Canada) were for a time numbered among its major newspaper publishers. The I.P.C. still owns the *Daily Times* which has the biggest daily circulation in the country and the *Sunday Times*, although in consequence of a deliberate policy of Africanisation both are under local Nigerian management and editorial control. Thomson ran the *Daily Express* and *Sunday Express* until lack of advertising decided him to close them down, although the daily had reached a circulation of 100,000.

However, private enterprise had from the start official competition. Each of the Regional Governments owns its own newspaper and the Federal Government is represented by the *Morning Post* and *Sunday Post* published by the Nigerian National Press Ltd with a first-class modern plant. Since the British-owned newspapers tended from the beginning to keep out of domestic politics and concentrate on human interest, the degree of political variety was a good deal less than it seemed even before the military coup of 1966 and the Biafran war. What controversy there was was provided by the Zik group whose *West African Pioneer* remained as radical, awkward and outspoken as in pre-independence days even when Dr Azikiwe himself had moved to higher realms as President of Nigeria. However, the *Pioneer*'s editor, along with two others, was arrested during the disputed elections and the political unrest that culminated in military government.

For the rest, in most of West Africa what was in the past a lively, if somewhat precarious, press tradition seems to have been put to sleep with the arrival of independence. Gambia has no press. Sierra Leone and Liberia have few newspapers worth reading. In Liberia, arrest—usually on the general charge of 'libelling the President'—or the smashing up of printing machinery have kept the press small and although the Thomson Group's *Liberian Star*, started in 1964, is slightly better produced than the rest, it carefully keeps away from political comment, as does the *Daily Mail*, owned by the I.P.C. in Sierra Leone.

The introduction of British capital and the know-how of large scale British publishing enterprises into African journalism cannot on the whole be counted a great success. No doubt it has brought some modern techniques and helped to make African journalism somewhat more professional. But it has been nothing like as important in this respect as have the professional training schemes fostered by the International Press Institute at centres in Nairobi and Lagos and for a time directed by Tom Hopkinson, one-time editor of *Picture Post* until, as recorded earlier, he resigned because of proprietorial interference, and the seminars organised by the International Federation of Journalists and by the African Journalism Institute it later started. On the whole the British-owned newspapers in newly developing African countries have tended to set a tone of political non-involvement and concentration on human stories which has been of no particular value in the development of a responsible indigenous journalism. Thomson, in fact, has probably done a good deal more for journalism in undeveloped countries through his Thomson Foundation with its Journalism Centre for overseas students in Cardiff and its Television Centre near Glasgow than by any of his newspaper enterprises in such countries, which have, as he took some pride in explaining to an International Press Institute Conference in 1965, always been run on the public utility principle: 'Nobody is asked to declare his political views before he can be supplied with water or electricity. . . . My newspapers have the role of common carriers. . . .'

British-owned newspapers inevitably bring with them memories of colonialism and although no doubt both Thompson and King, who was the chief influence behind all this at I.P.C., had the best intentions—or at least hoped that they might combine some good for Africa with getting for themselves an early stake in what they calculated would be a rapidly expanding market—the British-owned newspapers have tended, understandably enough, to try to keep out of trouble by keeping out of politics as much as they can, often leaning over backwards to stay out of controversy. Even this modest ambition has been less easy as the Africanisation of their staff—accepted by both as inevitable and desirable—has brought in editors who very properly hold convictions about their country's future. The problem of a developing press in a developing community, with all the pressures on it not to make national unity more difficult by 'irresponsible criticism', is to provide, in so far as it is able, a means through which the political dialogue can go on. It is by no means an easy one. It would seem unlikely to be made easier by newspapers which because of their foreign ownership often find it necessary to behave as though politics did not exist.

Nor, in fact, have such papers proved as profitable as their owners hoped. Perhaps they tended to think it possible to import a more sophisticated press structure into the countries they went into than conditions in fact permitted. I.P.C. has done reasonably well with the *Times* of Nigeria, or was doing so until the civil war between the Federal Government and Biafra impeded distribution. But Thomson's experience with the Nigerian *Daily Express* was not encouraging and even much older established 'white' newspapers like the *East African Standard* in Nairobi, with its local publishing companies in Tanzania, Uganda and Zanzibar, have, despite some attempt to widen their former colonial outlook, found the going tough as the European population has dwindled and advertisement revenue has declined. They are now, they claim, only able to continue because of financial support from ancillary activities like commercial printing. The *Mombasa Times* suspended publication in 1965 because it could no longer cover its costs. The most successful of foreign-owned East African newspapers are probably now the Nation Group owned by East African Newspapers Ltd, a newish company formed in Nairobi in 1959 with Michael Curtis, one-time editor of the London *News Chronicle*, as its chairman and some managerial and technical assistance from the Thomson Group. But the *Daily Nation*, which circulates in Uganda and Tanzania as well as Nairobi and has a number of smaller dailies in various languages in its stable, is a special case. It is aimed primarily at an Asian rather than an African readership and has as a major shareholder the Aga Khan, whose personal adviser Curtis previously was and many of whose Ismaili followers have settled in East Africa and make up a relatively prosperous middle class.

Over most of Africa the problem of creating an indigenous independent press arises not only from political instability, government pressures and the competition of government-owned newspapers, but from the absence of a sufficiently large commercial and professional middle class to find the necessary independent capital to finance the starting of a newspaper and to support it when it is started. The injection of foreign press capital on the I.P.C.-Thomson model seemed at one time to provide the answer to this. But it really does not do so since, as already pointed out, colonialism is too near and the reaction against it still too strong for such foreign-owned newspapers to meet the needs of societies deeply stirred by nationalist revolutionary spirit. Nations, particularly emergent nations, require their own newspapers rooted in their own soil.

In Africa the problem, if not yet the solution, is plain enough. In Latin America, that unawakened continent, it tends to be concealed by the show-cases of the great capital cities with their high material sophistication and justly famous newspapers of long tradition like *La Prensa* and *La Nacion* of Buenos Aires, *El Mercurio* of Santiago, *El Tiempo* of Bogota, *El Comercio* of Lima, *O Estado* of São Paulo and the vast Chateaubriand Brazilian newspaper chain with its headquarters at Rio de Janeiro. The newspapers in the windows are as well developed as any in the world. Behind, in the vast poverty-stricken hinterland, is a population as much bereft of means of communication as any in Africa or Asia. Only, perhaps, in Mexico with over 150 daily newspapers, has a regional press begun fully to develop. The roots of this expansion go back to the first days of the Mexican revolution and specifically to the social advances from 1920 onwards which followed the first military phase. There has been a new wave of advance in the sixties. Many more regional papers have been started: circulation is steadily increasing.

Like the Soviet revolution, which it pre-dated but from which it greatly differs, the Mexican revolution has made much of the press as an instrument of education in revolutionary social change. But the press has kept free for the most part from either government control or censorship and although there is one large privately owned newspaper chain, what strikes one most is the large variety of newspapers not only in Mexico City but all across the country. In the number of its competing dailies, the steady eruption of new ones, even although not all manage to survive, and in the steady rise in circulation, the Mexican press, in fact, reminds one of nineteenth century America. Compared with the silence in the hinterlands of most of the rest of Latin America it provides a remarkable example of how an active and lively press can both reflect and guide a country where ideas and aspirations are on the move, even although not all the newspapers are very good as some have been open to corruption by bribes.

CHAPTER TWELVE

What Place for Television?

This is the century of the common man with a transistor radio in his hand and a television set in his sitting room. It is broadcasting, or so it is said, that offers the true communications key in the second half of this century: a short cut to the future by which the rich may grow richer in spirit and the poor leap-frog the obstacles of isolation and illiteracy that stand in the way of modernisation. And, of course, there is a good deal in this. Broadcasting—mostly radio, but television when you can afford it or national pride demands it—is the obvious system of mass communication in underdeveloped countries, although even here, it is worth noting, China, like the U.S.S.R., still attaches more importance to an extensive web of press communications than it does to radio.

In all developing countries radio clearly has a major role in spreading information, even though in most of them it will be official or, at any rate, officially approved, information. It can help to get participation at local level in the economic developments, better hygiene and educational advances needed for the modernisation process. It can open new horizons for isolated local communities and make them aware for the first time of national and even international issues. Radio, in fact, is an essential information tool for societies trying to lift themselves with all speed out of a past economically and socially stagnant; television a more sophisticated but also much more costly tool of the same process.

Let no one underestimate them. But on the other hand let us

not overestimate them. They are wonderful. But they are not a substitute for newspapers. Like the young man who said, 'Damn. It appears to me now that I am just a being that moves in pre-destinate grooves—not a bus, not a bus, but a tram', these broad-casting services travel majestically from point A to point B along lines laid down by authority. Newspapers are more like buses—all the better, perhaps, when they are pirate buses. One serves the public need to know, the other the public right to know—and there can be a great deal of difference between the two as any student of public information services soon knows.

Discussing French broadcasting and de Gaulle's reorganisation of ORTF, the French television and radio organisation, after the revolution that never took place, the *Guardian* observed sternly that the freedom of the press must be construed to extend to broadcasting. 'Without an independent broadcasting system,' it declared, 'a country cannot be said to have in a full sense a free press.' One applauds the sentiment. But it has no relevance to the situation over most of the earth's surface. This is so not only in countries where the press itself is controlled, but in many where it is free. Not only in the official, but also in the public, mind there is a sharp distinction between the two. Even de Gaulle has not dared to lay a hand on the remarkably free French press. But the television producers and commentators who struck for greater freedom and were subsequently dismissed by the General for their presumption found to their dismay that most of the public was not with them. So long as it had its newspapers, it did not care that television was in chains.

In India even the mildest of government attempts to control the press for what it considers—mistakenly no doubt — reasons of the public interest have met with bitter, and successful, resistance at every turn. But no one objects to the fact that All-India Radio is an official monopoly controlled by the Ministry of Information and Broadcasting. At a 1965 meeting of the International Press Institute, Hilary Ng'weno, a Kenya journalist, claimed with pride that in Kenya 'freedom of the press is one of those rights entrenched in the country's constitution'. It would, he said, 'require virtually the unanimous approval of both Houses of the Kenya Parliament to remove or even qualify the clause guaranteeing this freedom'. And he claimed that although the good intentions found in the Constitution were not always matched by good deeds (a common malady in many new and some old countries) not only had no major inroad into this freedom been made but such attempts to infringe it as there had been had been repulsed without difficulty despite the hurt sometimes inflicted on the cause of press freedom by the foreign ownership of newspapers (to which I referred earlier) and the 'ludicrous attempts by non-African Kenya journalists to prove loyal by appearing even more African than the African himself'. Yet neither Mr Ng'weno nor anyone else seemed to think it the slightest bit odd that the Kenya Broadcasting Service should be a monopoly under the control of a Government Department.

One could multiply such examples almost indefinitely. In principle the freedom of the press ought to include broadcasting. But in practice it doesn't in more of the world than it does. And not only do principle and practice not coincide, but a good deal of public opinion seems well content that they should not. A double standard is accepted as natural.

Perhaps because broadcasting is so much newer a medium with none of the history of struggle for freedom that the press has behind it, perhaps because it is so eminently suitable an instrument of government information, education and persuasion in newly developing territories, perhaps because the cost of establishing broadcasting systems in a situation of undeveloped communications is so high that often only governments can undertake it, or because for technical reasons it is necessary to ration air waves, the fact is that nationally owned and controlled broadcasting is publicly acceptable where a nationally controlled press would not be. There is a clear distinction in the public mind between the functions, responsibilities and status of the two. And the public may be right.

In the whole of Africa not one single independent radio or television service exists. All are owned or controlled by governments, or in a very few instances, such as the Union of South Africa, Nigeria, Liberia and the tiny island of Mauritius, are operated under licence by public corporations on which the government is represented and which are required to keep clear of public controversy. In the whole of Asia only Japan, Hong Kong and the Philippines have independent, competitive non-government broadcasting systems. And although the Thomson Group and Rediffusion of London have gone into a few areas in both Africa and Asia with television services, they have done so as managers with a stake in advertising revenue, not as policy makers.

Even in Europe a great many radio and television services are state owned or subject to the exercise of state control. This is not only so in the Communist bloc but also in Austria, France, Finland, Turkey, Spain, Portugal and Greece—although admittedly one would not expect anything else in the last three. For the rest, apart from Luxembourg which operates both radio and television as revenue-earning services largely directed to external audiences for advertising purposes, broadcasting is in the hands of public corporations. Most of them are monopolies, although Britain, the initiator and exemplar of the public service broadcasting tradition, now has, of course, an independent commercial system to compete with the B.B.C. in television, although not in radio.

Only in North and South America and in Australasia is there a pattern of independently owned radio and television services at all comparable to that of the press. Even there broadcasting is for a number of reasons—some political, some commercial—a good deal less free in most instances than the press.

In such a situation it is idle to think of broadcasting as fulfilling over most of the world the same purposes as an independent press. It has other functions and they are important ones. But they do not include several that have come to be regarded over the last two centuries as among the most important responsibilities of newspapers. Moreover, where broadcasting services are government-owned as in Africa and Asia there is little inclination to alter them. On the contrary the tendency is to integrate them more completely into educational and information services the better to serve the modernisation processes of governments. Nor is it without significance, perhaps, that even in the private field the chief advocate of local newspapers as common carriers with the non-political functions of a public utility is Lord Thomson who originally learnt his journalistic philosophy running local radio stations in Canada.

In all underdeveloped countries the main official emphasis in mass communications is on broadcasting and for the most part, of course, because of cost, on radio. According to the latest returns available from UNESCO the number of radio transmitters in Africa increased by 156 per cent between 1950 and 1962, in Asia by 180 per cent. In the same period the number of daily newspapers in Asia increased by thirty-five per cent and in Africa by only twenty per cent. This disparity is natural enough. The money needed for broadcasting comes from governments, indeed, in most developing countries it is, having regard to the amount of capital involved, the only source from which it could come. That for press development comes in the main, despite some nationally owned newspapers, from private sources which are scarce and small. Moreover, broadcasting is a much more amenable instrument of information and education from the point of view of governments than is the press—particularly an independent press.

This is not to deny the great value of broadcasting as an instrument of modernisation. But it is to suggest that it is highly improbable that in the perceivable future broadcasting will provide any sort of substitute for a free press. Its function, important though it may be, is of a very different character. Indeed, the gap between state controlled monopoly broadcasting systems and the press is likely to become larger, not smaller, as time passes and the idea that the one is in any way a substitute for the other more mistaken.

In so far as it is true, as I believe it to be, that, in the words of the late Professor Cahn in *Confronting Injustice*, the essence of a democratic state is that the sense of injustice is given an opportunity to make itself heard and that for this reason the basic political rights are freedom of speech and of the press, it is to the press, not broadcasting, that we must look for the assertion of these rights.

Of course, it takes time for a free press to develop. But as the earlier historical chapters of this book have, I think, made plain, where societies are on the move and ideas are in ferment, independent newspapers always tend to come into existence. They rise in response to popular needs and give body to popular aspirations and there is nothing that can stop them. In a good many of the developing countries conditions now are to some extent comparable to those in the United States after independence. They are not, of course, economically so favourable, but they are likely to come closer to it as modernisation processes get under way and new sources of energy and initiative are released. Nations cannot lift themselves up by their bootstraps without producing the sort of forces—including an active middle class—out of which an independent press has always grown whatever the initial resistance from ruling groups, as in eighteenth century England and Colonial America. Even in authoritarian societies the head of steam generated by the stir of economic and political ideas cannot permanently be kept battened down by press censorship. Just as the first act of an authoritarian society, whether of the left, as in the Communist world, or of the right, as in Spain and Portugal and most recently Greece, is to impose press control, so the first act of liberalisation is, as in Czechoslovakia in July 1968, the end of press censorship, and the first counter attack against the press to restore it.

However much some of them might like to do so, few of Africa's or Asia's ruling parties outside China are in a position to develop the elaborately centralised machinery needed for permanent press control. Nkrumah tried. All he did in the middle run was to pile up opposition to his dictatorship, just as did Sukarno, that other fervent architect of a completely controlled and subservient press, in Indonesia.

The majority of Africa's and Asia's ruling parties are coalitions of convenience, just as Washington's first Cabinet was. They hold up umbrellas to cover conflicting opinions in the interests of national unity. But beneath the umbrella the debate goes on just as it did in revolutionary America and once the first pressure is over the press is its natural forum. To control braodcasting as a national service is easy—and on the whole respectable. It is less easy—and less respectable—to stop opinion from finding a voice in newspapers—especially when most of the opinions reside in the government anyway. And it becomes progressively less easy as economic and social standards rise and new energy appears in every aspect of the national life.

Moreover, in most developing countries it is still possible to start small local daily newspapers for very much the same sort of money as it took in early nineteenth century America. The vast capital conglomerations demanded by the sophisticated publications of modern Britain and America do not arise: 10,000 dollars or so will do. Circulation may initially be no more than a few thousands, or even hundreds. Such papers are common enough in the Middle East. They exist in almost excessive profusion on the tiny island of Mauritius in the Indian Ocean, which has more national dailies than Britain—in part because it has a considerable and active middle class. And even today small dailies with circulations between 5,000 and 10,000 or even less are common enough in many parts of rural America. Such American newspapers can, of course, draw on neighbourhood advertising to offset their running costs to an extent that is not possible for small papers in India and Africa. And they have easier access to news agencies and to relatively cheap and unrestricted newsprint supplies. The problems of small vernacular newspapers in developing countries are great, as Mr A. R. Bhat, President of the Indian Language Newspaper Association, showed in his study of *The Development of a Multi-Language Press*. Nevertheless, to take India itself as an example, despite all the difficulties and despite also a national broadcasting service able to convey news and information much more cheaply and quickly, the number of small Indian language newspapers is rapidly increasing. According to a report in May 1967 by a highly competent professional observer from Britain, Mr George Viner, Education and Research Officer of the British National Union of Journalists, by far the biggest advance in newspaper circulation in India over the next few years will come from such newspapers. In assessing the future of the press in all but a few economically highly developed countries, it is a mistake to think too big.

All the evidence suggests that despite its merits broadcasting is unlikely to become an acceptable substitute for newspapers in underdeveloped countries. Its advent has been of the greatest importance as a stimulant of new aspirations and a widener of horizons. It is a valuable means of communication between governments and people. But it has not dulled the appetite for newspapers among the literate, nor much affected either the role of the press or its traditional pattern of development.

Nor, of course, is it replacing the press in more affluent societies, despite some forecasts to the contrary.

It is not necessary to go all the way with Marshall McLuhan in his headlong rush on mass communications to agree with him that in so far as the press is concerned the medium is, indeed, the message to this extent at least: that it is the 'daily communal exposure of multiple items in juxtaposition that gives the press its complex dimension of human interest'. This is particularly so, of course, with popular newspapers. When Arthur Christiansen, Editor of the *Daily Express* during its quarter of a century of most rapid circulation rise, hit on the idea of using the front page—and later most of the other pages also—as a blank sheet of white paper to be treated as a foundation for horizontal designs in type far bolder and more attractive than the mainly vertical make-up that had formerly been common, he was recognising to an extent no one had previously done that to a mass readership not only is the appearance of the news as important as what it says, but that the impact of the one contributes to the impact of the other. He dazzled and seduced the reader by marrying content and display more skilfully than anyone before him. 'You cannot,' he told his staff, 'just put things into the *Daily Express*. By and large they must be projected.' And he constantly reiterated that 'contrast is the heart and soul of a newspaper'. McLuhan comes up with the conclusion that 'If we pay careful attention to the fact that the press is a mosaic, participant kind of organisation and a do-it-yourself kind of world we can see why it is so necessary to democratic government.' By the use of 'an individualistic technology dedicated to shaping and revealing group attitudes' newspapers have, he avers, a unique role in enabling Western man 'to accommodate himself to the electric world of total interdependence'.

Once one gets past the McLuhan trees there is a good deal in this. By their unique combination of immediate visual and cognitive appeal newspapers can, in fact, do much more than other mediums to impose a manageable pattern on events even if it is only a pattern achieved by cutting everything down to their own size in a unity composed of similar date-lines. To buy a newspaper is to hold the whole world in one's hand, at any rate the world of that one day. No other medium enables you to cover continents with a single glance in the same way; none offers so many intellectual, visual and even tactile satisfactions all at the same time and that time no longer than it takes to pick up the paper and open it.

Many newspaper publishers believed that radio would cut

newspaper circulations. This indeed, was the whole reason for
the long holding action fought by British newspaper publishers
against the B.B.C. in its early years, the attempt, for instance,
to stop it developing any news services of its own. Many thought
that television would do so to an even greater extent. They were
wrong. Throughout the broadcasting age newspaper circulations
have everywhere gone on rising. Indeed, so far from reducing
the demand for newspapers, broadcasting appears in a great many
instances to have increased it, stimulating an appetite for news
impossible to satisfy until one has read it and, as it were, felt it for
oneself on the pages of a newspaper.

The very nature of the newspaper, its physical shape, the
typographical mosaic of its pages with their juxtaposition of so
many varying happenings, the sense of interest and excitement
aroused by its headlines with their promise of instant satisfaction
of curiosity if one reads the type below set it apart from both radio
and television with their less complex appeals. But there are, of
course, other reasons than these why radio and television systems
cannot provide a substitute for the press and why, despite some
things they can do better, the responsibilities of the press remain
very much what they were before the communications revolution
came along.

In the first chapter of this book I suggested that traditionally
the press has three linked responsibilities over and beyond that
of entertainment. These responsibilities, I suggested, are to
collect and publish the news and instantly disclose, allowing so
far as possible no obstacles to stand in the way of telling the people
all they need to know; to interpret and comment on it; to act as a
guard dog ever ready to expose the arbitrary exercise of executive
power and investigate exploitation or corruption.

It can, of course, be argued that even if these responsibilities
exist at all, any statement of them is bound to be entirely subjective
and to beg more questions than it answers. Definitions of 'what
the public needs to know' are, for example, likely to vary widely
and in fact do so from newspaper to newspaper. So, too, do
definitions of the public interest and what is, or is not, an arbitrary
use of executive power, or, for that matter, what is exploitation or
even injustice. In fact, these responsibilities of the press are, it
may be said, no more than the inventions of journalists and

newspaper publishers to give themselves a status that their real business, which is selling newspapers, does not have—or at any rate does not have to any greater degree than that possessed by those who satisfy any other public need or taste as honestly as they can and hope to make a profit out of it. Or else, as Henry Mayer argues in his excellent book *The Press in Australia*, they are likely, if examined, to turn out to be no more than thinly disguised and quite arbitrary *a priori* assertions about what some particular person thinks the press should do. It can also be said that in any event no one asked the press to take on the responsibilities it claims to have. If they exist at all they were its own choice and not, as is the case, say, with judges or legislators, a matter of public decision. At their best they are simply a prop to newspaper egotism, a public relations front for what is basically as much a commercial business as any other; at their worst a cover for a liking for sensationalism and a desire to pry into other people's lives by men with a hankering for power without responsibility— even if it is only the power to give their own inflated sense of importance a free run. Nor can anyone deny that there have been many occasions when many newspapers have done their best to prove such critics right.

But even when all this is said and the element of truth in it acknowledged it remains the case, as I think the earlier chapters of this book have shown, that at all times and in all countries where a free press has existed, these are the things it has been expected to do. Indeed, it is usually because of the need that they should be done that the press has emerged.

No doubt newspapers attract egotists. But the egotists who become newspapermen and newspaperwomen do so because it is the reporting and uncovering of news, the chance to speak out, as they imagine, for ordinary men and women, that satisfies their egotism more than making money, or being Cabinet Ministers, or having their names up in lights on Broadway or in the West End of London. It may well be that some of the responsibilities the press regards itself as having were self-selected by ambitious and excitable men who turned to journalism because it suited their temperaments better than slogging away at running a business or government. But they are also self-perpetuating. Newspapers would not continue to exist if they did not have these responsibilities—the whole lot of them—or fancied they did, because without them they would neither get people to work for them nor read them. It is the fact—or sometimes, perhaps, the illusion—that this is what they are about that makes men and women want to work for newspapers; it is the fact—or sometimes, perhaps, the illusion—that, whatever their other preoccupations, newspapers will always be ready to rap the powerful over the knuckles and expose injustice when it comes their way or they can ferret it out that makes readers want to read newspapers. What I have called the responsibilities of newspapers are part of their compact with their staffs and with their readers: something the most commercially minded of newspaper owners or the most impersonal of publishing companies with a long list of corporate and individual shareholders without a thought in their heads except dividends has to recognise as in the nature of the newspaper animal. Plainly broadcasting systems directly owned or controlled by governments and employed by them as instruments of information and persuasion cannot carry these same responsibilities. They may, if they are fortunate, be able to honour the first, although even here they may be compelled to discriminate or suppress, as happens, for instance, in France, to take just one example of a society in which freedom for the written but not the spoken word is wholly accepted. But even if they are able to carry out this first function with only the most occasional limitations on their freedom they are unlikely to be allowed to honour the second, since independent interpretation and comment may well lead to conclusions contrary to those of Ministers. And it is extremely improbable that they will be allowed to honour the third, except perhaps as regards subsidiary levels of executive authority. This is so even if they are not employed as weapons of propaganda but simply as part of a legitimate system of education and information. What they are required to do may be both useful and honourable. But it is not what the press exists for.

The position is, of course, different in the case of independent broadcasting services whether owned by private or public corporations, although even these, coming as they did much later in the history of mass communications than the press, are subject in all countries to a good deal more regulation and supervision than the press through such bodies as the Governors of the B.B.C. with their Charter to guide them, or the Independent Television Authority which is required by Act of Parliament to exercise really quite considerable supervisory powers over the programme policies of the British independent television companies, or the Federal Communications Commission in the United States, or the Australian Broadcasting Commission and the Australian Broadcasting Control Board. However, it is not with the regulatory powers of such bodies as these that I am concerned in discriminating between radio and television and the press, but with the nature and limitations of the broadcasting medium itself and the economic and social climate within which even the most independent of broadcasting services operates.

In some ways broadcasting can do better than newspapers in covering the news—especially if it is action or event news. It can almost always beat the press to a dead line, for it is much quicker to get news to the microphone or on to the television screen than it is to print it—an obvious fact that many newspapers ignored for a long time and some still do. If the news is capable of visual coverage, as most event and action news is, then television can also frequently bring home what has happened much more vividly than the printed word—although it is surprising how often whose who have watched news on the television screen, particularly if it is of a shattering nature like the assassination of President John Kennedy, or Martin Luther King, or Robert Kennedy, or the horror of Aberfan, seem to need the printed word, with its less intrusive impact and its greater capacity to put raw material into shape, to grasp the full significance of what has happened. In news concerned with facts—even quite complicated facts of political changes or scientific achievements or economic developments—broadcasting can usually outpace the press with the facts themselves. It is not always so good in explaining them. It can, of course, bring experts to the studio to be interviewed about them, and tends to do so with almost excessive zeal. But anyone who has appeared on television with any regularity as a talking face and been stopped in the street by viewers afterwards will know how little gets across compared with what is read in newspapers. Television has a wide span. It tells viewers a great deal about a great lot. But it is doubtful whether much of it goes very deep. This is not only because the newspaper can be absorbed at one's own pace, whereas the broadcast must be absorbed at someone else's and with all the distractions of visual movement on the screen as well, but also because the very act of reading, if only because of the greater effort involved, tends to make for greater understanding than does the smooth continuous ripple of sound from the microphone or television screen. Listeners and viewers, in fact, are often better served by broadcasting in the getting of news than in the understanding of it.

However, to seek to diminish the value of radio and television as news mediums would be absurd. They reach many people who do not read newspapers or who only glance at them superficially, and if they do not go very deep at least they help great audiences to feel more at home in the world and more in touch with what is happening in it. Access to news is an essential part of the freedom of the press and this radio and television have greatly extended.

But with the remaining responsibilities of the press broadcasting is not so much at home—television perhaps even less than radio. It is, in fact, not allowed to be so as far as direct editorial comment is concerned. Because it has been generally accepted that air waves are part of the public domain all broadcasting services have been subject to some regulations, usually high among them the stipulation that permission to use this public domain does not carry with it the right to use it to put forward an editorial position. Unlike the press, broadcasting is in this respect a common service, a public utility. It carries the views of others, it is not permitted to have one of its own. In a large area where the freedom of the press has always been regarded as especially vital broadcasting has no place.

But, of course, opinion is not only formed by opinions or for that matter rejected because alternative opinions are formally put up against it. As all newspapers know, the investigatory side of a newspaper may be a lot more important than its editorial columns in influencing public attitudes. To this investigatory, public watch-dog side of the press, broadcasting has in some degree adapted itself. It can, and frequently has, disclosed conditions or exposed injustices with great skill and force and compelled public attention to be given to them, as British television has over housing conditions in London and as Columbia Broadcasting did over poverty in America, to quote only two out of many instances. It has forced public opinion both in the United States and in Britain to become more aware of racial problems. And it can on occasion, as Edward R. Murrow did in a famous exposure of Senator Joe McCarthy, do something to smash dangerous public images. However, it is probable that television's part in stopping McCarthy, who it should be remembered had had powerful opponents in the press much earlier, among them the *New York Times*, the *Herald Tribune*, the *Washington Post*, the Cowles and Knight newspaper chains and in his own state, the *Madison Capital Times*, came even more from its common carrier function when it gave an audience of 20,000,000 or more an opportunity to see the sort of man McCarthy really was when confronted by someone who was not afraid of him, in this instance a Boston lawyer, Joseph L. Welch, Army Counsel in the Army-McCarthy hearings.

Television is also, of course, a powerful instrument in giving ordinary men and women a much more intimate view of public men than they had before. Few public men can bring themselves to refuse an invitation to appear on television. They rush to the studio, convinced no doubt that they have only to be seen to be loved, and frequently succeed in damaging themselves almost beyond repair. To this extent television, which is better as an exposer of personalities than an explainer of principles, has undoubtedly had a large part in shaping political attitudes from time to time. It can convey a sense of personal participation in events, which although largely illusionary is not wholly so. It can bring the sounds and scenes of a distant war into millions of homes, as with Vietnam and so affect and perhaps change public opinion: as Margaret Mead has remarked, it is only because of television that most Americans know that American soldiers actually kill people. It can give a sense of large occasions and is often admirable in presenting the great figures of the age performing on their public platforms. It can help to create a climate of opinion which although likely to be basically self-satisfied and middle class may well be more sympathetic and open than it would otherwise have been.

But in many equally important matters such as the struggle against official secrecy, that ubiquitous pestilence, it cannot and does not serve the public right to know so well as the press does.

The Right to Know

It is true that, in Britain and the United States, nothing can happen anywhere without the appropriate Minister or public person appearing on television to be cross-examined, politely or aggressively according to the persona constructed for himself by the all-purpose interviewer. But such appearances are no more than public performances, exercises in histrionics, sometimes amusing, occasionally exciting, more often boring in their repetition of well-used techniques and over-exposed personalities. The talking faces talk furiously under the bright studio lights, the cameras zoom in for the kill. But the interviewer's knowledge is too much on the surface and the interviewed hold too tightly to their public images for more than a pretence of revelation. The public is given its necessary circus but the moments of genuine truth are rare.

Even less satisfactory as a means of illumination are most of those overseas forays by air-borne reporters which are so much a feature of modern television. All are conditioned by the necessity to interview in front of the camera only those who can discuss the situation, whatever the situation may be, in the language of the viewer at home, so that facility in a foreign tongue and a readiness to be questioned in it are more important than depth of knowledge. Moreover, as the interviewer knows, although the interviewee may not, what is said will in any event be cut and edited before transmission to fit its allotted time slot, just as the commentary itself must be married to visual content and length of shots. What the camera can find rather than truth unadorned—and so often unadornable—dictates the message. Television has opened many windows on the world. But they are mostly on public places and they often create the illusion that more is seen and known than is actually the case. For what goes on behind the arras the news-paper reporter, untrammelled by apparatus, able to delve and digest as experience and instinct alone direct, and unrestricted in his sources of information by any requirement to present them before a camera, still remains the best guide.

Television, of course, has thrown up a wide range of tele personalities who are sometimes thought to exercise great demagogic power. I doubt whether they do. It was my own feeling when I was appearing on television once or twice a week over a fairly long period, so that I became a tele personality of sorts and could not walk down the street or enter a pub or a restaurant without being recognised, that although this state was flattering enough in its way—but of diminishing attractiveness—the amount of influence it represented was a good deal less than politicians and others who worried themselves about television's impact were inclined to think.

Instead of giving even as much appearance of objective authority as does appearing on a public platform, television simply dumps one into the middle of the family circle in the sitting room. One becomes a one-dimensional next door neighbour to be taken neither more nor less seriously than any other. The smallness and intimacy of the actual viewing groups cuts one down to size and the very intimacy of the proceedings at the viewing end does away both with the possibility of demagogy and with the aura of special authority—a fact that politicians who thrive on their auras of authority often fail to appreciate.

Although I would not deny the incidental pleasures of broadcasting for one who likes talking and does not mind being paid for it, it soon seemed clear to me when I was doing it that if there was anything on which I really hoped to influence people it was much more likely to be done effectively by a public speech or a written article.

This, of course, was before the days when it became the habit to have captive studio audiences for televised interviews and discussions. By adding another dimension, that of a public meeting with an above normal amount of audience participation, to the proceedings, this may have altered the balance. What it has certainly done is increase ingredient E for Entertainment while reducing the smaller e for enlightenment. There is, of course, nothing wrong with entertainment. Television's major contribution to civilisation is that it has made the world a much more entertaining place for many millions of people who previously found it hard to fill in the time between coming home from work and going to bed without getting bored or bad tempered.

But the attitude of mind of those settling themselves down to be entertained is quite different from that of the same people getting ready to participate in serious business. Television is pre-eminently the medium of the tired businessman in all of us—a fact well understood by those who make money out of it. It has the same appeal as a detective story—it provides enough stimulation to take one's mind off other things, not enough to compel one to start thinking in real terms. Of course, the serious and the entertaining need not cut each other's throats. No one ever listened to a speech by Lloyd George or Winston Churchill or Aneurin Bevan or Adlai Stevenson without being entertained as well as made to think; no newspaper that does not entertain as well as inform is likely to last for long. But the key lies in the approach—in the mood in which one sets out to receive. It is not impossible to make those who come for entertainment stay to think. Bernard Shaw did it regularly in his plays. But it requires a lot of talent and wit—more than anyone can be expected to offer for sale each week. And the whole pressure of television's demand for large audiences, instantly hooked, is against it.

The difficulty about using relaxed programmes of the Jack Parr, David Frost type as vehicles for serious current affairs controversies or interviews with public figures is that despite the superficial attraction of ready-made audiences for top people, entertainment must always come first. Moreover, although the resident hero has to be sharp-witted, he must also be naive so that the audience can identify with him. He must ask the questions they would have liked to ask, whether they are the right ones or not.

Basically such programmes live on the fallacy that everything is easy to understand. A good deal in the world is not, even with the help of Mr Frost, who has many of the qualities, good and bad, of the newspaper tycoons. Frost is as much at home in his medium as Bennett, Pulitzer and Northcliffe were in theirs. He is currently the international champion in this field, commuting between New York and London with zestful nonchalance, because just as they did, he believes in what he is doing and ordinary people recognise that he does. For him, as for them, life, one suspects, is genuinely simple. Energy is all. His programmes have, in consequence, no hard core of philosophy other than the conviction that what goes well with the studio audience must be right. Each programme lives by and for the moment. Whether it is the Israeli-Arabic war or the pleasures and pressures of identical twins the high pitched giggle never fails. It is what can be got out of the situation in audience entertainment not the situation itself that matters.

What Place for Television ?

Thus on the famous and much criticised occasions when Dr Savundra and Dr Petro appeared before him on the British screen after being the subject of long investigation by newspapers and also by the time he got to them the subject of police inquiries subsequently leading to arrest—no thought of fairness deterred him although in other more agreeable situations his desire to be fair shines out untarnished through innocent eyes. These were men morally on the run. His studio audience were baying for blood and he gave it to them. On the other hand, the Archbishop of Canterbury evoked from his audience and therefore from him a genuine human warmth and so did Mr George Brown. When a young woman who had abandoned her baby in a ladies' lavatory was invited to the programme Frost and audience wallowed together in a warm bath of sickly sentimentality. With Denis Healey, the Defence Minister, it was different again. On this occasion it was the audience who had to save David, sent reeling to the ropes by someone who was not only much tougher than it is proper for Frost interviewees to be but had brought with him a battery of well directed arguments that revealed both the mediocrity of the programme's intellectual foundations and the paucity of its facts. They gave help gladly, loving him the more because he needed them, hating Healey with a greater intensity because he had dared to crack the image of the hero.

Such programmes have their place in television's ethos. Like *Daily Mirror* leaders, they provide mass audiences with the assurance that there is no need to be lonely, there is someone on their side. In a world where a feeling of disassociation and of the gulf between 'them' and 'us' is a perilous reality for many people, this is a useful function to perform, although it sometimes brings with it the inflation of dangerous myths. But as genuine exercises in understanding current affairs and in sustaining the public right to know on serious issues such programmes have little more relevance than had William Randolph Hearst at an earlier stage in mass communications.

Even serious current affairs programmes like the B.B.C.'s *Panorama* and those occasionally available among the advertising wastes of American television suffer from the weakness inherent in the television medium. They must seek to be visually compelling and when, as in interviews or discussions, the only visual components are talking heads, the compulsion must be injected by the expectation that the heads will be knocked together at any moment. Entertainment must be made manifest by the technique of the duel or joust so that every discussion is a confrontation. Tension is all.

Not that I am in any position to be high and mighty about this. Just after I had written this comment my sister showed me a page of the *Sunday Times* of 20 April 1958 which she happened to have kept because it contained some information on antiques in which she was interested and had been left between the pages of a book on Georgian furniture. On the back of it was an article by the paper's television critic on television interviewing which referred bitingly to the habits of television interviewers of the time 'led by that redoubtable jack-in-the-box Francis Williams' (a reference no doubt to the fact that I was apt to pop up on a considerable number of public affairs programmes at this time). He continued sharply, 'These household gods are all the same. They put their victims on trial for treason even when all that is at stake is the butter content of ice cream.' I can only assume that there is something in the medium that corrupts even the best of characters!

It is possible, although it seems increasingly unlikely, that ultimately the broadcasting media will find an idiom that serves the public right to know not just intermittently or on small matters, as for instance the Braden Show on A.T.V. did for a time in Britain, but continuously and on great ones. But the conformist advertising pressures on American television and the conformist establishment pressures on British television, the two television systems that at one time seemed most likely to achieve this, do not give much hope. So far as the B.B.C.—always bolder than commercial television in these areas—is concerned, such hope was further reduced by a statement on 'Broadcasting and the Public Mood' by its Board of Governors in August 1968, presumably under the inspiration of its new Chairman, Lord Hill. After observing sadly that 'an interviewer who by tendency or technique unnecessarily incurs hostility involves the B.B.C. in that hostility' and that a reporter should not incur 'unnecessary indignation against the B.B.C.' (necessary indignation is presumably permissible) this concluded with an ecstatic explosion of double think. The B.B.C.,' it mused, 'has at once to be alert and deaf, to listen to silences as well as clamour, to have a skin thick and sensitive, to step boldly and delicately.' I cannot think that in the days when Barbara Wootton and I were Governors of the B.B.C. and Sir William Haley was Director General we would have been willing to sign our names to such a tin of glucose.

No doubt television will continue to be of service in public affairs as will, also, radio in between the soothing music. Indeed, on both sides of the Atlantic there are some indications that despite an excessive dependence on breathlessness, radio may be returning to some of the adult assumptions that belonged to it in the first fine flowering of American news radio. But, as Mr Charles Curran the new Director General of the B.B.C. declared, when interviewed on his appointment, 'Broadcasting is first and foremost an entertainment medium.' This is so whether it is run by a public corporation like the B.B.C. or depends on advertising for its living. It is not to be criticised for that, though one could wish the entertainment were a little better. But is does mean that it is unlikely that broadcasting can ever provide a substitute for the press in the constant scrutiny of public affairs or take over a good many of the responsibilities that have, sometimes by intent, sometimes almost by accident, accrued to newspapers over the years.

CHAPTER THIRTEEN

The Plague of Secrecy

The question is can the press do what is expected of it? Or, perhaps, not so much expected, since what's expected is usually the worst, as hoped. There are many intelligent critics of the press, like Raymond Williams, who seem to think not—or at any rate not without changes in structure and control that seem improbable. Some years ago, before its own immersion in the modern world, *The Times* turned its attention in a leading article to the future of the British press. It concluded magisterially, 'It can safely be said that if it continues its present course it will regain neither status nor authority. The race for mammoth circulations has led in some instances to a disgraceful lowering of values. The baser instincts are being pandered to not only in lasciviousness—the influence of this can be over-rated—but in social attitudes and conduct as well. Envy, jealousy, intolerance, suspicion are all too often being indirectly fostered. Irresponsibility is rife. . . . The tone of voice is a perpetual shriek. So-called brightness is all.' It added, 'By no means all popular papers are thus (it is in fact deplorable that some of the worst examples should be classed as newspapers at all), by no means all the journalists on even the worst newspapers wish them to be thus. But the turning of the press into predominantly a business enterprise, the fact that in the present state of newspaper economics readers have to be fought for by the million to make popular journalism viable, have engendered forces greater than the journalists.'

This was in 1955. Over the next eight years the warning was to be amply justified. But at the time of writing the onslaught brought an angry response from the National Council of the Press, then in its second year and without the independent chairman

276

and lay members it subsequently acquired. The Council saw the British popular press through spectacles very differently coloured from those of *The Times*. It was, it declared in terms that must have made many newspaper staffs blush before nausea turned them green, 'invariably on the side of patriotism and legality, of courage and chivalry', and trumpeted, 'To expose injustices, to right wrongs, to give advice, to befriend the friendless and help the helpless—these are among the services which these newspapers are constantly rendering to people who could not otherwise obtain them.'

More detached observers found it hard to go all the way with either. If *The Times* seemed too lurid, the Press Council was too much like a doting mother with a child accused of delinquency. But this was a bad period for the British press. Not quite so bad as *The Times* made out although it was to get worse, and not so bad as during the frenzied circulation wars of the thirties. Not so bad, either, as American journalism had been in the days of Hearst. But a lot worse than most post-Hearst American journalism than most popular journalism elsewhere. The end of the cushioned circulations of the war and immediate post-war years with their newsprint rationing and small papers had brought a competitive struggle in which almost anything went. It was frequently accompanied by a vast clamour about press freedom of the kind that made William Allen White of the *Emporia Kansas Gazette* declare in 1939 that although it was not a universal rule it was a fairly workable one 'that a newspaper which is eternally agonising about freedom of the press is a newspaper which is endangering the freedom of the press by abusing it'.

The bad period extended into the sixties and was particularly exemplified in the operation of some leading gossip writers who took as their journalistic models the cheapest kind of American private eyes in the cheapest kind of American thriller.

One example of their methods will perhaps suffice: that of a young couple both of whom subsequently made substantial reputations for themselves as serious writers who asked me if I could publicly expose the kind of treatment to which they were being subjected for refusing to play the cafe society role some newspaper gossip columnists had picked for them. They were repaid for being rude to the gossip writer by paragraphs hinting that the young man had married his wife only for her money. There were suggestions that the marriage was breaking up (they are still happily together some ten years later) and pictures 'carefully designed to suggest that we are being unfaithful to each other'. A cameraman armed with a telescopic lens was posted in an upstairs window overlooking a small house in an unfashionable area to which they moved to get away from the glossy life, and neighbours were bribed to discover malicious tit-bits about their private lives if they could. All these charges and others I carefully investigated and found to be in the main true, indeed, for the most part they were under-statements of what was actually being done. This was only one case among many.

This sort of journalistic activity has now been ended. The gossip writers who lived so lush a life during the fifties and early sixties have been sacked. Their end was in part hastened by an article by Penelope Gilliatt published by the *Queen* magazine in 1960. This turned some of their own weapons against the gossip columnists by describing the lives, backgrounds and methods of the principal amongst them in devastating detail, and did so in a medium to which they were particularly vulnerable because it circulated amongst their social victims and admirers.

Miss Gilliatt saved others. She could not save herself. In the latter part of 1961 she and John Osborne, the playwright whom she subsequently married after a divorce, became the targets of a remarkable newspaper campaign which used most of the methods formerly employed by the gossip writers but translated them to the news columns. Posses of reporters were posted outside Mr Osborne's flat in London to report on his and Miss Gilliatt's movements. When they left for Mr Osborne's house in Brighton they were followed by a cavalcade of cars, and reporters invaded the garden and hid among the bushes, noting breathlessly in which windows lights appeared. When the two went for a walk the next morning every look they exchanged, every stop they made was eagerly reported to waiting news editors. They were followed into every shop they visited. Their meal in a cafe was described in minute detail. They walked arm in arm along the sea front. Reporters raced for telephone booths. They bought an ice-cream. Every lick was recorded. Mr Osborne was cornered on the lawn of his house and had the impertinence to be rude to reporters.

The Plague of Secrecy

They retaliated with an even closer day and night watch on his and Miss Gilliatt's movements.

Some time previously the American Society of Newspaper Editors had ruled for the guidance of its members that 'a newspaper should not invade private rights or feelings without sure warrant of public right as distinguished from public curiosity'. Except in the offices of *The Times*, the *Guardian* and the *Herald* which took no part in this detective work, this raised laughter in Fleet Street which was echoed by the members of the as yet unreformed Press Council—on which most of the editors concerned were represented—when it was asked to sit in judgment on the matter.

It was a shoddy affair, the more painful for those directly concerned because, as John Osborne, speaking, I am sure, for many said in a letter in which he thanked me for exposing the treatment to which he and Miss Gilliatt had been subjected, 'It is very difficult indeed to fight back on one's own behalf in this kind of distasteful situation without fear of doing more damage.'

It was this sort of behaviour duplicated over many years that provided the background to the public response to the imprisonment of two newspaper reporters for their refusal to disclose their sources of information to the tribunal appointed in November 1962 under the chairmanship of Lord Radcliffe to inquire into the circumstances surrounding the Vassall case: the arrest and sentencing of a clerk in the Admiralty as a Russian spy, which had led to a spate of newspaper stories of inefficiency or worse by Ministers and others.

Most newspapermen anticipated that their own reaction to the prison sentences on the two reporters would be matched by equal public indignation. The contrary proved the case. The punishment proved widely popular. In so far as the press could claim that it was doing no more than its proper duty by serving the public right to know it seemed to be a right in which the public were no longer interested.

In a leading article, which the *Daily Mirror* at once sought permission to reprint in full the next day so that it should reach a mass audience as well as a quality one, *The Times* thundered against 'the degree of ignorance, complacency and apathy towards the particular dangers perpetually threatening every free society' that this public attitude revealed. The public responded with a happy smile that newspapers were at last getting what had long been coming to them. Although regrettable it was an understandable response in view of many newspaper methods.

The Tribunal's report published in April 1963 disclosed for example that the Tribunal had analysed some 250 separate newspaper stories and given the writers of the most substantial every opportunity to substantiate them. Not one story had stood up to serious inquiry. One in the *Daily Mail* was described as 'in all essentials a piece of fiction'. Another in the *Daily Mirror* and the *Daily Herald* as 'also fiction and not based on any information that could support the story'. One which was given great prominence in the *Daily Express* under the by-line of its Chief Crime Reporter and subsequently incorporated in a political story by its Political Editor was reported to be 'completely false'. Of another in the *People* the report said, 'We are satisfied there is no truth in it.'

These were only a few among many other examples of the way in which the wildest speculation had been presented as known truth. Tiny scraps of fact had been exaggerated out of all recognition. When all else failed news editors and reporters had simply sent to the library for the cuttings from other newspapers, most of which had no foundation in the first place, and let their imaginations run riot without regard for public reputations.

The Tribunal's report was all the more damning in that it went out of its way to emphasise that it had fully taken into account the fact that much of the work of a reporter, and still more that of a political or diplomatic correspondent or crime reporter, could not proceed on the factual basis that would justify an assertion before a court of law but must often by its nature be based on intelligent conjecture supported by inquiries which could not be definitive.

Newspapers came little better out of the inquiry into the Profumo Affair by Lord Denning later that year.

The Profumo Affair during which the Secretary of State for War, Mr J. P. Profumo, resigned after first denying to the House of Commons and then admitting a liaison with a prostitute, Miss Christine Keeler, who was also conducting an affair of sorts with an Assistant Naval Attaché in the Russian Embassy, Captain

The Plague of Secrecy

Eugene Ivanov, uncovered a sordid story of vice and procuration centering around a well known London osteopath, Mr Stephen Ward. Ward subsequently committed suicide while standing trial on a charge of living on the earnings of prostitutes and the whole business brought to a high pitch both the British public's taste for scandal and its hyprocrisy. Piquancy was added by the fact that Mr Profumo first met Miss Keeler in the swimming pool of Lord Astor's house, Cliveden, famous as the resort of the Cliveden Set at an earlier period in British political history. Here she was enjoying herself with Mr Ward, who had a cottage in the Cliveden grounds, and Captain Ivanov.

In uncovering this story and disclosing the possible, although in fact unsubstantiated, security risks of Mr Profumo's association with Miss Keeler the press played a part of some value. But when the Master of the Rolls, Lord Denning, was asked by the Prime Minister, Mr Macmillan, to investigate the wider rumours in circulation, many of them involving other Ministers, his report showed that not only were no other Ministers involved but that most of the rumours were lies. It did not increase newspaper credit when he declared that he was satisfied that many of the worst of them had come into existence only because their perpetrators hoped to sell them to newspapers: the cupidity of such peddlers of fiction had no doubt been aroused by the report that before his arrest Stephen Ward was negotiating to sell his story to a newspaper for £50,000 while Christine Keeler had actually already sold hers to the *News of the World* for £23,000.

Lord Denning concluded with these words, 'Scandalous information about well-known people has become a marketable commodity. True or false, actual or invented, it can be sold. The greater the scandal, the higher the price it commands. If supported by photographs or letters, real or imaginary, all the better. Often enough the sellers profess to have been themselves participants in discreditable conduct which they seek to exploit. Intermediaries move in, ready to assist the sale and assure the highest prices. The story improves with the telling. It is offered to those newspapers— there are only a few of them—who deal in this commodity. They vie with one another to buy it. Each is afraid the other will get it first. So they buy it on the chance that it will turn out profitable. Sometimes it is no use to them. It is palpably false. At other times it is credible. But even so, they dare not publish the whole of the information. The law of libel and the rules of contempt of court exert an effective restraint. They publish what they can but there remains a substantial part which is not fit for publication. This unpublished part goes round the world by word of mouth. It does not stop in Fleet Street. It goes to Westminster. It crosses the Channel, even the Atlantic, and back again swelling all the time. Yet without the original purchase it might never have got started on its way.'

All this was only some five years ago. It is not surprising, therefore, that statements about the importance of the press in a parliamentary democracy and its position at the heart of the struggle for the public right to know sometimes produce raised eye-brows and rude laughs among British readers. But although a few Sunday papers, notably the *News of the World*, since acquired but not improved by Fleet Street's newest minder, the Australian Robert Murdoch, remain in the market for criminal confessions and inside stories of the notorious, the British press as a whole has very considerably altered its character since those days.

The events of 1962 and 1963 forced newspaper owners and editors to recognise how low they had sunk in public esteem and the total loss of public confidence that lay ahead if they did not change course. The Daily Mirror group—the *Daily Mirror*, the *Daily Herald*, the *Glasgow Daily Record*, the *Sunday Mirror*, the *People*, and the *Scottish Sunday Mail*—issued a statement that 'pimps, prostitutes and perverts should not profit from their notoriety and degradation'—which might have amounted to no more than the pious assurance that, like President Coolidge's clergyman, it was against sin but for what had gone before. Newspaper staffs generally received warnings from editors to be more careful of their facts and not to intrude on private lives unless there was very strong public reason. The National Union of Journalists reminded its members of the Union's code of conduct. And after resisting change for ten years newspaper proprietors accepted the need for a reformed Press Council with a proportion of lay members and an independent Chairman—a constitution originally proposed for it by the first Royal Commission on the Press in 1949 and re-asserted by the second Royal

The Plague of Secrecy

Commission on the Press under Lord Shawcross in September 1962.

All these and the realisation forced by events that much of the press had got out of touch with popular opinion and that scandal, irresponsibility and intrusion were no longer quick ways to fortune have brought substantial changes in the past five years. Under Lord Devlin the Press Council has taken on new force as a stern mentor when need be, but also as a strong defender of legitimate interests of the press when defence is called for. A detailed analysis of its decisions prepared by Mr H. Philip Levy, principal legal advisor to Daily Mirror Newspapers, has provided editors with a case history to which they can refer whenever they feel the need to check their own judgments against those of men whom they can respect.

Yet although the public standing of the press has improved a good deal it would be absurd to pretend and foolish to expect much mutual love between newspapers and politicians. By mid-1967 relations between press and government in Britain had in fact become worse than for decades. Nor was this only so in Britain. Relations between the two were equally bad, if not worse, in America where what came to be known as the credibility gap between President and press had reached such a stage that the two were hardly on speaking terms any longer—certainly not on polite ones.

A machinery of relationship between government and press has been a part of American government much longer than in Britain, as long, indeed, as American government has existed. The Presidential News Conference has been an accepted part of the administrative system since Woodrow Wilson. These relationships have had their ups and downs. They ran into frustration in Wilson's second term, were banal under Harding, dull under Coolidge, colourful and significant under Roosevelt, useful but tetchy under Truman, benevolent but vague under Eisenhower ('If you listen carefully you think maybe you understand what he means,' said a prominent White House Correspondent to me. 'It's when you check against the written record that you find you can't understand a damn thing'), glamorous and factual but contrived under Kennedy, intimate and expansive at first under Johnson but later a cause of hostility and mistrust. Presidential press relations have always, of course, been subject to a pull of forces: the newspaperman's desire to find out what he thinks the public wants to know, or anyway ought to know, the President's anxiety to use the press as an instrument of government. They have been fraught always with the sort of stresses indicated by Arthur M. Schlesinger Jr., not in reference to Presidential press conferences but to those of the Secretary of State, but as true of one as the other, in an article in the *Reporter* as long ago as March 1953:— 'Washington newspapermen today hardly know whether to believe the Secretary of State because they do not know if he is speaking to them as reporters or seeking to use them as instruments of psychological warfare.' Schlesinger went on to ask, 'What is the responsibility of a newspaperman when he discovers that some rumoured development of policy is really only a psychological warfare trick? Should he print the truth at the risk of wrecking the plans of the Secretary of State? Or should he suppress the truth and betray himself and deceive the American people?'

It is a dilemma that constantly confronts newspapermen in contact with Presidents, Prime Ministers, Secretaries of State and Ministers of all sorts and is far from being confined only to foreign policy. Usually, however, it is a dilemma both sides manage to live with by judicious compromise: the recognition by Ministers that they must not push their use of the press too far but must be willing to give out and discuss genuine information on occasion, even if they would prefer not to; the recognition by newspapers that although all governments like to conceal too much there are some things about which to be secretive is a public duty.

It is significant of our age, of the pre-occupation on the one hand with the need for secrecy born out of the national security problems of the cold war but avidly adopted in other areas of government where no such excuse exists and of the equal pre-occupation on the other of politicians with their need to foster a good public image, that such compromises have become very much more fragile. To political leaders the press has become at one and the same time and to a degree much greater than ever before something to be guarded against and something to be courted; guarded against for fear it finds out too much, courted for fear it doesn't give good publicity.

The Plague of Secrecy

President Johnson and Mr Wilson both became victims of these dual preoccupations. Both began their administrations with a rush of good will to and from the press. Both courted the press and courted it, moreover, in a peculiarly personal and intimate way. One could say of both that what happened in the end could not have happened to nicer men.

'No President in the history of the Republic,' declared Mr James Reston in *The Artillery of the Press*, 'has ever devoted so much time to reporters, editors and commentators as President Johnson. He sees them individually and at such length that the reporters themselves are often embarrassed to intrude so much on his other duties. It was not unusual last year for the President to sit casually in his rocking chair talking steadily to a reporter for a couple of hours and sometimes even much longer than that.'

Mr Wilson was equally forthcoming in his first year of office. He had not long been in Downing Street before he was loved ardently by all the Political Correspondents, irrespective of the colour of the papers they worked for. He took them into his confidence. He delighted in swopping ideas with them. He gave them an almost unending supply of news. Other Prime Ministers had treated them somewhat as if they were upper servants. He talked to them as if he and they were members of the same senior common room at one of the older universities.

The difficulty is that frankness on this level is not really pos-sible—or is only possible in brief snatches—between President or Prime Minister and the press. It establishes a confidential, personal relationship that is basically fraudulent although neither side may want it to be. Unless President and Prime Minister are unfit for their jobs there are bound to be many occasions when the frankness can only be an appearance of frankness, not a reality. Unless the reporter has forgotten his job he must always have his ears a-cock for news. As the going became tougher for both President Johnson and Mr Wilson and the political and economic decisions they had to take became harsher and more complicated they found themselves at one and the same time under greater temptation to try to use the friends they had made among news-paper men to sell a bill of goods and more eager to be written about nicely. As for the reporters, after finding themselves misled on more than one occasion they reacted as men do who think they are being used. The beautiful friendship was over. The reporters did not get confidences when they most wanted them. The politicians got criticism when they most looked for understanding. Both sides became hypersensitive. Reston records an occasion when he went to see the President on an important matter and was met with an outburst of self-pity because *Time* Magazine had printed a sharply edged account of an incident when Mr Johnson was said to have driven his car at more than eighty miles an hour along a Texas highway with, according to some reports, a paper cup of beer beside him.

'I have only one thing I want to do,' said the President. 'I want to unify the country.' But, he went on, he was not going to be allowed to because there was a group of papers and writers determined to make him look like 'an irresponsible hick'. This was because he was a Southerner and they were still not 'far enough away from Appomattox' for a Southern President to be allowed to unify the nation. 'I went away,' says Reston, 'sad and astonished.' It was after such incidents as this, says Mr Reston, that an attitude of caution and reserve began to permeate the Johnson regime in place of the early expansiveness.

Mr Wilson reacted in similar fashion to personal stories about himself. Both followed news reports closely. President Johnson, for example, was not only an avid newspaper reader but had Associated Press and United Press International News ticker tape machines installed in a small cubby hole off his main office so that he could follow their news files every hour of the day. And he installed three television sets in his office and three in his bedroom so that he could follow all three television networks at once. Mr Wilson was scarcely less news conscious. But as each persuaded himself that despite all his attempts at good will the press was gunning for him the flow of news and background dried up, caution and suspicion took over. Governments take their tone from those at the top. A similar attitude spread through all branches of administration. Even the illusion of frankness disappeared. Closed mouths became the fashion, greatly to the satisfaction of all those in official places with a congenital dislike of publicity.

Both President Johnson and Mr Wilson had a genuine case against the press. Once the first friendliness went, the personal press campaigns against both of them reached almost unbelievable levels of innuendo and dislike. And the campaigns were curiously similar. When I was in the U.S. in the Spring of 1967 I made a small collection of anti-Johnson smears. Three months later almost all of them were in circulation in London in almost identical form except that Johnson's name had been altered for that of Wilson.

Yet it is significant that the low point of Mr Wilson's relations with the press came as a result of one of the big security non-events of the year—the D notice affair. It began with the publication by the *Daily Express* on 21 February 1967 of a story by its Defence Correspondent, Chapman Pincher—for long a thorn in the thumbs of Ministers and civil servants by reason of his excellent sources of information—headlined 'Cable Vetting Sensation'. This declared that 'thousands of private cables and telegrams sent out of Britain from the Post Office or from Commercial Cable Companies' were regularly being made available to the security authorities for scrutiny.

It was in many ways a somewhat silly story and not up to Mr Pincher's usual high standard of revelation. In the first place the procedure so sensationally described had been in existence as a routine security matter for more than forty-five years, having originally been authorised under an openly debated section of the Official Secrets Act of 1920. In the second place it was not even very secret. The cables—only a very small percentage of the total at any one time—were collected by vans of the Ministry of Public Buildings and Works quite openly each day in plain view of anyone interested. It would have had to be a very dull secret agent who did not know about it. Pincher was told of it by a former telegraphist at Commercial Cables and Western Union who had learned of the procedure in the ordinary way of his duties without going to any special pains to find it out. However, it was written up in the *Daily Express* as a sensational 'Big Brother' intrusion into privacy with political overtones, including the implication that it was being used by the Labour Government to obtain 'advance information of confidential trade negotiations and private deals'—a suggestion without any truth in it whatever even although the basic facts in the story were—if very old—true enough.

The Right to Know

Questions followed in the House of Commons. The earlier Mr Wilson would, one suspects, have dismissed the political implications of the story for the nonsense they were, pointed out that there had been no change whatever in the procedures followed for many years under many different governments, although for obvious security reasons it was impossible to go into details, and perhaps have poked a little gentle fun at the *Daily Express* and Mr Pincher for their passion for old hares.

The Mr Wilson battered by press criticism, 'let down' by his friends of the Lobby, persuaded by intimates that newspapers were interested only in damaging stories and were best excluded from government confidences, reacted very differently. With all the paraphernalia of a Prime Ministership defending the most solemn national interest he denounced the Pincher story as 'sensationalised and inaccurate' and a grave danger to national security, declared that the story had been published in direct contravention of the request of the Services, Press and Broadcasting Committee, commonly known as the D Notice Committee (a joint body of Civil Servants and newspaper representatives to advise newspapers by the issue of 'D Notices' concerning the publication of matters that might involve security), was 'a clear breach of two D Notices' and 'utterly wrong; a wicked thing to do'. After this he announced with great solemnity the appointment of a Committee of Privy Councillors consisting of Lord Radcliffe (who had been Chairman of the Vassall Tribunal and also of a Committee on Security Procedures in the Public Service) and two former Defence Ministers, Mr Emanuel Shinwell and Mr Selwyn Lloyd, one Labour, one Conservative, to investigate the matter. This distinguished Committee could, he declared with a flourish, claim the confidence of the whole House, and the Government 'would rely on their judgment in all these very difficult matters'.

The Committee met for more than two months and saw twenty-four witnesses. Its investigations disclosed a number of curious incidents. Among them was a lunch at the fashionable restaurant, *L'Ecu de France*, at which Colonel Lohan, the Secretary of the D Notice Committee, was the guest of Mr Chapman Pincher. When first approached on the telephone Colonel Lohan had said that he saw no particular significance in the story and knew of no D Notice that would apply. However, when officials of the Foreign

288

Office and the Defence Ministry heard of the story events took a very different turn. Colonel Lohan was ordered to suppress the story at all costs. An amiable man, he promised to do his best and over lunch tried hard to persuade Mr Pincher that two D Notices applied. Mr Pincher who knew as much about D Notices as anyone in the country was friendly but unconvinced. He refused to give any promise.

The inquiry also disclosed that at one stage public relations officers in both the Ministry of Defence and the Post Office, instead of being told to say nothing, were instructed that if approached by Mr Pincher or anyone else they were to say that the report that cables were collected and vetted was 'untrue' and 'ludicrous'. This was a deliberate lie and must have been known to be so by those giving the instructions—surely the absolute negation of sound public relations. Finally in the most bizarre incident of all it was disclosed that the Foreign Secretary, Mr George Brown, had been persuaded by his officials late one night to intervene in the matter. Instead of having a word with the editor, which would have been the proper course, he decided to approach Sir Max Aitken, Chairman of Beaverbrook Newspapers Ltd., the owners of the *Daily Express*, with whom he had a slight acquaintance. Sir Max was at a dinner at the Garrick Club at the time. However, he was finally reached with a message at 10.15 in the evening and took the Foreign Secretary's call in the porter's box in the hall of the Club. Thereupon, since he had never heard of the story and Mr Brown did not like to describe it in any detail on a public telephone, there followed a conversation of farcical incomprehensibility in which Sir Max could not understand what Mr Brown was talking about and Mr Brown jumped to the conclusion that since their conversation, if confused, had been polite and friendly, all was well.

After examining this and much other evidence, including that of high officials of the Ministry of Defence and the Foreign Office, the three Privy Councillors published their conclusions. The principal ones were: 'That the *Daily Express* article was not inaccurate in any sense that could expose it to hostile criticism on that score'; that there was 'no evidence to indicate that the editorial decision to publish the article was taken with a deliberate intention of evading or defying D Notice procedure or conventions'; and that 'it would not be right to say that the article amounted to a breach of the D Notices'.

Having announced when appointing this Committee of distinguished Privy Councillors that the Government would rely on their judgment the only thing left seemed to be for the Prime Minister to express his regret for having being misled in the first instance and to do his best to kiss and be friends. However, in his then mood such a procedure by no means commended itself to him. Instead, a Government White Paper was issued rejecting the Privy Councillors' main conclusions and sticking to the original charges—a course which not unnaturally led to highly critical debates in both Houses of Parliament and strong condemnation by all newspapers. Relations between government and press were further worsened when Colonel Lohan was forced to resign, subsequently taking on a job as 'Food Spy', for the Beaverbrook *Evening Standard*, reporting on restaurants.

Apart from these immediate consequences, the affair was important for the light it threw on the then attitude of Ministers and higher civil servants towards information to the press and to what has been referred to during this book as the public right to know. It seemed, indeed, to many people to confirm conclusively the view expressed some two years previously by a Joint Working Party of newspaper representatives and members of the law reform organisation known as Justice, under the chairmanship of Lord Shawcross, a former Minister and a most distinguished lawyer, that the Official Secrets Act on which the D Notice system rests was being too much used by governments for the purpose not of legitimate security, but for suppressing the ventilation of matters which governments or government departments thought were politically embarrassing. A position had already arisen, said this Joint Working Party, most of whose investigations took place before the Wilson administration was formed, in which 'The disclosure or improper use of the most harmless document can lead to a prosecution. We feel this does not make for good government: it can lead to protection of inefficiency and malpractice, stifle the needful exposure of public scandals and prevent the remedying of individual injustices.'

The change since my own post-war days at 10 Downing Street in governmental attitudes—both Conservative and Labour—in this matter of D notices and their use for all sorts of purposes was for me piquantly illustrated when Earl Attlee came to sit beside me in the tea room of the House of Lords at the height of the D Day affair. 'Tell me, Francis,' he said, 'what is all this D Notice business? I never remember the things even being mentioned during all the time I was P.M.' It also became quite clear during the Privy Councillors' investigation that high officials in both the Foreign Office and the Defence Ministry had got into the habit of assuming that the press ought to behave as an ally of government and was very naughty if it did not. In particular it became plain that they took it for granted that although the Services, Press and Broadcasting Committee had been set up as an independent body with a majority of press members on it for the purpose of ensuring that only such requests for non-publication were issued as the press were convinced were genuinely necessary on security grounds and had operated on this basis throughout the much more difficult security conditions of the war, when first Lord Radcliffe and then I myself were in charge, it was now being treated by Ministers and civil servants alike as an official government organisation entirely subject to their will. The Secretary of the Committee, so far from being any longer the servant of an independent committee, was regarded as a civil servant of comparatively low status required to do exactly what they told him.

This affair has been recalled in some detail because it so clearly demonstrates the need for extreme watchfulness in matters affecting the public right to know and the ease also with which governments, even when they start out with the best intentions, can slip into the habit of thinking that the press should do only what they want it to do. It demonstrates, too, the ease with which political leaders can—as both President Johnson and Mr Wilson came to do—persuade themselves that the newspapers are their enemies if they insist on their independent right to publish what their readers ought to know. Some, of course, are. It would be silly to underestimate the sheer malice of which a few newspapers are capable when someone to whom they are politically opposed is in office—or even for more personal reasons.

But even where malice does not exist—and for the most part it does not—the fact is that there is, and must be, a difference of interest between government and press and it is well that this should be recognised by both. They can be friends but they can rarely be allies. It is a newspaper's business to disclose. It is there to publish as much as it can. In a democracy this ought, of course, to be the aim of government too—after full account has been taken of genuine security needs and of the essential confidences necessary to the process of reaching decisions. But it rarely is and seems to be becoming less so.

Even in Washington, which to envious journalistic visitors from other countries seems to be the most open town on earth, the shutters are coming down. As long ago as 1960 Joseph and Stewart Alsop were commenting sadly in their book *The Reporters' Trade* on the change that had come over the scene since they first began as political columnists. In those earlier days, they observed, no one doubted that the people's government was the people's business and a reporter, being charged with the task of describing the government to the people, had an unqualified right to ask about any aspect of the people's business which he thought interesting or significant. But this, they reported, had become progressively less so. One reason, they decided, was the proliferation of 'classification stamps'. Two decades ago such things had scarcely existed. 'But today all papers in all government departments are classified —except the toilet paper and there are probably "Confidential" Men's Rooms in the Pentagon.' Moreover, there had, they noted, been an increasing effort to cover up internal arguments, although earlier the public had been helped to understand great issues of principle by the very openness of the disputes about them and the ability of newspapers to report both sides of them. In this respect the real rot began, the Alsops concluded, in the first Eisenhower administration, when the so-called 'team' he had gathered around him with Secretary of the Treasury George M. Humphrey at its head behaved more and more 'like the executive hierarchy of a self-satisfied (because monopolistic) industrial corporation in a one-company town'—an echo to British ears of conditions under Mr Neville Chamberlain who was once described to me by one of his Ministers as conducting himself like the Chairman of a private company in which he held all the shares. Journalistic curiosity which went beyond the official press release was, said the Alsops, 'even thought to be a mark of subversive tendencies'; for the team also held 'that the country only needed to have faith in Eisenhower, presumably because it was well known that he walked on the water-hole at the Burning Tree golf course'. By the time the Eisenhower administration was ended, not only had the problems of defence and foreign policy led to 'a whole elaborate system of secrecy . . . charged with limiting the people's knowledge in these areas' but 'the habit of secrecy had spread by a sort of noxious contagion, to other government agencies and departments that have no shadow of an excuse for secretiveness'.

The Kennedy administration was not much better in this respect despite its appearance of openness and President Kennedy's own liking for social occasions with newspapermen. Consider, for example, the pressure which was unfortunately only too successful as President Kennedy himself ruefully admitted later, to persuade the press to keep quiet about the preparations for the abortive Bay of Pigs invasion of Cuba. Similar pressure was put on the British press to stop it disclosing what the British Government was up to during the Suez crisis of 1956. When it failed Sir Anthony Eden actually went to the length of asking the Lord Chancellor to prepare an instrument to take over the B.B.C. to prevent it giving publicity to newspaper editorials in its news broadcasts. He might have got his way if the B.B.C. had not been warned in advance by his Press Secretary, William Clark, who resigned.

British and American governments, in fact, both seem to have become progressively more sensitive to press attempts to explore issues while they are still in process of making up their own minds—although this is, in fact, the only stage at which public opinion can have any genuine part in decision making.

According to Reston, Bill Moyers, when President Johnson's Press Secretary, expressed the philosophy behind this in this way, 'It is very important for a President to maintain up until the moment of decision his options, and for someone to speculate days or weeks in advance that he is going to do this and this is to deny the President the latitude he needs in order to make in the light of existing circumstances the best possible decision.' Carried to its logical conclusion—and it is frequently carried well beyond it by some Departments—this means that all public speculation in the press or elsewhere ought to stop until a decision is actually taken and the President has sent a message to Congress, or, in London, the Whips have been put on. But in a democracy decisions ought to be taken in the daylight after there has been an opportunity for public opinion to express itself. So far from this happening it would seem to have become the accepted practice, to judge from the instructions given to the public relations officers of the British Defence Ministry and Post Office in the cable vetting affair already referred to, not merely to keep quiet or refuse comment, but to lie quite deliberately in order to keep press and public in the dark. Moreover, if Sigma Delta Chi, the professional association of American journalists, is to be believed, this is a matter on which American and British officials see eye to eye. In November 1967 it issued a statement declaring that 'High officials have been deliberately misleading the public, the press and Congress through flat lies, through half truths and through the clever use of statistics that distort.' It accused the State Department of 'misusing a claim of national security for purposes of hiding or obscuring the record' and the Pentagon of 'pouring out inaccurate information on everything from the controversial TFX plane matter to the question whether there was Joint Chiefs' disagreement over the conduct of the Vietnam war.'

Public criticisms of governmental secrecy come most often from journalists. They after all suffer most professionally from its impact. They may be thought to be interested and perhaps prejudiced witnesses. But consider the restrained testimony of the highly respectable Fulton Committee on the British Civil Service in its Report of June 1968 after more than two years' examination of the processes of administration.

'We think that the administrative process is surrounded by too much secrecy. The public interest would be better served if there were a greater amount of openness. The increasingly wide range of problems handled by government, and their far-reaching effects upon the community as a whole, demand the widest possible consultation with its different parts and interests. . . . It is healthy for a democracy increasingly to press to be consulted and informed. There are still too many occasions where information is unnecessarily withheld.'

The Fulton Committee went on to argue that in the process of stimulating the flow of information the traditional anonymity of the British Civil Servant was likely to be eroded, and to add that it saw no reason why it should not be. On the contrary, it said, 'We think that administration suffers from the convention, which is still alive in many fields, that only the Minister should explain issues in public and what his department is or is not doing about them.' It dismissed as no longer tenable the old thesis that the Minister alone must answer for his department in public. 'The Minister and his junior Ministers cannot,' it declared, 'know all that is going on in his Department, nor can they nowadays be present at every forum where legitimate questions are raised about its activities. The consequences is that some of these questions go unanswered.'

To many these will seem no more than truisms, although truisms backed in this instance by a dozen highly eminent people headed by Lord Fulton himself with a host of public appointments that fills getting on for half a page of *Who's Who*, and leading businessmen, university dons, public administrators, MPs and Fellows of the Royal Society as his colleagues. Yet when less than two and a half years previously the *Sunday Times* had the same idea and thereupon appointed a highly intelligent and responsible journalist, Mr Anthony Howard, formerly of the *New Statesman* and later Washington Correspondent of the *Observer*, to be its Whitehall Correspondent to seek to break down exactly those barriers of Civil service secrecy and anonymity to which the Fulton Report refers, it brought down on his and its own head such bitter antagonism as to force it to abandon the whole project within a matter of months. Like the Fulton Committee, the *Sunday Times* pointed out that increasingly decisions were made by civil servants rather than Ministers and it was desirable for the public to know about them. 'It is the business of a newspaper,' it said, 'to go where power is.' The civil servants saw things differently. Mr Howard was frozen out by such a snowfall of bureaucrats as has never been seen before or since. The day after the announcement of his appointment there was a hurried get-together of the principal heads of departments led by the mandarins of the Foreign Office and Treasury. Instructions were given that anyone seen talking to Mr Howard would no longer be regarded as a member of 'the club'; instructions conveyed to lower members of the hierarchy that he was a man it would be wise for the ambitious not to know. Telephones were unanswered when he rang, doors closed. No one was ever free for lunch. Eventually Mr Howard and the *Sunday Times* were forced to give up as foredoomed the attempt to do what the Fulton Committee was later to recommend with such conviction, and Mr Howard left for America.

These brief examples have been given to indicate the stubborn resistances to the public right to know that still exist in what have some claim to be considered the two most free and democratic countries in the world. Such resistances were well characterised in the report of the Special Sub-Committee on Government Information (the Moss Sub-Committee) of the Congressional Committee on Government Operations in 1955. They represented, it said, 'An attitude novel to democratic government—an attitude which says that we, the officials, not you, the people, will determine how much your are to be told about your own Government.' The intervening years have strengthened, not reduced, this attitude. It is no longer novel. It is accepted procedure.

CHAPTER FOURTEEN

Public Interest and Commercial Ownership

A hundred years or so ago Francis Lieber, the American writer on government and politics, wrote, 'Publicity informs of public matters; it teaches and educates and binds together. There is no patriotism without publicity and though publicity cannot always prevent mischief, it is at all events an alarm bell which calls the public attention to the spot of danger.' As a short, plain statement it is hard to better this.

Of course, newspapers are not the only instruments of this publicity. But even in Britain where Question Time in the House of Commons and to a lesser extent in the House of Lords has a role for which there is no American counterpart—although it should also be said that there is nothing in Britain to match the Congressional Committee as a means of extracting information—the press is the most consistent and regular of these instruments. Indeed, a large proportion of the questions put to Ministers by MPs would never be brought but for newspaper stories.

It is not necessary to pretend that the newspaper's role in all this is entirely high-minded. When in reply to questions during a survey of *Newsgathering In Washington* by Professor Dan P. Nimmo for the American Political Science Association an irritable civil servant snapped that there was a good deal of hypocrisy about talk of the public right to know, all that the newspaperman was usually concerned with was his own story, he had a point. Few newspapermen go about their business of news gathering with their minds exclusively on the public interest. They are on the look out for a good story. They may well serve the public interest in getting it, but that is incidental to their main purpose which is to get ahead of the competition if they can. But although the public interest may be incidental to, indeed often no more than a by-product of, journalistic competition, nevertheless the newspaperman's nose for news, his professional involvement in finding out, does serve the public interest and has served it fairly consistently over the years.

The history of the press like that of all human activities is a chequered one. It has frequently fallen well behind the aspirations of the most intelligent of its members. But despite the periodic misuse of its investigatory functions and publicity powers for purposes of mere sensation or the inflation of the personal egotism of individuals, the major compulsions behind its development have almost always been, as I think the earlier chapters of this book have shown, the urge to satisfy the public right to know and to provide a platform for public anxieties and aspirations which might otherwise have been denied a means of expression. This is natural, for it was in response to such needs that newspapers came into existence and it is by the satisfaction of them that they live, despite all the ancillary functions of entertainment and so on they have taken over. News is their trade. It is what their readers expect and require of them: the hard, indispensable core of the newspaper life.

In all ages and in all countries newspapers, of course, have had to match their publics. Yet the remarkable similarity in pattern of newspaper development suggests that the needs to which they respond are timeless and universal. The differences in character between individual newspapers is substantial, between those serving a 'quality' readership and those serving a 'popular' one, often startlingly so. Yet their basic similarities are so much more profound than their differences that there is nothing illogical in talking of them as part of one institution.

Yet if they are united as regards their basic purposes, it is also the case that this generic quality makes them very capable of injuring each other. The excesses of the worst reflect upon the best. It was not simply the reputation of a few individual British newspapers that was tarnished during the absurd frolics of the thirties or the contemptible excesses of the fifties and early sixties but that of 'the press' as a whole. And American newspapers still carry in many foreign eyes not merely the insignia of irresponsible sensationalism won in some of the worst of recent trials by newspaper like the Dr Sam Sheppard case, or in their irresponsible scramble that followed President Kennedy's assassination and Oswald's arrest, but even those pinned on them long ago by Randolph Hearst.

What conception the press of Western countries has of its duties is important not only because of its own role in the increasingly complicated—and increasingly secretive—operations of government in Western societies themselves but also because the course taken by the Western press will have a profound effect on that of the newly developing countries of Asia and Africa. As has, I think, been shown earlier, it has always been the case that journalistic experience in the more developed countries has affected that in the less developed. Newspapers mirror the social, economic and political patterns of their own societies. But because they also reflect and respond to needs that are universal they form part of an international fraternity in which the professional and economic norms of the most advanced, their status, public position and relation to governments, have great effect in determining the position of newspapers in less developed societies.

In the new societies of Africa and Asia newspapers will be helped or hindered in their movement to independence by what image the independent privately owned press of the West throws across the world. This image has not always been such as to inspire new nations with the desire to emulate them. It was accidental that some of those now running affairs in former colonial territories got their main impression of how a privately owned independent press might be expected to behave from the goings on of Lord Beaverbrook and the first Lord Rothermere while learning their politics at the London School of Economics in the twenties and thirties. But it has had its effect in making some of them more reluctant to accept the risk of an independent press than they might otherwise have been.

Like democracy independent private ownership of the press has, of course, its imperfections. All one can say of both is that in the long run they have shown themselves more likely to serve the public interest than any alternatives. But neither can any longer assume that it will be taken for granted. Both respond to fundamental human needs and for this reason tend to be paid lip service

299

even when they are ignored in practice. But both are still on trial and the verdict will be determined by the evidence. So far as freedom of the press is concerned not all the efforts of the International Press Institute, Unesco, the International Federation of Journalists and many American universities and private bodies, like the Thomson Foundation, to improve the technical and professional equipment of journalism in developing countries—excellent and admirable although these efforts are—will do the trick if the end product of press freedom in the highly developed countries themselves seems to be no more than the personal power of a few individuals or large profits for business organisations with not a thought in their heads beyond their balance sheets.

For this reason the rift—or what sometimes seems to be the rift—between the press as business and the press as public service, particularly exemplified by the almost universal trend in economically developed societies to larger press units and greater monopolisation traced earlier in this book, has a much larger than local significance, considerable although that is in itself. There is nothing to be gained from deploring this trend. It is here. It is likely to increase rather than diminish. The whole weight of economic circumstance is behind it.

Indeed, it must be expected to increase. It has probably gone as far as it can in New York. Even that city is not likely, one would think, to find life possible with less than two morning papers and one afternoon one, although conceivably the increasing advance of the suburban daily press could in the end put the *New York Post* —none too happy even now—out of business. But even if contraction has gone as far, or almost as far, as it can well go in New York the trend to monopolisation and the killing of independent newspapers in the rest of America is still proceeding. In Britain, the *Sun* and the *Daily Mail* are still vulnerable, the *Daily Sketch* only a little less so than it was. On a purely accountancy judgment it is difficult to see all three surviving indefinitely, although the *Mail* still has resources of past financial strength to fall back on and the *Sun* has a few more years to fight in on time bought for it by the *Mirror* group. Both have done a good deal—although so far without much effect on their budgetary position—to improve themselves journalistically and deserve success more than they did at one time. Both, also, are helped to survive by the fact that although it costs money to continue, it is also very costly to close down. Some time ago Mr Cecil King, who no doubt had gone carefully into the matter having in mind his then responsibilities to the *Sun*, estimated that with redundancy payments and one thing and another the cost of shutting down a London daily could well come to close on £2,000,000. Closure is not an operation to undertake lightly.

The *Guardian* also is still vulnerable, although less so than it was. It has been helped by the general and long overdue rise in the price of British daily newspapers. This has somewhat reduced its dependence on advertising and it has made economies in production costs with the intelligent co-operation of the printing unions. Its prop, the *Manchester Evening News*, is also stronger.

In Germany Herr Springer has resisted attempts to reduce his press empire by the ingenious argument that although it is true that the West German constitution guarantees the individual right to seek information unhindered from 'generally accessible sources' it does not stipulate how many such sources there should be. Meanwhile increasing production costs seem likely to bring a reduction in the highly important provincial press. So, too, in France rising costs and the increasing competition of television advertising are already threatening the existence of some newspapers both in Paris and in the provinces and seem certain to stimulate further the movement to bigger newspaper groups that has already begun.

Moreover, although technological developments in newspaper production may in the end make it much cheaper to produce newspapers for minority publics and open the way in Britain to national newspapers which will be able to get along comfortably enough on a circulation of 100,000 or so, the road there is hazardous and expensive in the extreme. In the initial stages only the financially strongest national newspapers are likely to be able to afford the capital expenditure which may be involved in switching over to computer setting, and web-offset printing in perhaps eight or ten regional centres serviced with editorial pages transmitted photographically by wire from a central composing centre, thereby making it possible to offer both colour advertising and local editioning to match the advertising appeal of colour television. Those who wish to get ahead of their newspaper competitors and keep abreast of television by such methods will probably have to spend in the region of £35,000,000—and there is always the fear that by the time the money is spent new processes will already have put the expensive plant out of date, so rapid are the technological changes now coming after a century during which basic printing processes have hardly altered at all.

Technological developments do not, of course, necessarily affect the editorial quality of newspapers either way. The development of the electric telegraph in the last century did so because it fundamentally altered the speed of news collection. So did the development of the rotary press because for the first time it enabled newspapers to be printed at a speed and in a quantity that made it possible to develop large readerships which in their turn required a different mode of reporting and writing from that of the former minority minded newspapers. No doubt colour printing will have some similar editorial consequences, although hardly of the order that these earlier developments did. But where it will have an enormous effect—or so it is believed—is on advertising revenue. It will enable the daily paper to compete on equal terms, especially in consumer advertising, with the glossy magazines and commercial colour television. In view of the large dependence of all newspapers on advertising revenue this is bound at first to make the strong who can afford the huge capital costs, stronger and the weak weaker by drawing more and more advertising to the strong at the expense of the weak. That at least is the current thesis. I, myself, believe that although the impact may be serious for popular newspapers it may not much affect the quality ones. I cannot believe that the appeal of the *New York Times* or the *Guardian*, for example, would be much enhanced by colour printing—any more, for that matter, than the readers of *Le Monde* have been upset because it does not print pictures. And ultimately it is readership—its quality as well as its quantity—for which the advertiser pays. However, this is a personal and quite possibly prejudiced view which may well be proved wrong: after all, the *Sunday Times* although a quality newspaper gained very greatly in circulation from providing a glossy colour supplement and the *Observer* was forced to follow its example. The London *Times* has colour high among its current priorities.

Decentralisation, with regional printing of national newspapers may hit provincial morning newspapers and put some out of existence, not only in Britain but also in West Germany where Springer is well poised for multi-centre printing of this kind. In France Hachette could well decide to embark on such a programme. Such developments could even lead to a national press in the United States and competition for some of the larger regional newspapers. But the absence any longer of a New York based newspaper industry at all comparable to that of London, West Berlin or Paris makes this less likely. The great newspaper barons of Washington, Chicago and Los Angeles are hardly likely to fall before a New York invader and State loyalties make a strong regional press a natural reflection of American life.

However, there seems little doubt that one way and another technological developments will bring larger newspaper units and a greater commercial domination of the press. It is within this context that the newspaper as a public service has now to learn to live. It is not a new dilemma. It has had to be coped with in varying degree ever since newspapers began. In one sense it is not a dilemma at all for if an element of public service is demanded by all newspaper readers, then it is no more than commercial commonsense to see that they get it. But the matter is not as simple as that. There is the question of balance, of priorities. Newspapers must pay their way and make a profit if they can. But this is a very different thing from seeking to maximise profits as commercial television has for example in the United States to the grave damage of its public service responsibilities.

Some twenty years ago Arthur Hays Sulzberger was asked by the American Society of Newspaper Editors to address them as president and publisher of the *New York Times* on the relation between a newspaper's freedom and its responsibilities to the public. These are some of the things he said.

'As I see it we as a newspaper have one paramount responsibility and that is to the public. I, in turn, as a publisher, have a second great responsibility and that is to the staff. As a newspaper we live under certain guarantees of freedom, and it is important to point out that there is no *quid pro quo* written into the constitution. Freedom is granted—responsibility is not required. Despite that, more and more of us have come to recognise that responsibility is the Ruth to freedom's Naomi.'

The Right to Know

He went on, 'I would define a responsible press as one which admits that the manner in which it covers and presents the news is a matter of legitimate public concern. It seems to me that the public has a right to demand this. It has a right to protection from unscrupulous advertising; it has the right to demand as accurate, full and impartial a news service as the public itself is prepared to support. It has this right because freedom of the press is one of its own fundamental freedoms which, in effect, it vests with a relatively small number of its citizenry. And the press suffers, and freedom everywhere suffers, where a community fails to demand and receive its rights in this respect. ✦ . . I hold that it is the duty of every newspaper of general circulation to inform its readers on all sides of every important issue and that it fails in its responsibilities when it does not do so. . . . We believe it to be our duty to give all available sides to a story and to present the news without any criterion except objective news judgment. . . . We recognize the difficulties in obtaining strictly factual information although we constantly try to achieve it. . . . Always we make the distinction between interpretation and opinion and we earnestly seek to exclude the latter from our news columns.'

Fundamental to this picture, said Mr Sulzberger was 'the fact that in this country and in many other lands the press is privately owned and sincerely good democrats can well ask how any industry vested with so much public interest can proceed with fairness to the community without some form of governmental control. Of course the answer is that governmental control would destroy freedom and the question these people ask is actually an impossible one—you cannot have outside control of a free press and have it free. Control must come from within. . . .'

This is a fine statement. It does Mr Sulzberger credit and is worthy of the attention of all involved in the editing and publishing of newspapers. But it contains one proviso which is worth noting when considering the press as a whole and leaves one question unanswered. The proviso comes in the last eight words (which I have underlined) of the reference to the public's right 'to demand as accurate, full and impartial a news service *as the public itself is prepared to support*'. Not all newspaper publics are prepared to support as full a news service as that of the *New York Times*. Many want something a great deal shorter, lighter, more 'human.' The newspapers that supply this need and the many other varying levels of need and interest that exist, are not open to criticism because they are not like the *New York Times*. It is fallacious to compare the popular and the quality press to the detriment of the first. Each newspaper can only do—and if it is a good newspaper only wants to do—what is appropriate to its own circumstance. All that anyone is entitled to ask is that within its own context it shall be honest, fair and reliable.

The unanswered question comes from Mr Sulzberger's emphasis on impartiality and objective news sense. It sounds admirable. But what is objectivity? Is it ever attainable? Judge Learned Hand gave the best reply perhaps in the course of a famous judgment in an anti-trust action against the Associated Press of America which followed protests by Mr Marshall Field concerning the barriers to membership of the A.P. erected against his *Chicago Sun* when it was founded in competition to Robert R. McCormick's *Chicago Tribune*, which was already a member.

In the course of this judgment which found against the A.P., Judge Learned Hand said, 'News is history; recent history it is true, but veritable history nevertheless; and history is not total recall, but a deliberate pruning of, and culling from, the flux of events. Were it possible by some magic telepathy' (for which word one may perhaps be forgiven for substituting in these days television, having regard to the undigested quality of some of television's instant news programmes) 'to reproduce an occasion in all its particularity, all reproductions would be inter-changeable, the public could have no choice, provided that the process should be mechanically perfect. But there is no such magic and if there were its result would be immeasurably wearisome and utterly fatuous. In the production of news every step involves the conscious intervention of some newsgatherer and two accounts of the same event will never be the same. Those who make up the first record—the reporters on the spot—are themselves seldom first hand witnesses; they must take the stories of others as their raw material, checking their veracity, eliminating their irrelevances, finally producing an ordered version which will evoke and retain the reader's attention and convince him of its truth. And the report so prepared when sent to his superiors they in turn "edit" . . .

personal impress is inevitable at every stage, it gives its value to the dispatch, which without it would be unreadable. . . . But these are not all: the same personal choice which must figure in preparing a dispatch operates in deciding what events are important enough to appear at all: and about that men will differ widely . . . and even though the whole dispatch be printed verbatim its effect is not the same in every paper; it may be on the front page or it may be in an obscure corner; depending upon the importance attached to it. The headlines may plagently call it to readers' attention or they may be formal and unarresting. There is no part of a newpaper which is not the handiwork of those who make it up; and their influence is often most effective when most concealed.'

These are the reasons why it is always best to suspect claims of objectivity—even when they are made by the *New York Times*. The thing is not possible. One should always be on guard against those who claim to have achieved it. Even the attempt to do so can be dangerous. The American obsession with newspaper objectivity—British newspapers have never fallen for this desiccated female in the same way—certainly served to support the cause of lies and distortion during the era of Senator Joe McCarthy as Mr Douglass Cater, at that time the distinguished Washington Editor of the *Reporter* Magazine, points out in his book, *The Fourth Branch of Government*.

He quotes Mr Dean Acheson's bitter comment to the American Society of Newspaper Editors at the height of the McCarthy assault on the State Department: 'Now I don't ask you for sympathy. I don't ask you for help. You are in a worse situation than I am. I and my associates are only the intended victims of this mad and vicious aberration. But you, unhappily—you by reason of your calling—are participants. You are unwilling participants, but nevertheless participants. And your position is far more serious than mine.'

Mr Cater goes on to say, and anyone who was there at the time will agree, that 'The McCarthy era came as a deeply unsettling experience to many Washington Correspondents. The demagogue has been defined as the undetected liar. Yet all the elaborate reporting mechanisms of the press seemed unable to detect and communicate the basic fact of McCarthy's lies. . . . More than at any time in the past this experience led to re-examination of the iron clad concepts that rule the so-called 'objective' or 'straight' reporter. 'The job of the straight reporter,' a wire service editor once defined for me, 'is to take the place of the spectator who is unable to be present. Like the spectator he does not delve into motives or other side issues except as they become part of the public record. Unfortunately the spectator is a casual witness, usually bewildered by any unexpected event. The reporter who limits himself to this role becomes frequently an unwitting agent of confusion.'

He certainly became so in the hands of Senator Joe McCarthy. Objectivity, the blindfolded virgin, served McCarthy well, because under her influence newspapers reported his lies straight as if they were facts. The statement was the news, not the truth of the statement. As Eric Sevaried wrote, 'Our rigid formulae of so-called objectivity, beginning with the wire agency bulletins and reports—the warp and woof of what the papers print and the broadcasters voice—our flat one-dimensional handling of news, have given the lie the same prominence and impact that truth is given . . .'

This dangerous tradition of objectivity according to which the reporter's greatest sin is to inject an assessment of the value of what is being said or done into his story—opinion is for editorial writers and columnists, not for the news reports people read first and most—is fortunately, of course, always in some jeopardy from human nature, as Judge Learned Hand pointed out. But these checks and balances—the differences between one man's view and another's—only operate if there is variety of reports. They are defeated if by reason of monopoly only one version is made available to public scrutiny.

In that same judgment Judge Learned Hand also had this to say about the weight that should be given to the commercial interests of newspapers—in the case under review their commercial interest to refuse to a rival a news service to which they belonged or to make him pay through the nose for permission to take it.

'Neither exclusively, nor even primarily,' he said, 'are the interests of the newspaper industry conclusive, for that industry serves one of the most vital of all general interests: the dissemination of news from as many different sources and with as many different facets and colours as possible. That interest is closely akin to, if indeed it is not the same as, the interest protected by the First Amendment: it presupposes that right conclusions are more likely to be gathered out of a multitude of tongues than through any kind of authoritative selection. To many this is, and always will be, folly, but we have staked our all upon it.'

There has, perhaps, never been a better statement of the case against newspaper monopoly—or against the proposition that the commercial interests of newspaper owners come first. But the laws of economics have a force that sets aside the profoundest judgments of the wisest judges and if, as Arthur Hays Sulzberger declared—and I actively agree—the only free press is one free from any form of government control, then we must pay the price exacted and accept that commercial interest must be served, at least to the extent that newspapers can only exist if they can be made reasonably profitable. And the hard fact is that today the commercial circumstances of newspaper life have already produced a monopoly situation for most of the provincial press of both Britain and the United States and are everywhere working for a reduction in the number of newspapers and the greater concentration of those that remain into fewer hands.

Various proposals for checking this tendency have from time to time been made.

There have been suggestions that public corporations should be set up nationally or locally to print newspapers under contract on a cost plus basis in order to reduce the capital investment required for the launching of new papers. Where it can be shown that significant local groups are being denied expression or representation because of the absence of a newspaper to serve them and where those concerned represent a sufficiently serious local interest to be able to guarantee the payment of printing charges for a minimum period, there may be some merit in this.

The suggestion has also been made—I myself have made it and therefore, not unnaturally, see merit in it—that because of the immense technological changes that lie ahead in the newspaper industry and the disadvantage under which these may, for reasons earlier described, put newspapers which although excellent in themselves are not linked to large organisations with massive financial resources, a government research institution should be established to advise on the most practical line of technological advance over the next five or ten years. This done a national newspaper finance corporation should be set up to make loans at low interest rates—or possibly even interest free—to enable newspapers without massive capital resources of their own to re-equip to meet the technological challenges of the time. This would mean doing no more for the newspaper industry than many governments are already doing on a vastly greater scale for the aircraft industry—and if it is a national interest to keep an effective aircraft industry in being, it is no less one to keep an effective press alive.

Because the nub of the economic problems that affect newspapers in economically developed countries such as Britain and America, France and Germany lies in their great and increasing dependence on advertising revenue, there have also been many proposals for somehow spreading advertising more evenly. It is certainly the case that the free play of market forces as it at present operates can produce some strange results—forcing in Britain, for example, the closure of many excellent newspapers with circulations which in any other country in the world would have assured them of success. Indeed, these market forces can have the effect of making insufficient for survival in one part of England a circulation which would in another part assure prosperity. Thus in 1963 the *Manchester Evening Chronicle* was compelled to close, although it had a circulation of over 250,000 which was two and a half times that of the average circulation of provincial evening newspapers in Britain. This large sale and the paper's manifest popularity with a great number of readers proved useless in attracting advertising because it consistently ran second in circulation to the *Manchester Evening News*. As a result its advertising revenue fell to a level where it was operating at a loss of over £300,000 a year. Similar circumstances brought evening paper closures in Birmingham and Nottingham in the same year. If you can only run second you might as well not run at all.

Dependence on advertising is moreover much greater for quality papers, those with a high percentage of what may be described as public service content, than for popular newspapers, those with a much higher percentage of entertainment content.

Quality national newspapers in Britain get seventy-six per cent of their gross revenue from advertising (a percentage very close to that in the American press as a whole), popular newspapers only forty-six per cent. In fact, if costs attributable to advertisements, that is to getting them, servicing them, printing them and transporting the extra bulk of pages on which they are printed, are taken into account, the difference is even greater. After such costs the average net revenue of quality newspapers from advertising is around sixty-five per cent of their total net revenue, that of popular large circulation newspapers only twenty-four per cent. Quality newspapers have the advantage of drawing more of their total advertising revenue from classified advertising than do the popular newspapers and are not quite so dependent on display advertising where competition is most severe. Nevertheless they are extremely vulnerable to any economic recession and a general fall-off in advertising.

This vulnerability has been the greater in Britain because of the tradition of cheap newspapers that came with the ending of the newspaper stamp taxes in the fifties of the last century and the rush of new papers that followed and with Northcliffe's deliberate policy of producing a newspaper at a cut price—'a $1d$ paper for a $\frac{1}{2}d$'—in order to create a market that would attract advertisers. British newspapers were for years sold at prices well below their counterparts in other countries in the conviction that advertising would fill the gap.

Because of this vulnerability—and particularly the vulnerability of what the educated and influential tend to regard as the most important part of the press—a number of ingenious proposals for correcting the balance have been advanced from time to time. The best known of these is that put forward by Nicholas Kalder and his fellow economist, Robert Neild. This proposes a levy on advertising revenue imposed at a percentage rate which would rise with a newspaper's circulation and the proceeds of which would be distributed to assist newspapers of less circulation and consequently with smaller revenue from advertising. The second Royal Commission on the Press which considered this proposal agreed that such a scheme could be made to change the market forces affecting newspapers in a way which would provide more opportunity for the survival of a number of independent newspapers and also give some encouragement for the establishment of new ones—although most probably by established groups or chains. But it rejected the scheme both because of the practical difficulties involved and because it felt that the thesis that newspapers of high circulation—in British terms this would have meant chiefly the *Daily Express* and the *Daily Mirror*—should be required to subsidise those of lower circulation was in principle wrong.

It also rejected two other proposals. One was that a statutory restriction should be placed on the proportion of a newspaper's space that could be devoted to advertising on the thesis that those at present selling more than this proportion would have to compensate for loss of revenue by raising their rates for the space they were allowed to sell and this in turn would encourage some advertisers to buy space in currently neglected newspapers. Another was that an excise duty comparable to that paid by the commercial television programme companies and rising progressively by stages should be imposed on the gross advertising revenue of any newspaper or periodical where this exceeded £2,000,000 annually. The purpose of this levy would not be, as with the television advertisement levy, to raise revenue for the Exchequer although it would make some such contribution, but to discourage newspapers from seeking advertisements above a certain level and thus to divert more advertising to the less successful, more vulnerable newspapers.

As already noted, none of these proposals found favour with the Royal Commission and I cannot but think they were right to reject them. Although one may sometimes wish that advertisers would exercise their rights with greater discrimination and concern for the effect on the medium as a whole, the freedom of the press includes the freedom of advertisers to advertise where they wish and for readers to read the advertisements as well as the news they want to do. It is still the case that as David Stuart, editor of the *Morning Post*, first said in 1795, 'Advertisements act and react. They attract readers, promote circulation and circulation attracts advertisements.' To many readers advertisements are news. There is no more case for denying access to the one than the other. Suggestions for curtailing them are, one suspects, often as much motivated by a general moral dislike by the high-minded for the whole business of advertising as for more concrete reasons. But although the excesses of the admass world are sometimes morally revolting, advertising can probably claim to have done more than many more highly regarded expressions of human enterprise to change social conditions by infusing the underprivileged with the determination to change intolerable economic conditions in order that they, too, may benefit from the goodies spread so lavishly before them in the advertisements. One might like some of the goodies to be better. But the social stimulus has been profound.

In so far as the over excessive dependence of newspapers on advertising revenue can be broken and the vulnerability of the weakest reduced, a proper balance can be more satisfactorily restored by raising the selling price of newspapers and therefore the percentage of their income from sales. Nor is it sensible to insist—as used to be the case in Britain—that there should be only a minor differential between the selling prices of different classes of newspapers. This is not the case among magazines. Readers expect to pay more for an expensively produced magazine than they do for a less expensively produced one, a higher price for a magazine appealing to a minority market of which they are a part, than for a mass market. The same principles should apply to newspapers. Readers should expect to pay more—perhaps a good deal more—for a 'quality' newspaper than a popular one.

To some extent this is now happening in Britain although the first effect has been a fairly general fall in sales. Prices have increased, the need for a price differential between different classes of newspaper accepted—although it is still far smaller than it ought to be. According to Mr Cecil King, and some others, safety through price increases and price differentials is an amateur notion because its only result can be further to reduce the sales of the weak compared with those of the strong. But there is no strong evidence either way in the results of such price rises as there have already been and the King thesis presupposes a lack of discrimination among readers, a readiness to go entirely by the price tag, which would deny among other things the whole reason for the success of the *Mirror* itself which was not due to price but to character. It seems extremely unlikely that those who want serious, well informed, comprehensive newspapers are as miserly as Mr King presumes. In any event one lesson of the current phase of

newspaper development is that those who want the best newspapers must be ready to pay for them. An English jam maker has
made a success out of advertising 'The Most Expensive Jam
in the World'. Perhaps some publishers should try a similar
line.

What stand out after all the ideas on how to improve the current
economic condition of newspapers in the West are considered is
that the real problem for the foreseeable future is that of coming
to terms with monopoly in many areas and with commercial
values in all. The answer lies, I am convinced, in strengthening
the professional element in the press. I do not believe the journalism departments of universities are likely to be much help in this
although university education in the liberal arts may be. Most of
them—in the United States anyway, Britain has none to offer—
are stuck with gentility. Their only ambition is to be accepted as
academic by academics. 'The first question I asked,' said Wilbur
Schramm of Stanford explaining about communications research
(in which he happens to be, unlike many, very good), 'was "How
can journalism schools behave like university people?" The answer
was research.' Journalism departments might have done more for
journalism if they had asked how they could behave like newspapers. As it is too many spend their time producing busy little
research workers who would faint at the sound of a printing press.
It is as though law schools were dedicated to the proposition that
only dropouts practise law.

This problem of values was solved in earlier, easier days by the
fact—particularly in America—that the newspaper builders were
editors who required no great capital to found their newspapers
and developed commercial skills as they went along while remaining faithful to their editorial loyalties—even if, as in Joseph
Pulitzer's case, it was only a death-bed repentance, somewhat
prolonged, that brought them back to their original editorial
visions. It was solved, remarkably, in the case of the London
Times in its greatest days by the self denying but also shrewd
acceptance by the early members of the Walter family of the
advantages to be gained from sticking to the business side of their
paper and leaving its editorial control to independent editors;
Barnes first, Delane second. It was evaded in part in the second
half of the nineteenth and the early part of the twentieth century

by an unnatural division between popular and quality newspapers in which the popular went out after circulation and advertising while the best of the quality newspapers became the privileged and subsidised possession of rich men who were content to foot the bill and take such credit as came to them while their editors were left in control. But that was no real solution and certainly is not one available today. The problem was turned upside down in the period of the great individualistic owners—the press barons—who used their newspapers for their own personal or political purposes as Hearst and Northcliffe and Beaverbrook did. They made money out of them, although in Hearst's case only after a long spending spree, because they happened to be great popular communicators with a flair for the interests and aspirations of their time. But they were not primarily interested either in business or in traditional editorial values and used editors as no more than hired technical assistants. That period, too, is over.

Moreover, during most of these periods you had to try very hard in both the United States and Britain to avoid making money out of newspapers. They operated on a rising market. Readers proliferated as social and economic frontiers widened. Advertisers tumbled over themselves to advertise. Until 1945 there was nowhere in Britain except newspapers, magazines and the hoardings on which you could advertise and even in America the share of radio was still relatively small. There was money in plenty to go round. You did not need to be a good businessman to make a newspaper pay.

All this is ended. Newspapers have now to fight for their lives. They fight by developing monopoly situations where they can. Where they can't, except for those like the *New York Times* and a few of its major contemporaries who have had the luck to possess both dedicated and commercially intelligent publishers, they huddle into groups with others—or with concerns with quite different interests. And many, of course, have died.

If the press were ordinary business all this perhaps would not matter much. Change and transition is normal. It is the tendency in all modern industries for the weak to go to the wall, or lose their identity in something larger, and for the successful to grow bigger. But newspapers contain the quite separate element of a particular and vital, not generalised but quite specific, public interest that

314

sets them apart from other businesses. If the freedom of the press, which can be eroded from within as easily as it can be attacked from without, is to survive and the public right to know is to continue to be served in the way that only a free press can serve it, then newspapers have not only to be watchful of governments, they have also, which is harder, to come to terms with their own condition.

This I believe can only be done—as I have already said—by a great strengthening of the professional element in the press, the recognition by both sides of the newspaper industry that the public service element in newspapers is the business of the journalist and that he must have the independence and authority to look to it all the time. This is not because journalists are necessarily more intelligent or more concerned with the general public good than businessmen, but because this is their trade and should be their vocation. It is not in human nature to be wholly objective. But by training and experience the journalist's concern is, as near as he can get, with the impartial, disinterested handling of news, its collection, assessment and interpretation and with the regular study of public affairs—just as a lawyer's is with the law or a university teacher's with learning. The better a businessman is at his business the more he will look and should look at all issues that arise in the light of how they will affect his shareholders and those he employs and the economic climate in which he must conduct his company's affairs. But to the journalist everything that happens must, or ought to, be looked at in the light of a more general interest. He is in a sense a man disassociated. He must be concerned not with what will affect dividends or his private interests or ambitions, but with what will interest and entertain his readers and with what they need to know, irrespective of what apple-carts their knowing may upset. The more divorced he is from even the most legitimate preoccupations of the businessman, except in the general sense that he has always to bear in mind that even the best newspapers must be economically viable, the better journalist he will be. His interest is at once wider and narrower than that of the businessman. Wider because it must, in so far as he is capable of doing so, embrace the public interest as a whole and not simply particular sections of it, narrower because in reaching his judgments he must seek to exclude all such extraneous values and side effects as may well be the proper concern of the businessman.

His loyalties are, of course, to his paper. But they should be professional, not business loyalties. Such a relationship between journalist and proprietor or publishing executive is a delicate matter requiring understanding on both sides. But as newspapers become more businesslike organisations, concerned as they must be with their balance sheets and profit potentials in a hazardous world, the independence of the editor, the integrity of the professional element in the press, becomes of increasing importance if the responsibilities of a free press to the public interest are to be maintained. Fortunately as earlier chapters have shown there is an increasing recognition of this fact. It is to be found in the best parts of the American press—it is surely not accidental that although in the organisation of the *New York Times*, which has always been blessed with owner publishers with no outside interests, the publisher remains supreme, the authority and scope of the professional editor has lately been increased. It is to be found in the French press—notably in *Le Monde* but increasingly among others as a consequence of *Le Monde*'s example. It has long existed in some parts of the British press such as the *Guardian* and the *Observer* with their trusts defining editorial independence, it was specifically documented by the Monopolies Commission in its report on the *Times–Sunday Times* merger, which for this reason, if no other, may become an important landmark in British newspaper history, and was wholly accepted by Lord Thomson. And, indeed, it is not only in the public interest that the division between commercial and editorial responsibilities is desirable, but in the commercial interest of newspapers themselves. The most successful newspapers have always been those with strong editors enjoying continuity of office. The least successful have always been those that changed editors with each proprietorial whim.

Professional values are the red corpuscles in the blood of a newspaper. They give it life. If the historic role of the press is to continue in the changing commercial conditions of our time editorial independence must be accepted by managements and constantly defended by journalists and their professional associations. And it must be given the powerful buttress of public opinion.

The independence of the editor, the recognition of the importance of the professional element, in newspapers will become even more essential as monopoly conditions become more general. The temptation in such circumstances to take the easy neutralist way to good profits is strong. It is for the editor to learn to live with monopoly and to make sure that within it there is vigour and variety. American newspaper readers have the advantage even in many of their monopoly papers of a large variety of syndicated interpretations of, and views on, national and international affairs. A man whose local paper sets regularly before him the opinions of Walter Lippmann, Joseph Alsop, James Reston, Drew Pearson and half a dozen other national columnists cannot complain that he is being given only one side of any question. But a similar variety and debate in state and city affairs by no means follows, unless the editor deliberately causes it to do so. French, German and English provincial newspapers with monopolies lack the advantage of such columnists—although this lack is offset in Britain by the universal presence of the national press. If they are properly to fulfil their professional function they need a strong determination by their editors not to relax on the feather bed of monopoly, however strong the commercial urge to do so in a non-competitive situation may be.

They need, too, the lively involvement of reporters conscious that they belong to a trade which is best perhaps when not too respectable. Of course, more highly educated journalists are required in the conditions of today. Specialists are needed to treat with the specialists of governments and public corporations on equal intellectual terms. Yet there is disadvantage as well as advantage in turning journalism into a profession to which only university graduates need apply. Reporters, said Mencken, are better taking in worldly wisdom from a police lieutenant, a bartender, a shyster lawyer or a midwife than listening to balderdash from a pedagogue, and the strength of journalism has always come in the past from the openness of the trade and from the fact that any good news-room might expect to find on its staff men from every conceivable social background who did not need official reports to tell them how the poor lived because they had been down there among them and knew.

One final question remains. Does the press with all its changes and all its problems still matter as it did? Or are we moving

The Right to Know

through the medium of television, radio and space communication to what McLuhan has called the 'global village' in which we shall all feel and think alike without benefit of newspapers? I do not think so. As a concept the global village puts too much weight on the technology of mass communication, too little on the existence of societies and governments determined to preserve their own frontiers. We do not move into one tribe, but rather away from it, to a world in which, to give only one example, men have been prepared to die and let their children die for the right to be Biafrans instead of Nigerians. Humanity still has a compulsive urge to build frontiers round itself and gather together in its own familiar groups. In such circumstances it is the newspaper speaking from within, much more than the space message from outside, that will continue to influence men's alives and the nature of their societies.

Newspapers are the ground troops of democracy, the infantrymen and the G.I.s. Their equipment may alter. But whatever may take place in the skies above them they will continue to be needed on the ramparts of civilisation.

Note on Sources and
Brief Bibliography

This book is the product of a good deal of thought about news-papers and their readers during some forty-five years as a news-paperman in almost every capacity from junior reporter on a local weekly to Editor of a London national daily with pauses along the way as a general reporter, sub-editor, crime reporter, labour reporter, book reviewer, feature writer, political correspondent, Washington Correspondent, financial editor and foreign corre-spondent and columnist, and with forays into radio and television as a roving reporter and commentator and as a Governor of the B.B.C. There were also two periods of government service as war-time controller of news and press censorship with Winston Churchill and as advisor on press and public relations affairs to the Prime Minister, Clement Attlee, in the post-war Labour Government and two very agreeable excursions into academic life as Regents' Professor at the University of California, Berkeley and Kemper Knap Professor at the University of Wisconsin, Madison, in both instances as a result of invitations from their schools of journalism. For some years, also, I wrote, at first in the *New Statesman* and later in *Punch*, a weekly column on newspaper affairs: 'Fleet Street'. This brought me letters and reports from newspapermen all over the world as well as invitations to lecture in many countries.

The book, therefore, draws not only on much newspaper experience but on discussions with newspapermen of a great many countries whom I have been proud to know as members of the same craft. It extends, and I hope develops, themes which concerned me in two previous books on the press, both now out of print, *Press, Parliament and People* and *Dangerous Estate: The Anatomy of Newspapers*. But since I have aimed here at a com-parative history of the development of newspapers across the world and especially in Britain and the United States, the scope of this book is much wider than either of these two previous

Note on Sources and Brief Bibliography

volumes of mine. So too, of course, is the possibility of error and although I have done my best to avoid this I would not swear to have succeeded all along the line. For such mistakes as may be found I can only apologise.

Where I have quoted directly from published sources, or from individuals I have given the reference in the text. But of course any writer on the press who is not inordinately egotistical or extremely lazy must be aware of his indebtedness to many fellow writers. Without attempting a full bibliography the following are among the publications which have given me most pleasure and on which I have most drawn.

AINSLIE, ROSALYNDE, *The Press in Africa*, Gollancz, 1966.

ALSOP, JOSEPH and STEWART, *The Reporter's Trade*, Reynal (New York) 1958; Bodley Head (London) 1960.

BRADDON, RUSSELL, *Roy Thomson of Fleet Street*, Collins, 1965.

BRIGGS, ASA, *History of Broadcasting in the United Kingdom*, Vol. 1. *The Birth of Broadcasting*, Vol. 2. *The Golden Age of Wireless*, Oxford University Press, 1961, 1965.

BROWN, FRANCIS, *Raymond of The Times*, Norton, 1951.

CATER, DOUGLASS, *The Fourth Branch of Government*, Houghton Mifflin, 1959.

Commission on Freedom of the Press, *A Free and Responsible Press*, University of Chicago Press, 1944.

CRUIKSHANK, R. J., *Roaring Century 1846–1946*, Hamish Hamilton, 1946.

CUDLIPP, HUGH, *Publish and Be Damned*, Andrew Dakers, 1953. *At Your Peril*, Weidenfeld and Nicolson, 1962.

DRIBERG, T., *Beaverbrook*, Weidenfeld and Nicolson, 1956.

EMERY, E. and SMITH, HENRY L., *The Press and America*, Prentice-Hall, 1954.

FRIENDLY, FRED. W., *Due to Circumstances beyond our Control*, MacGibbon and Kee, 1967.

GOLLIN, A. M., *The Observer and J. L. Garvin, 1908–1914*, Oxford University Press, 1960.

Note on Sources and Brief Bibliography

Government Pressures on the Press, International Press Institute, 1955.

HALEY, SIR WILLIAM, and others, *C. P. Scott. 1846–1932; The Making of the Manchester Guardian*, Muller, 1947.

HARRIS, H. W., *J. A. Spender*, Cassell, 1946.

HERD, H., *The March of Journalism*, Allen and Unwin, 1952.

History of The Times.
    Vol. 1. *The Thunderer in the Making 1785–1841*,
    Vol. 2. *The Tradition Established 1841–1884*,
    Vol. 3. *The Twentieth Century Test 1884–1912*,
    Vol. 4. *The 150th Anniversary and Beyond 1912–1948*,
    The Times, 1935, 1939, 1947, 1952.

KING, CECIL, *The Future of the Press*, MacGibbon and Kee, 1967.

KOBLER, JOHN, *Henry Luce*, Macdonald, 1968.

LEVY, H. PHILLIP, *The Press Council*, Macmillan, 1967.

MATHEWS, T. S., *The Sugar Pill*, Gollancz, 1957.

MAYER, HENRY, *The Press in Australia*, Angus and Robertson, 1964.

MERRILL, JOHN G., BRYAN, CARTER R., and ALISKY, MARVIN, *The Foreign Press*, Louisiana State University Press, 1964.

MINNEY, R. J., *Viscount Southwood*, Odhams, 1954.

MORRISON, S., *The English Newspaper*, Cambridge University Press, 1932.

MOTT, FRANK L., *American Journalism*, The Macmillan Co., New York, 1950.

NELSON, HAROLD L., *Freedom of the Press from Hamilton to the Warren Court*, Bobbs-Merrill, 1967.

NIMMO, DAN D., *Newsgathering in Washington*, Atherton Press, 1962.

POLLARD, JAMES E., *The Presidents and The Press*, The Macmillan Co., New York, 1947.

POUND, R. and HARMSWORTH G., *Northcliffe*, Cassell, 1959.

RESTON, JAMES, *The Artillery of the Press*, Harper & Row, 1967.

Note on Sources and Brief Bibliography

RUCKER, BRYCE W., *The First Freedom*, Southern Illinois University Press, 1968.

SCHRAMM, WILBUR, *Mass Media and National Development*, Stanford University Press, California and Unesco, Paris, 1964.

SCOTT, GEORGE, *Reporter Anonymous*, Hutchinson, 1968.

STEED, H. W., *The Press*, Penguin Books, 1938.

STOREY, G., *Reuter's Century, 1851–1951*, Parrish, 1951.

SOMMERLAD, E. LLOYD, *The Press in Developing Countries*, Sydney University Press, 1966.

SWANBERG, W. A., *Citizen Hearst*, Longmans, 1962.

TEBEL, JOHN, *The Compact History of the American Newspaper*, Hawthorn Books, 1963.

UNESCO, *The Daily Press*, Unesco, 1953.
World Communications, Unesco, 1964.

VAN DEUSEN, GLYNDON, *Horace Greeley; Nineteenth Century Crusader*, University of Pennsylvania Press, 1953.

WADSWORTH, A. P., *Newspaper Circulations 1800–1954*, Manchester Statistical Society, 1955.

WEISBERGER, BERNARD A, *The American Newspaperman*, University of Chicago Press, 1961.

WILLIAMS, DAVID, *Not in the Public Interest*, Hutchinson, 1965.

WILLIAMS, FRANCIS, *Press, Parliament and People*, Heinemann, 1946.
Transmitting World News, Unesco, 1953.
Dangerous Estate, Longmans, 1957.

WILLIAMS, RAYMOND, *Communications*, Penguin Books, 1962.

WOOD, ALAN, *The True History of Lord Beaverbrook*, Heinemann, 1965.

WRENCH, JOHN EVELYN, *Geoffrey Dawson and Our Times*, Hutchinson, 1955.

I am also much indebted to many publications and reports of the International Press Institute, the Commonwealth Press Union and the International Federation of Journalists, and to the Annual

Note on Sources and Brief Bibliography

Reports of the British Press Council; to the Reports of the Royal Commissions on the Press 1947–1949 and 1961–1962, the Vassall Tribunal, 1963, the Privy Councillors' Committee on 'D' Notice Matters, 1967, Lord Denning's investigation into matters arising from the Profumo Affair 1963 and to the Report of the Monopolies Commission on the proposed merger of *The Times* and *Sunday Times* 1966. I have also been helped by many articles on the press in newspapers and magazines in many parts of the world and particularly by the writings of Ben H. Bagdikian on the American Press. To the many publications of my friends of the Center For The Study of Democratic Institutions, Santa Barbara, California, I owe much. Nor must I forget my debt to professional and trade publications such as *Journalism Quarterly*, *The Journalist*, *World's Press News*, *U.K. Press Gazette* and *Editor and Publisher*. To all these I give my thanks.

INDEX

331